Garfield
feeds the kitty

BY JIM DAVIS

Ballantine Books • New York

2018 Ballantine Books Trade Paperback Edition

Copyright © 1999, 2018 by PAWS, Inc. All rights reserved.
"GARFIELD" and the GARFIELD characters are trademarks of PAWS, Inc.

Published in the United States by Ballantine Books, an imprint of Random House,
a division of Penguin Random House LLC, New York.

BALLANTINE and the HOUSE colophon are registered trademarks of Penguin Random House LLC.

Originally published in slightly different form in the United States by Ballantine Books,
an imprint of Random House, a division of Penguin Random House LLC, in 1999.

ISBN 978-0-425-28569-5
Ebook ISBN 978-0-425-28570-1

Printed in China on acid-free paper

randomhousebooks.com

9 8 7 6 5 4 3 2

First Colorized Edition

PRACTICAL USES FOR GARFIELD'S HAIRBALLS

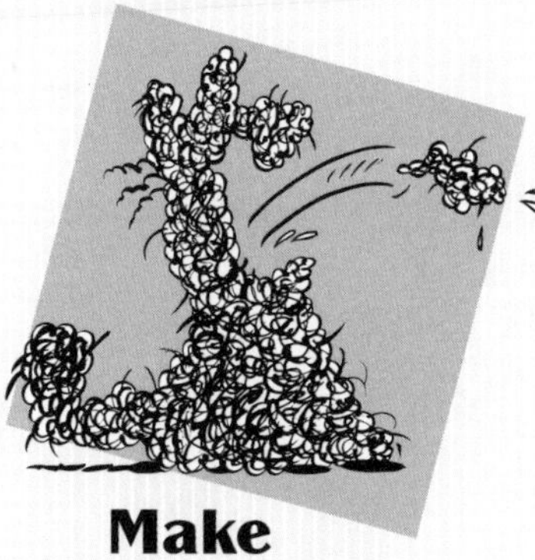

Make Another Cat

Unique Sweaters

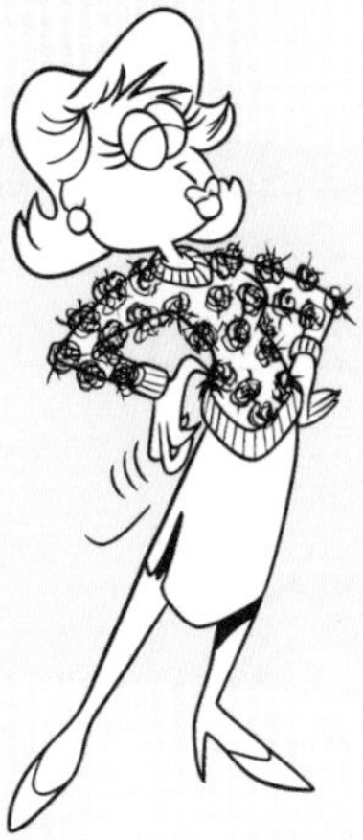

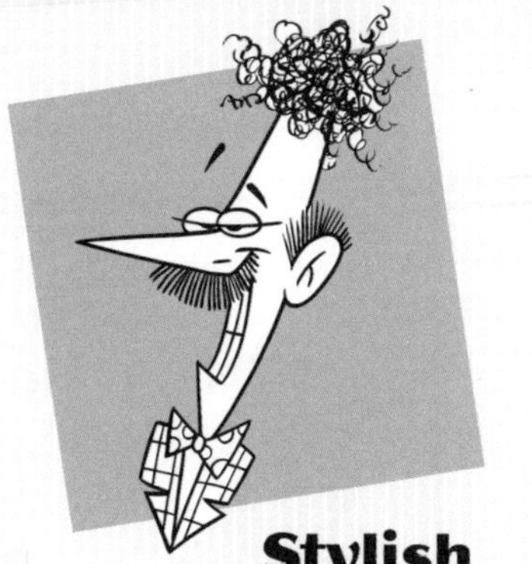

Stylish Toupees

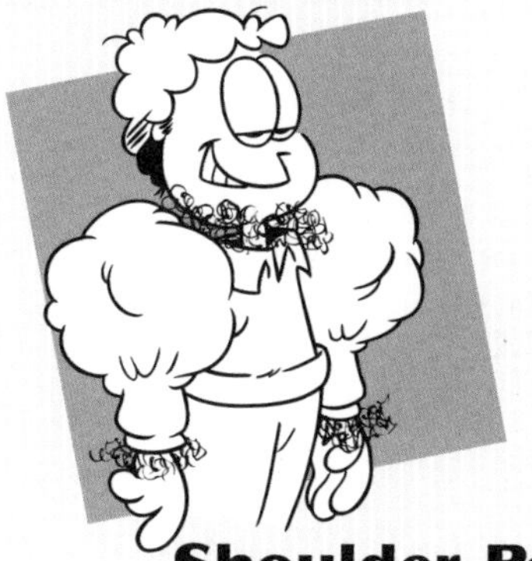

Shoulder Pads

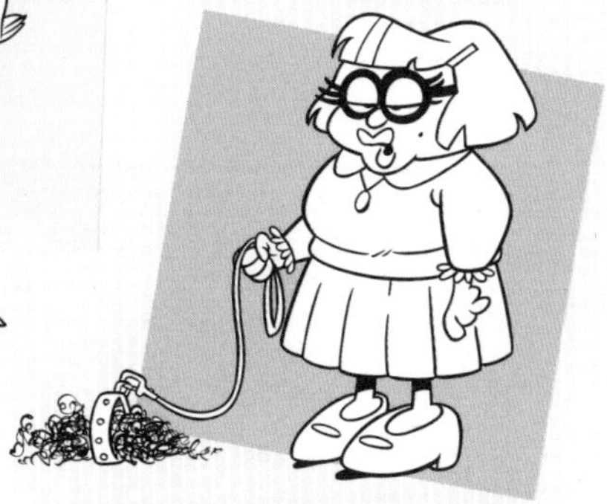

Maintenance-Free Pets

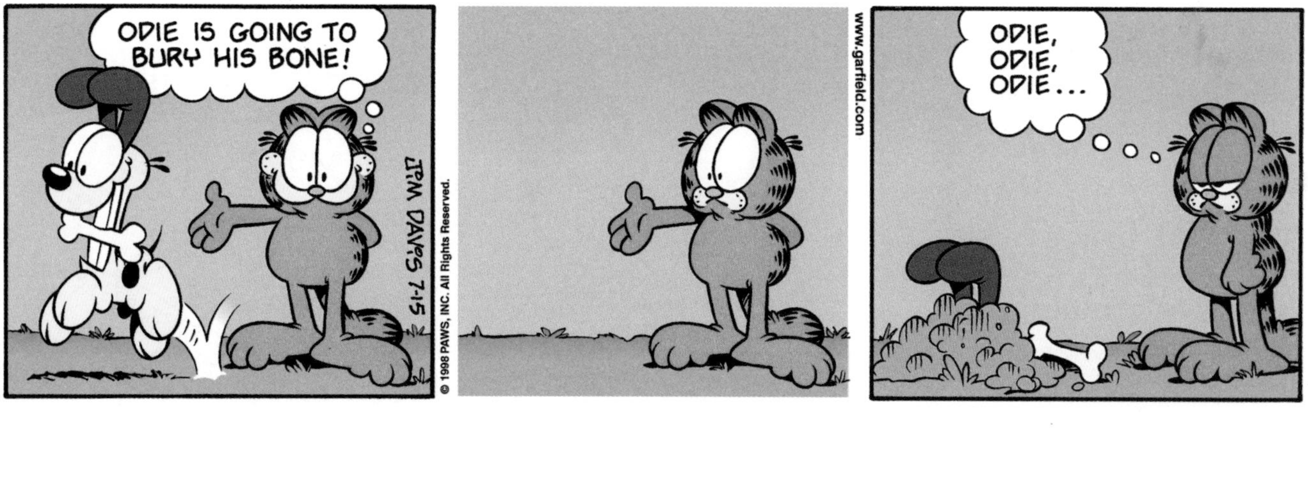
ODIE IS GOING TO BURY HIS BONE!
JIM DAVIS 7-15
© 1998 PAWS, INC. All Rights Reserved.
www.garfield.com
ODIE, ODIE, ODIE...

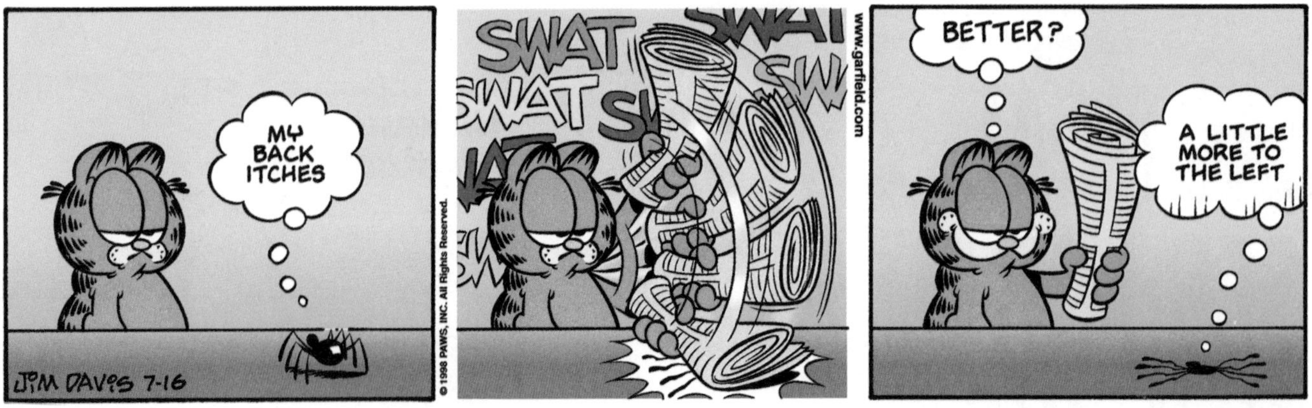
MY BACK ITCHES
JIM DAVIS 7-16
© 1998 PAWS, INC. All Rights Reserved.
SWAT SWAT SWAT SWAT
www.garfield.com
BETTER?
A LITTLE MORE TO THE LEFT

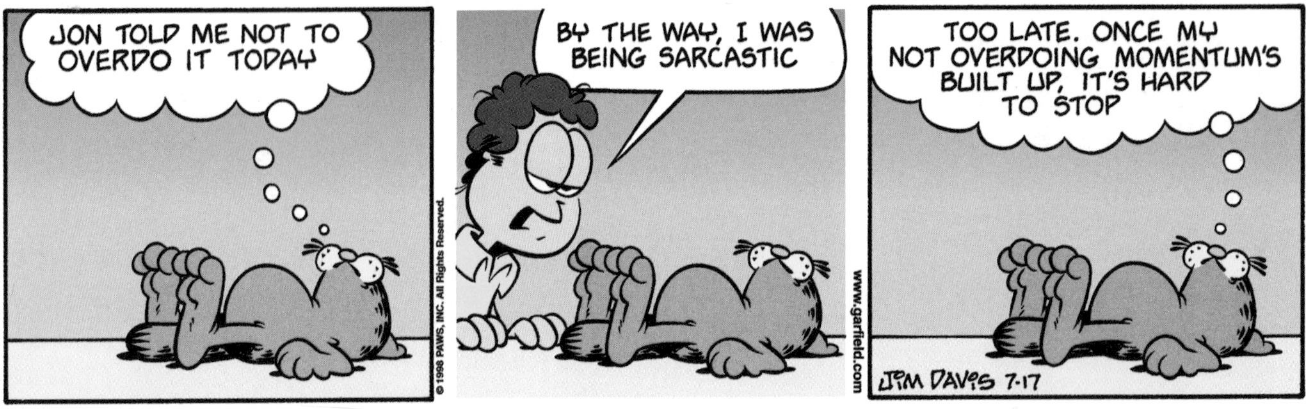
JON TOLD ME NOT TO OVERDO IT TODAY
© 1998 PAWS, INC. All Rights Reserved.
BY THE WAY, I WAS BEING SARCASTIC
www.garfield.com
TOO LATE. ONCE MY NOT OVERDOING MOMENTUM'S BUILT UP, IT'S HARD TO STOP
JIM DAVIS 7-17

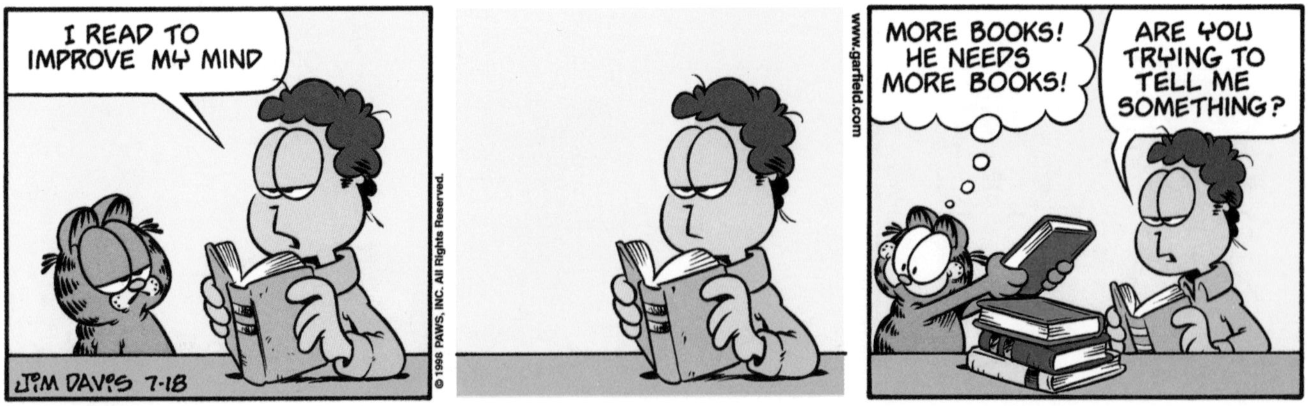
I READ TO IMPROVE MY MIND
JIM DAVIS 7-18
© 1998 PAWS, INC. All Rights Reserved.
www.garfield.com
MORE BOOKS! HE NEEDS MORE BOOKS!
ARE YOU TRYING TO TELL ME SOMETHING?

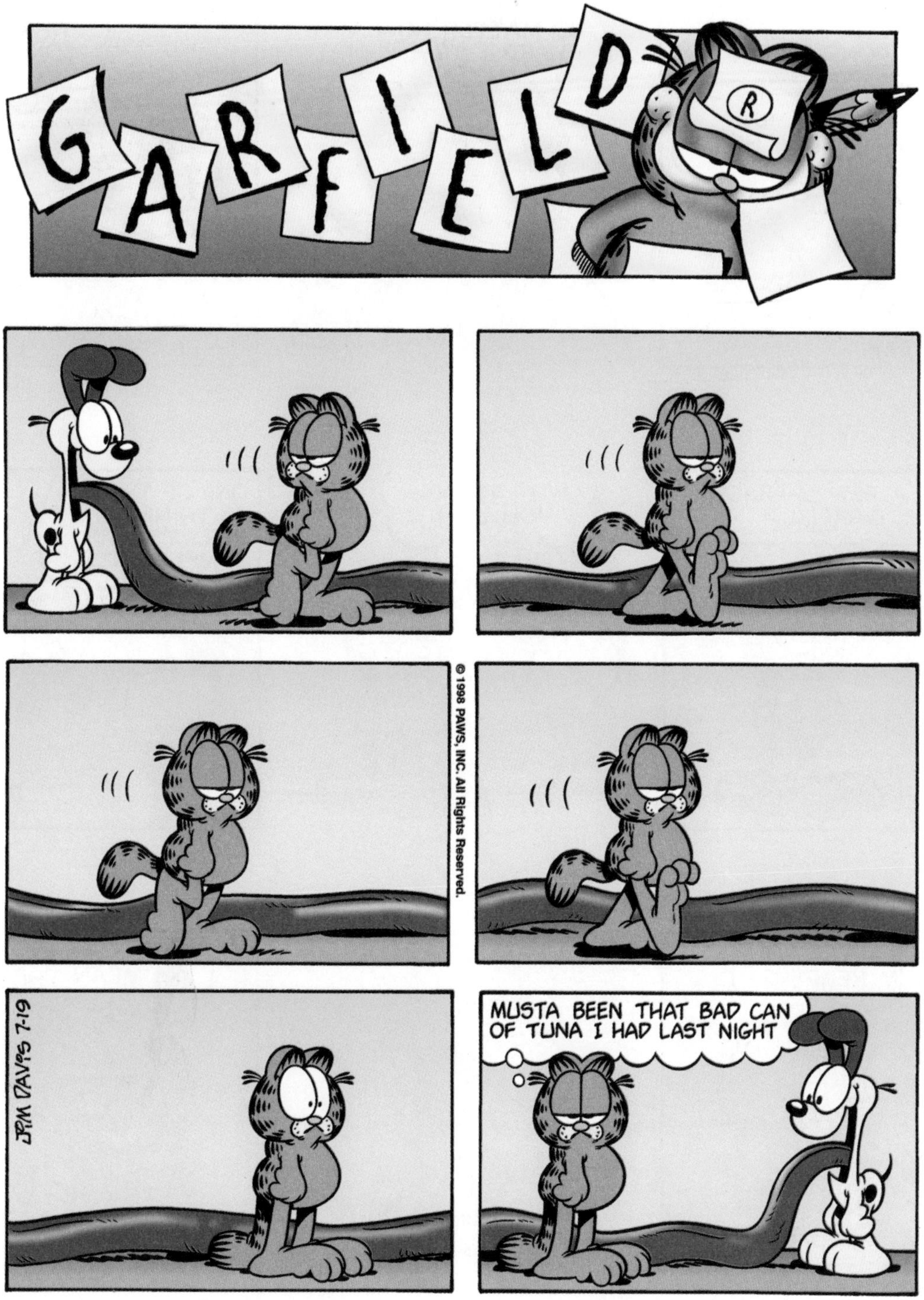
GARFIELD
JIM DAVIS 7-19
MUSTA BEEN THAT BAD CAN OF TUNA I HAD LAST NIGHT

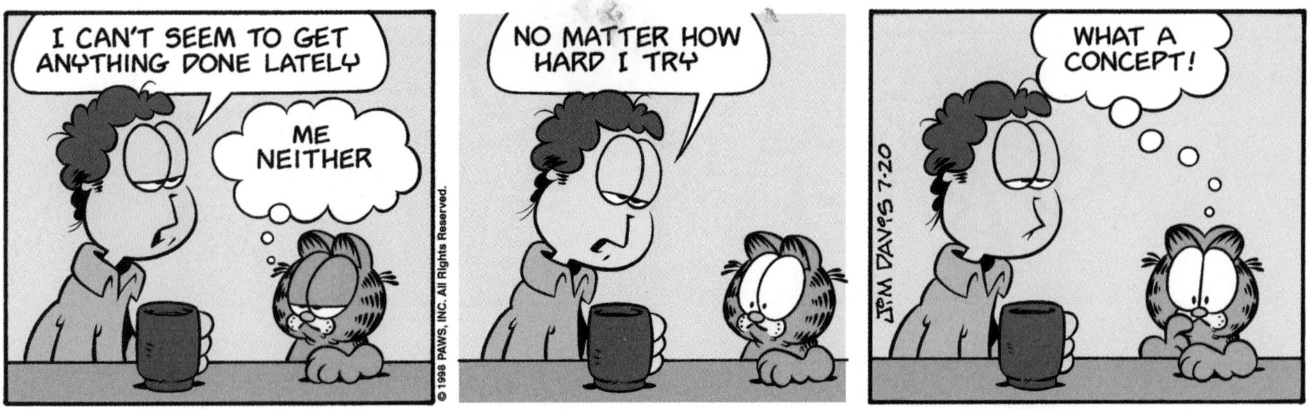
I CAN'T SEEM TO GET ANYTHING DONE LATELY
ME NEITHER
© 1998 PAWS, INC. All Rights Reserved.
NO MATTER HOW HARD I TRY
JIM DAVIS 7-20
WHAT A CONCEPT!

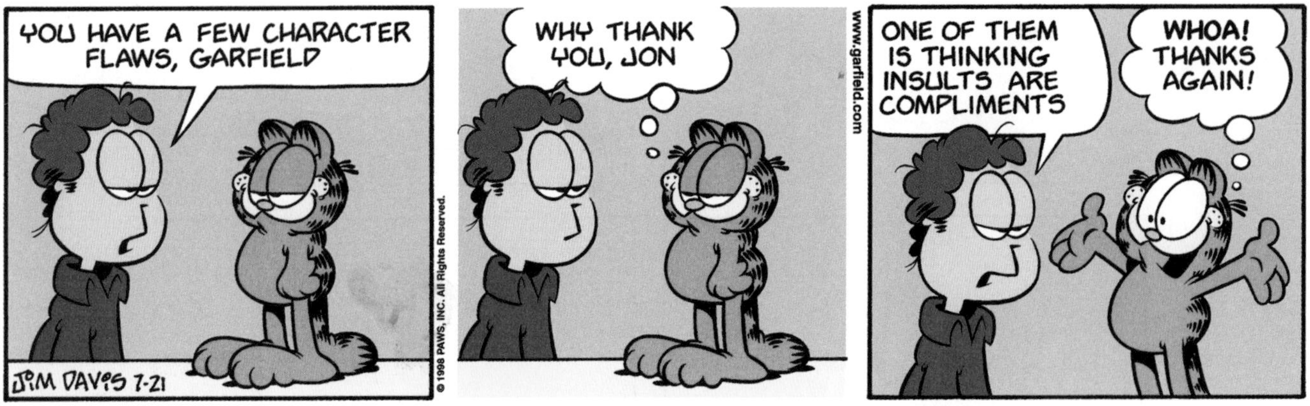
YOU HAVE A FEW CHARACTER FLAWS, GARFIELD
JIM DAVIS 7-21
© 1998 PAWS, INC. All Rights Reserved.
WHY THANK YOU, JON
www.garfield.com
ONE OF THEM IS THINKING INSULTS ARE COMPLIMENTS
WHOA! THANKS AGAIN!

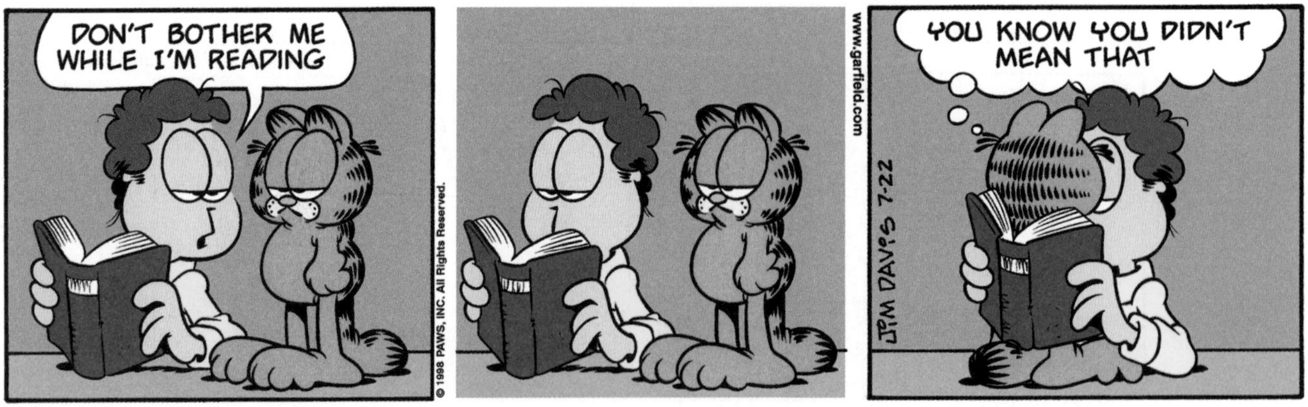
DON'T BOTHER ME WHILE I'M READING
© 1998 PAWS, INC. All Rights Reserved.
www.garfield.com
JIM DAVIS 7-22
YOU KNOW YOU DIDN'T MEAN THAT

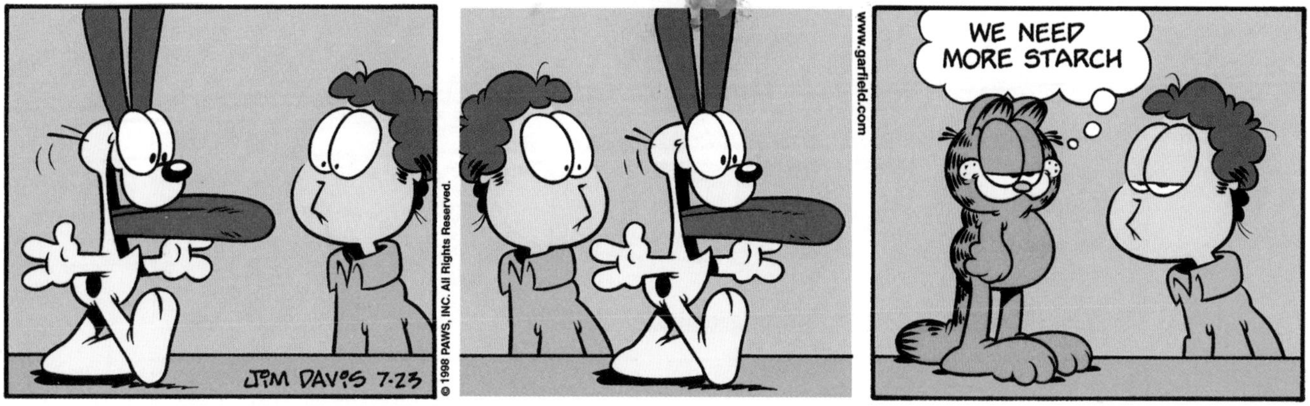
JIM DAVIS 7-23
© 1998 PAWS, INC. All Rights Reserved.
www.garfield.com
WE NEED MORE STARCH

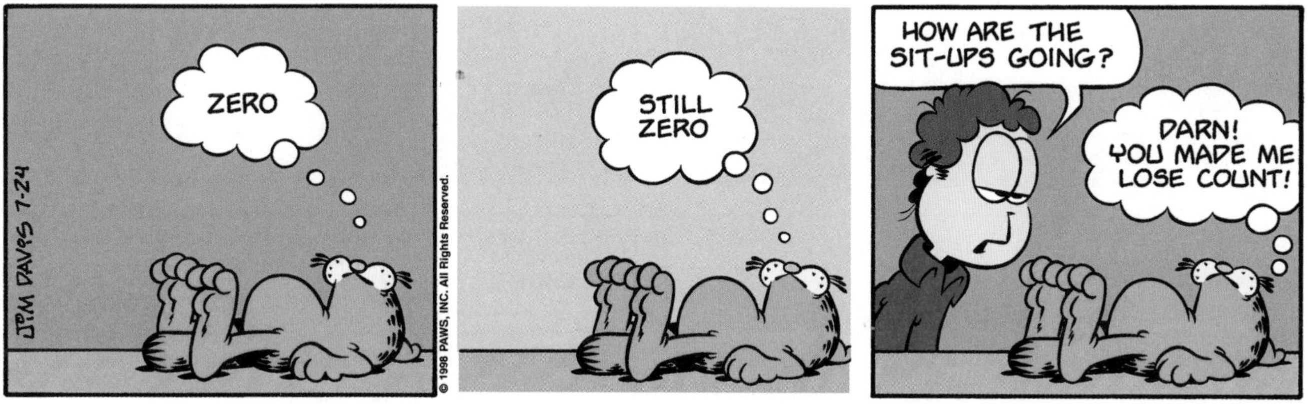
JIM DAVIS 7-24
ZERO
© 1998 PAWS, INC. All Rights Reserved.
STILL ZERO
HOW ARE THE SIT-UPS GOING?
DARN! YOU MADE ME LOSE COUNT!

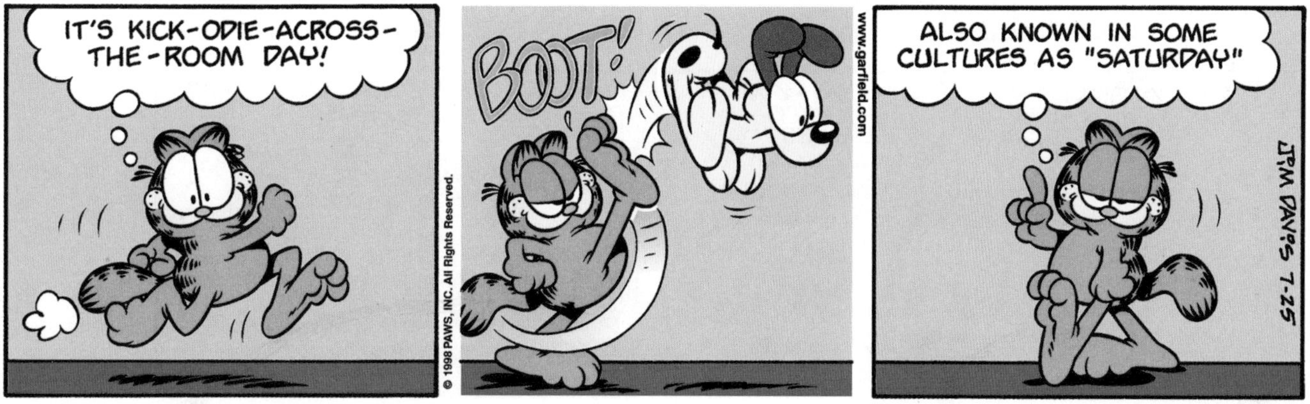
IT'S KICK-ODIE-ACROSS-THE-ROOM DAY!
© 1998 PAWS, INC. All Rights Reserved.
BOOT!
www.garfield.com
ALSO KNOWN IN SOME CULTURES AS "SATURDAY"
JIM DAVIS 7-25

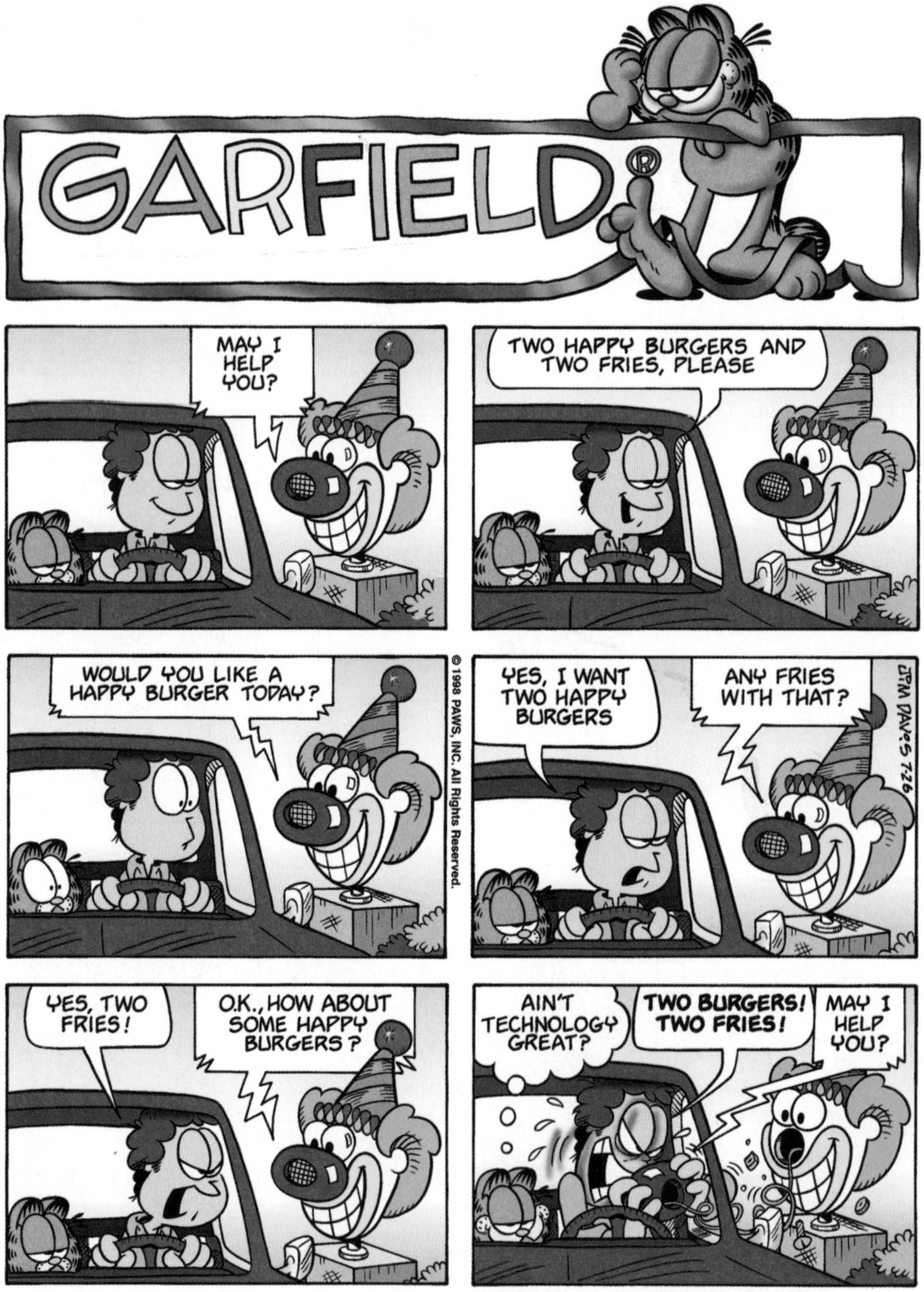
GARFIELD®
MAY I HELP YOU?
TWO HAPPY BURGERS AND TWO FRIES, PLEASE
WOULD YOU LIKE A HAPPY BURGER TODAY?
YES, I WANT TWO HAPPY BURGERS
ANY FRIES WITH THAT?
YES, TWO FRIES!
O.K., HOW ABOUT SOME HAPPY BURGERS?
AIN'T TECHNOLOGY GREAT?
TWO BURGERS! TWO FRIES!
MAY I HELP YOU?
JPM DAVIS 7-26
© 1998 PAWS, INC. All Rights Reserved.

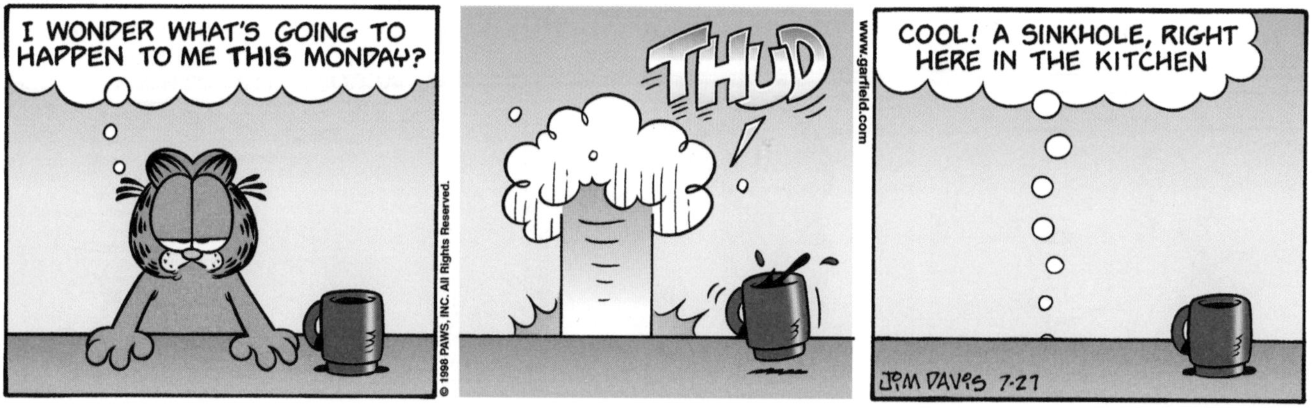
I WONDER WHAT'S GOING TO HAPPEN TO ME THIS MONDAY?
THUD
COOL! A SINKHOLE, RIGHT HERE IN THE KITCHEN
JIM DAVIS 7-27
© 1998 PAWS, INC. All Rights Reserved.
www.garfield.com

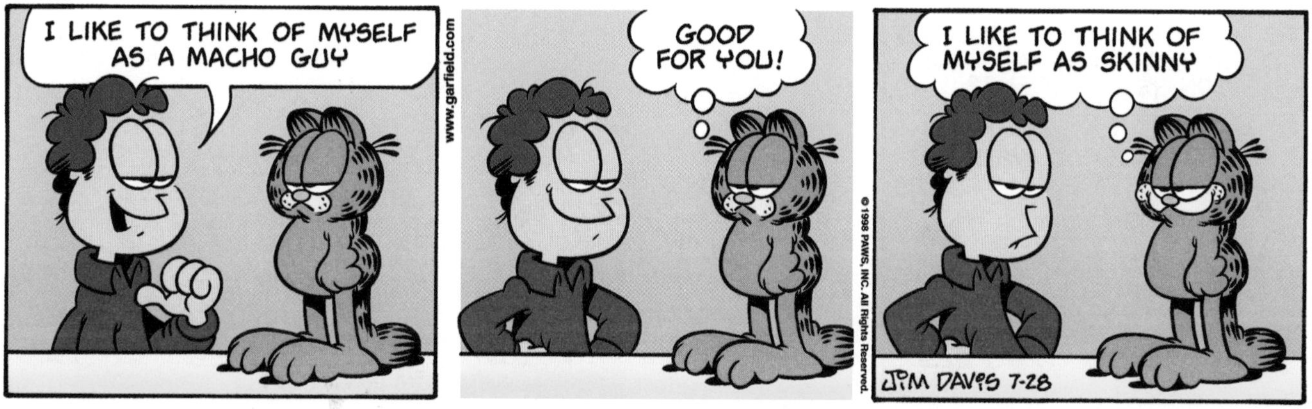
I LIKE TO THINK OF MYSELF AS A MACHO GUY
GOOD FOR YOU!
I LIKE TO THINK OF MYSELF AS SKINNY
JIM DAVIS 7-28
www.garfield.com
© 1998 PAWS, INC. All Rights Reserved.

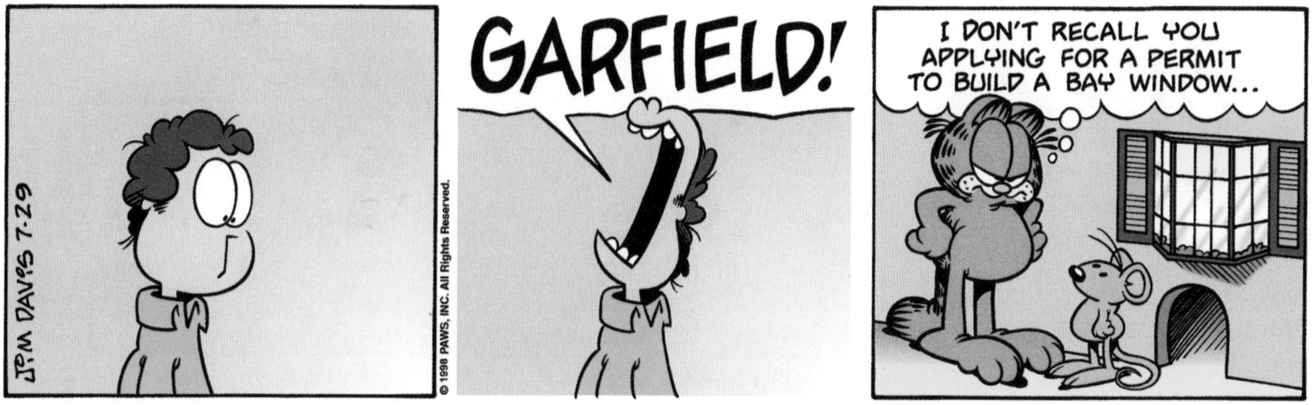
JIM DAVIS 7-29
GARFIELD!
I DON'T RECALL YOU APPLYING FOR A PERMIT TO BUILD A BAY WINDOW...
© 1998 PAWS, INC. All Rights Reserved.

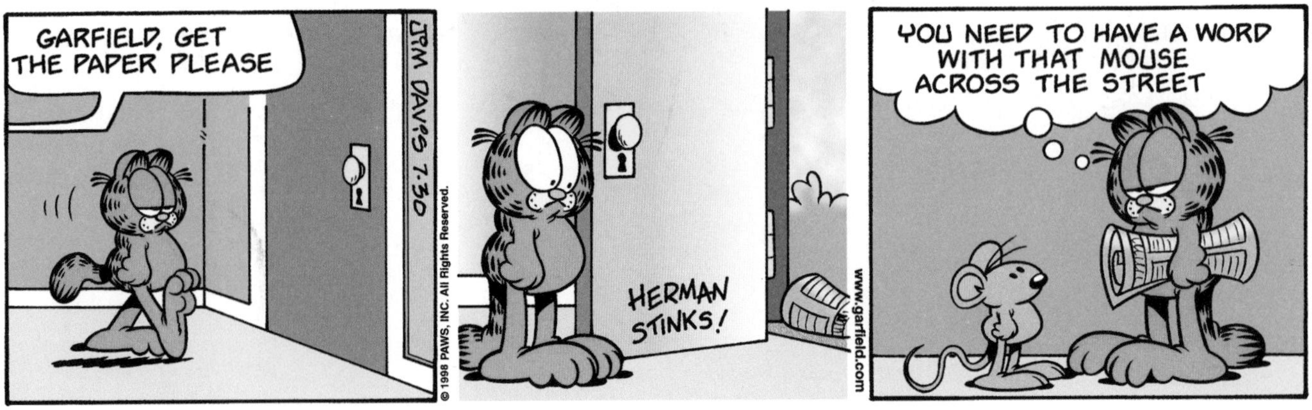
GARFIELD, GET THE PAPER PLEASE
JIM DAVIS 7-30
© 1998 PAWS, INC. All Rights Reserved.
HERMAN STINKS!
www.garfield.com
YOU NEED TO HAVE A WORD WITH THAT MOUSE ACROSS THE STREET

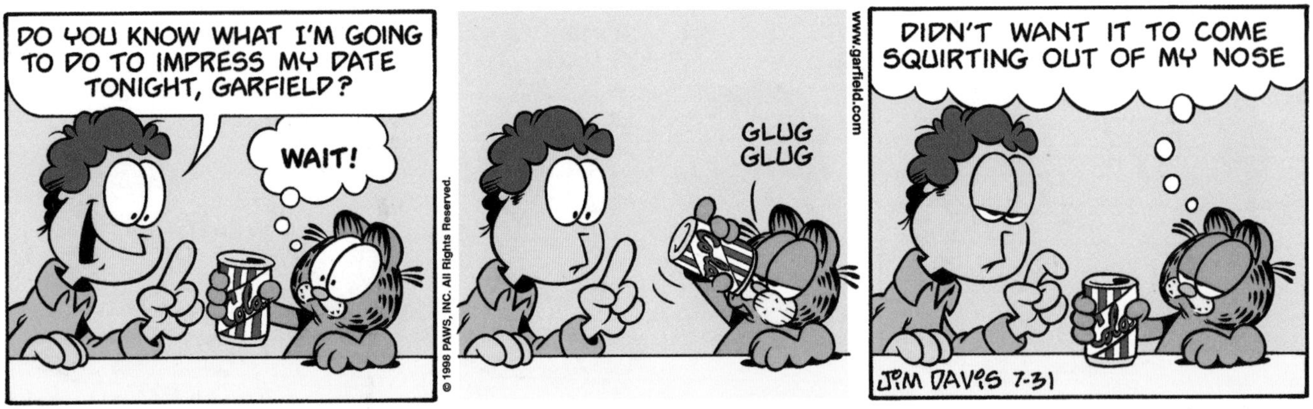
DO YOU KNOW WHAT I'M GOING TO DO TO IMPRESS MY DATE TONIGHT, GARFIELD?
WAIT!
© 1998 PAWS, INC. All Rights Reserved.
GLUG GLUG
www.garfield.com
DIDN'T WANT IT TO COME SQUIRTING OUT OF MY NOSE
JIM DAVIS 7-31

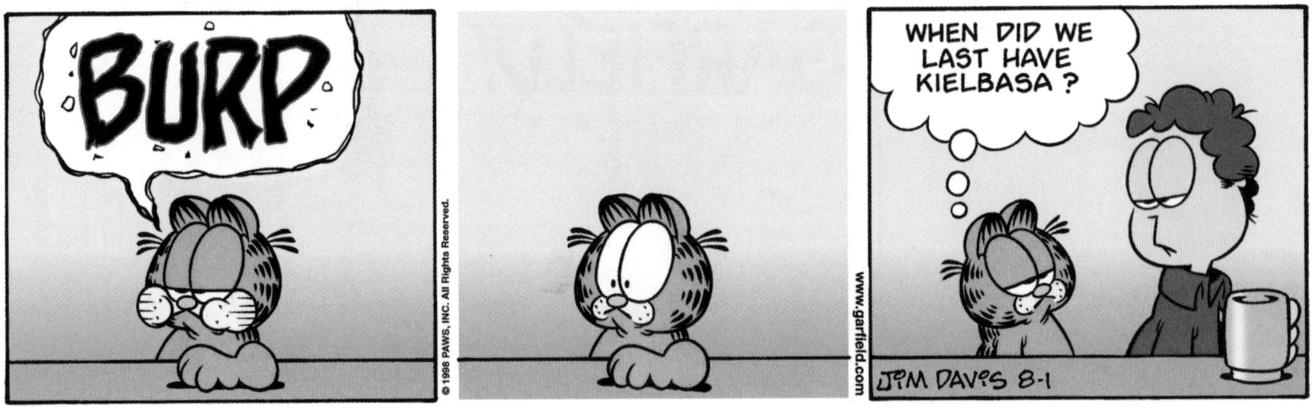
BURP
© 1998 PAWS, INC. All Rights Reserved.
www.garfield.com
WHEN DID WE LAST HAVE KIELBASA?
JIM DAVIS 8-1

GARFIELD®
AND NOW...
CLICK
COMING UP NEXT...
CLICK
PRESENTING...
CLICK
HERE'S...
CLICK
JIM DAVIS 8-2
WELCOME TO...
CLICK
ANYTHING GOOD ON?
CLICK
HOW SHOULD I KNOW?

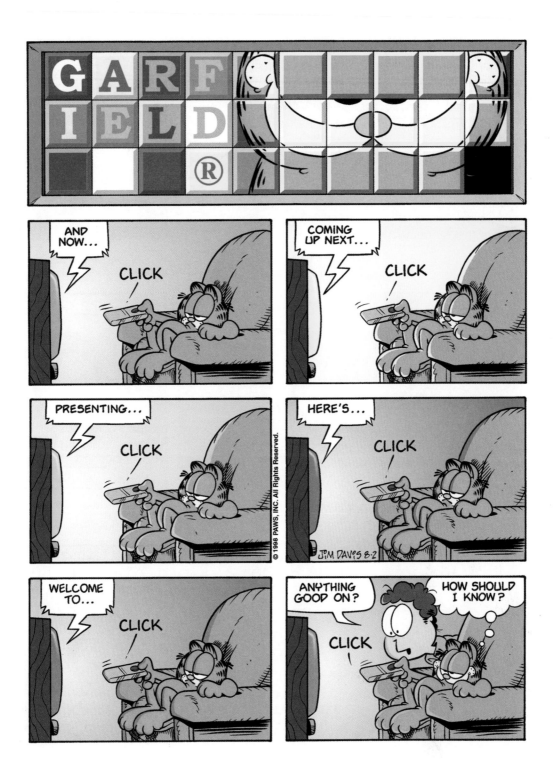

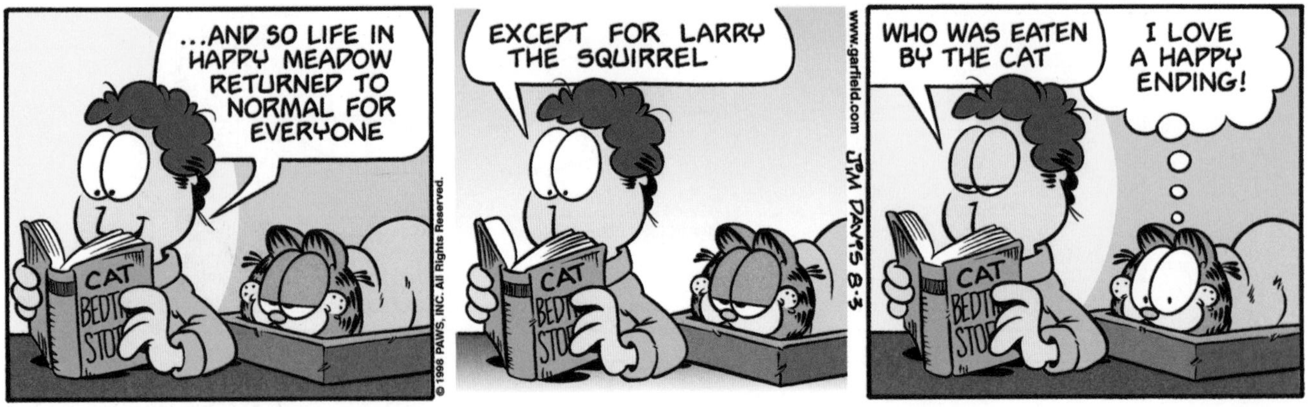
...AND SO LIFE IN HAPPY MEADOW RETURNED TO NORMAL FOR EVERYONE
CAT BEDTI STO
© 1998 PAWS, INC. All Rights Reserved.
EXCEPT FOR LARRY THE SQUIRREL
JIM DAVIS 8-3
www.garfield.com
WHO WAS EATEN BY THE CAT
I LOVE A HAPPY ENDING!

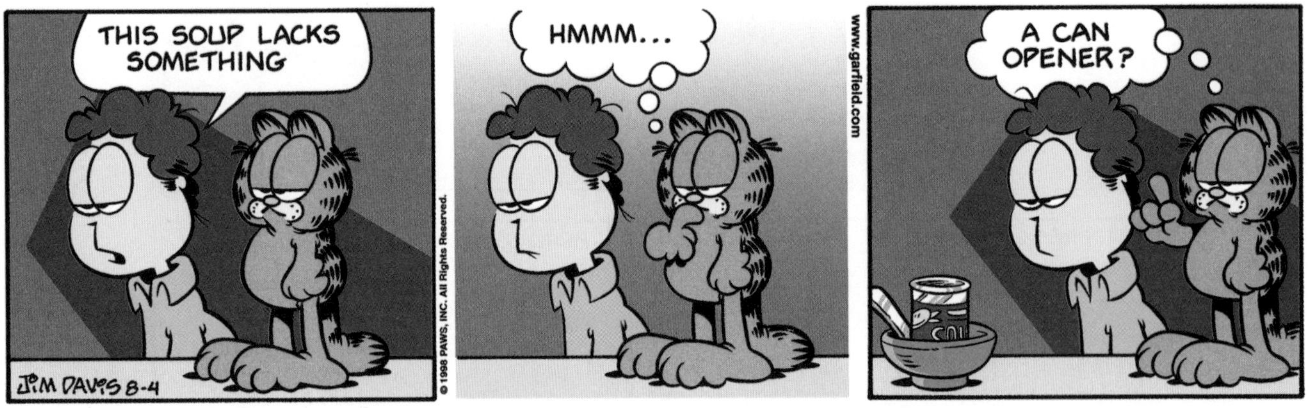
THIS SOUP LACKS SOMETHING
JIM DAVIS 8-4
© 1998 PAWS, INC. All Rights Reserved.
HMMM...
www.garfield.com
A CAN OPENER?

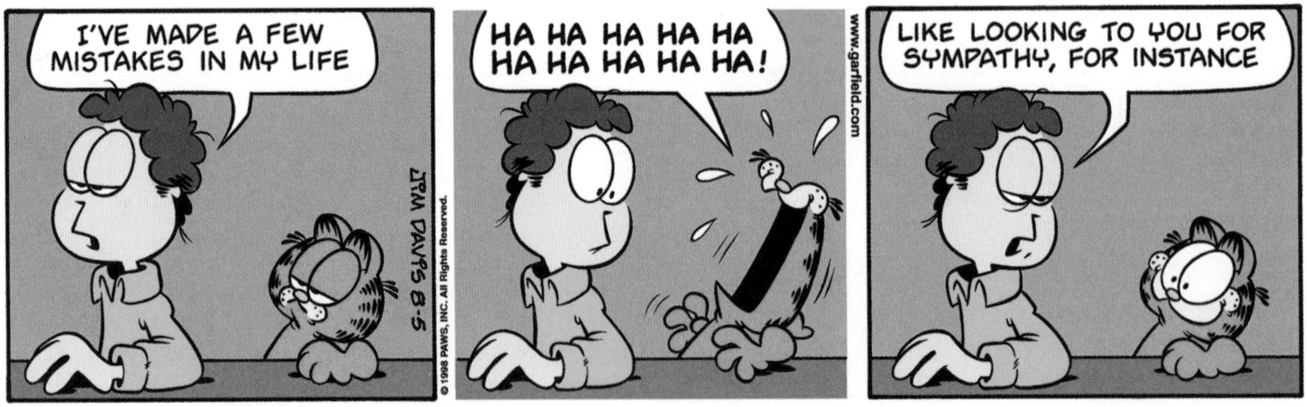
I'VE MADE A FEW MISTAKES IN MY LIFE
JIM DAVIS 8-5
© 1998 PAWS, INC. All Rights Reserved.
HA HA HA HA HA HA HA HA HA HA!
www.garfield.com
LIKE LOOKING TO YOU FOR SYMPATHY, FOR INSTANCE

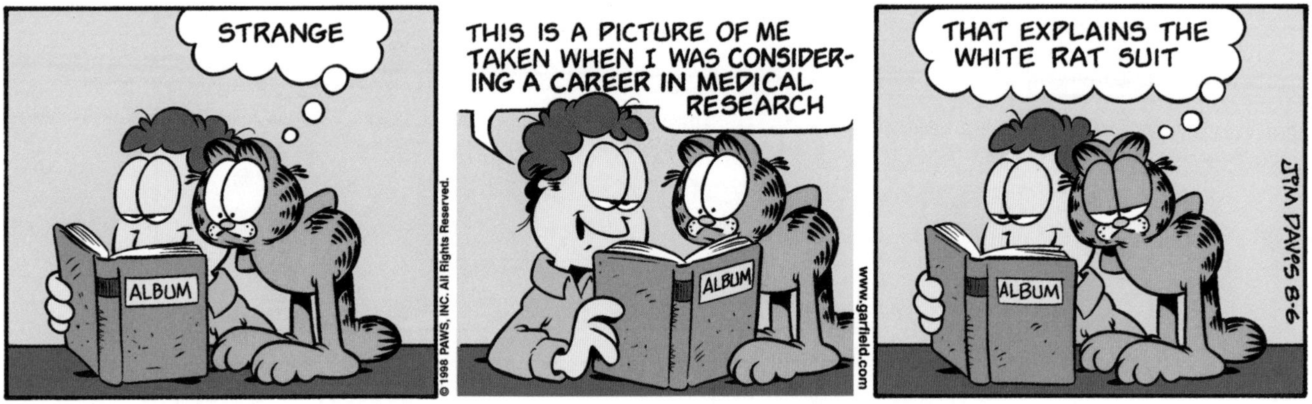
STRANGE
THIS IS A PICTURE OF ME TAKEN WHEN I WAS CONSIDER-ING A CAREER IN MEDICAL RESEARCH
THAT EXPLAINS THE WHITE RAT SUIT
ALBUM
JIM DAVIS 8-6
www.garfield.com

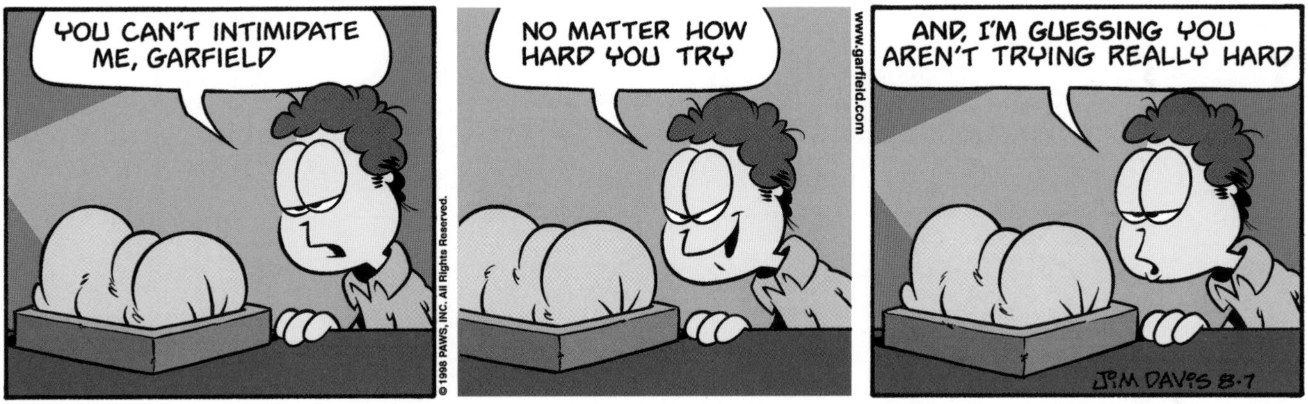
YOU CAN'T INTIMIDATE ME, GARFIELD
NO MATTER HOW HARD YOU TRY
AND, I'M GUESSING YOU AREN'T TRYING REALLY HARD
JIM DAVIS 8-7
www.garfield.com

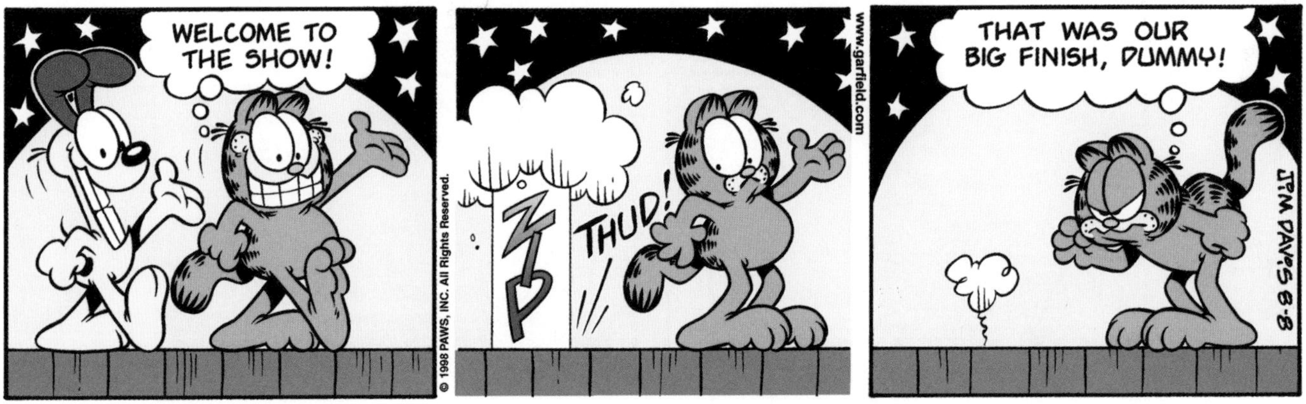
WELCOME TO THE SHOW!
ZIP
THUD!
THAT WAS OUR BIG FINISH, DUMMY!
JIM DAVIS 8-8
www.garfield.com

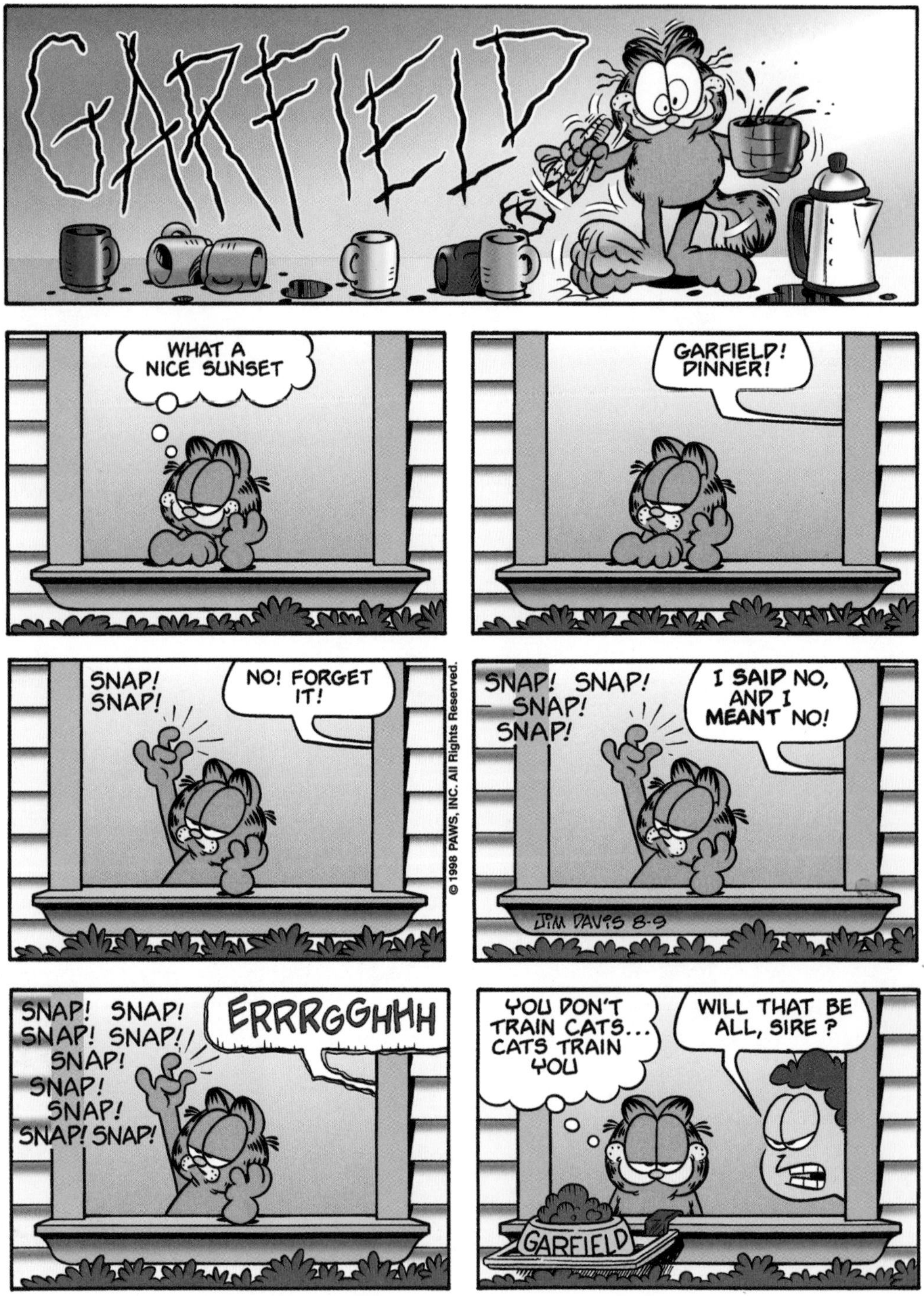
GARFIELD
WHAT A NICE SUNSET
GARFIELD! DINNER!
SNAP! SNAP!
NO! FORGET IT!
© 1998 PAWS, INC. All Rights Reserved.
SNAP! SNAP! SNAP! SNAP!
I SAID NO, AND I MEANT NO!
JIM DAVIS 8-9
SNAP! SNAP! SNAP! SNAP! SNAP! SNAP! SNAP! SNAP! SNAP!
ERRRGGHHH
YOU DON'T TRAIN CATS... CATS TRAIN YOU
WILL THAT BE ALL, SIRE ?
GARFIELD

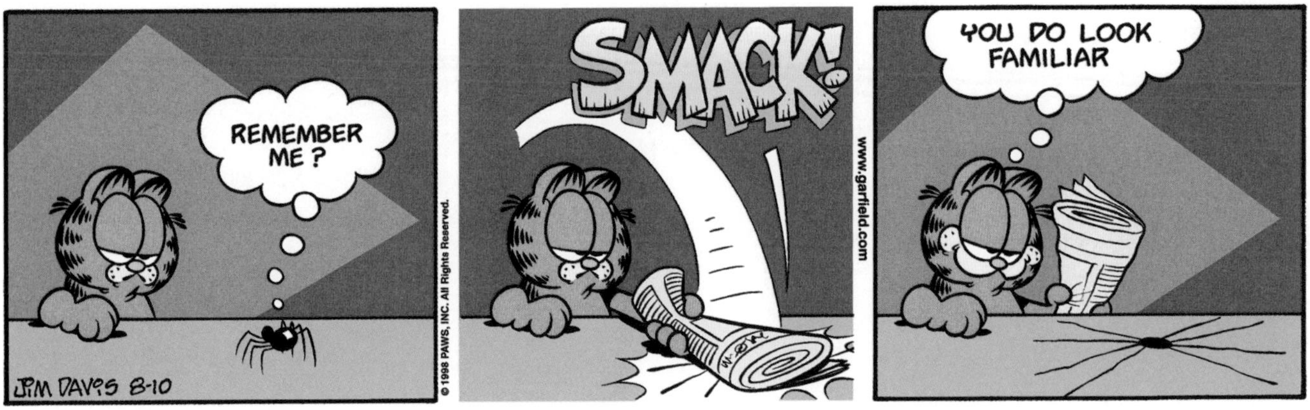
REMEMBER ME?
JIM DAVIS 8-10
© 1998 PAWS, INC. All Rights Reserved.
SMACK!
www.garfield.com
YOU DO LOOK FAMILIAR

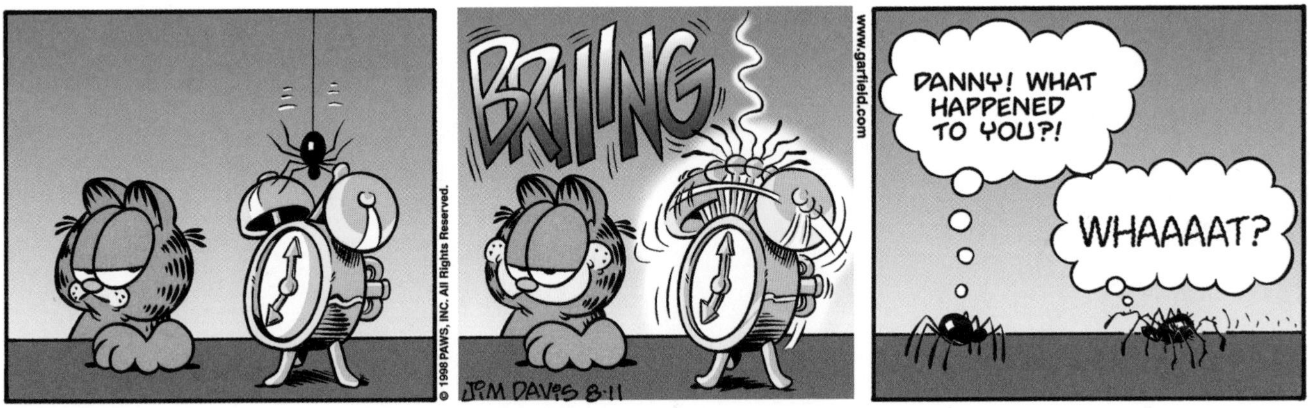
© 1998 PAWS, INC. All Rights Reserved.
BRIIING
JIM DAVIS 8-11
www.garfield.com
DANNY! WHAT HAPPENED TO YOU?!
WHAAAAT?

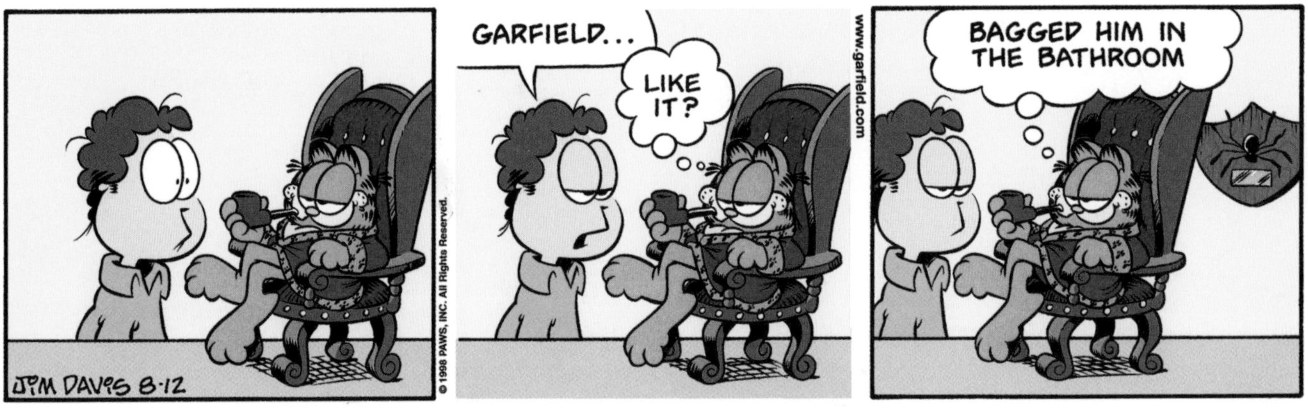
JIM DAVIS 8-12
© 1998 PAWS, INC. All Rights Reserved.
GARFIELD...
LIKE IT?
www.garfield.com
BAGGED HIM IN THE BATHROOM

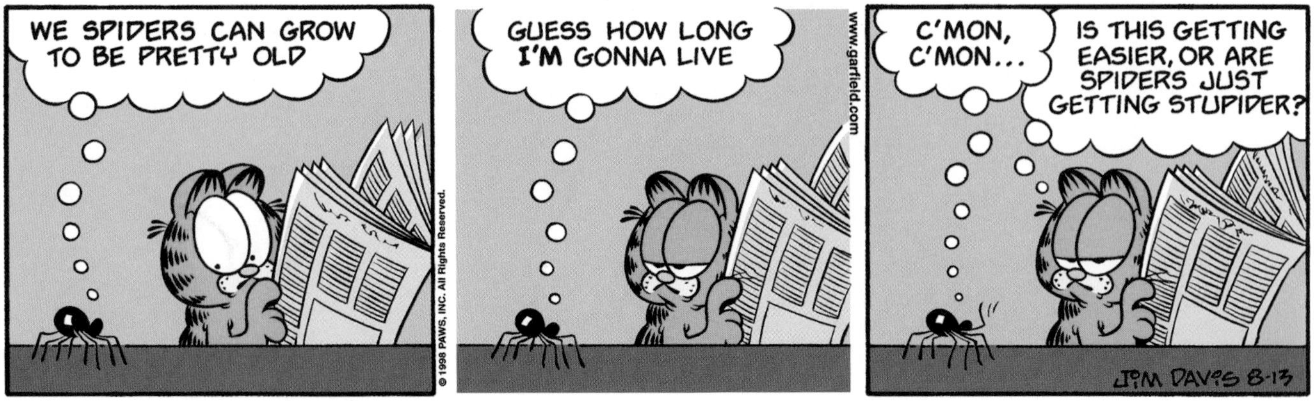
WE SPIDERS CAN GROW TO BE PRETTY OLD
© 1998 PAWS, INC. All Rights Reserved.
GUESS HOW LONG **I'M** GONNA LIVE
www.garfield.com
C'MON, C'MON...
IS THIS GETTING EASIER, OR ARE SPIDERS JUST GETTING STUPIDER?
JIM DAVIS 8-13

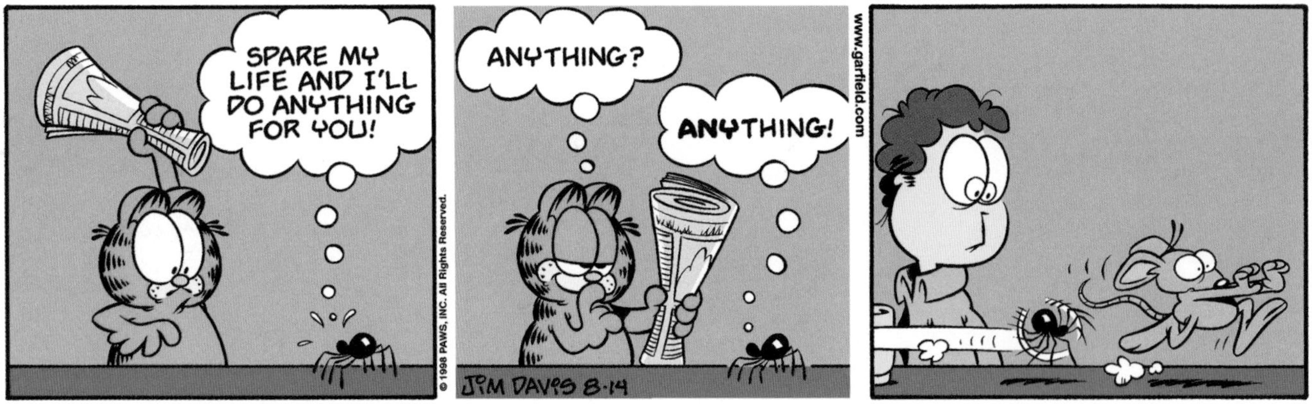
SPARE MY LIFE AND I'LL DO ANYTHING FOR YOU!
© 1998 PAWS, INC. All Rights Reserved.
ANYTHING?
ANYTHING!
JIM DAVIS 8-14
www.garfield.com

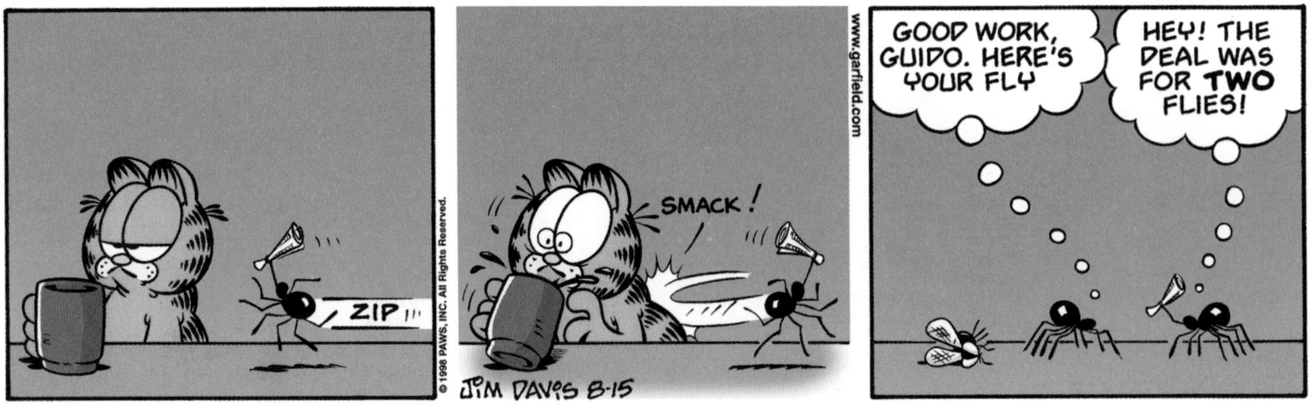
ZIP
© 1998 PAWS, INC. All Rights Reserved.
SMACK!
JIM DAVIS 8-15
www.garfield.com
GOOD WORK, GUIDO. HERE'S YOUR FLY
HEY! THE DEAL WAS FOR **TWO** FLIES!

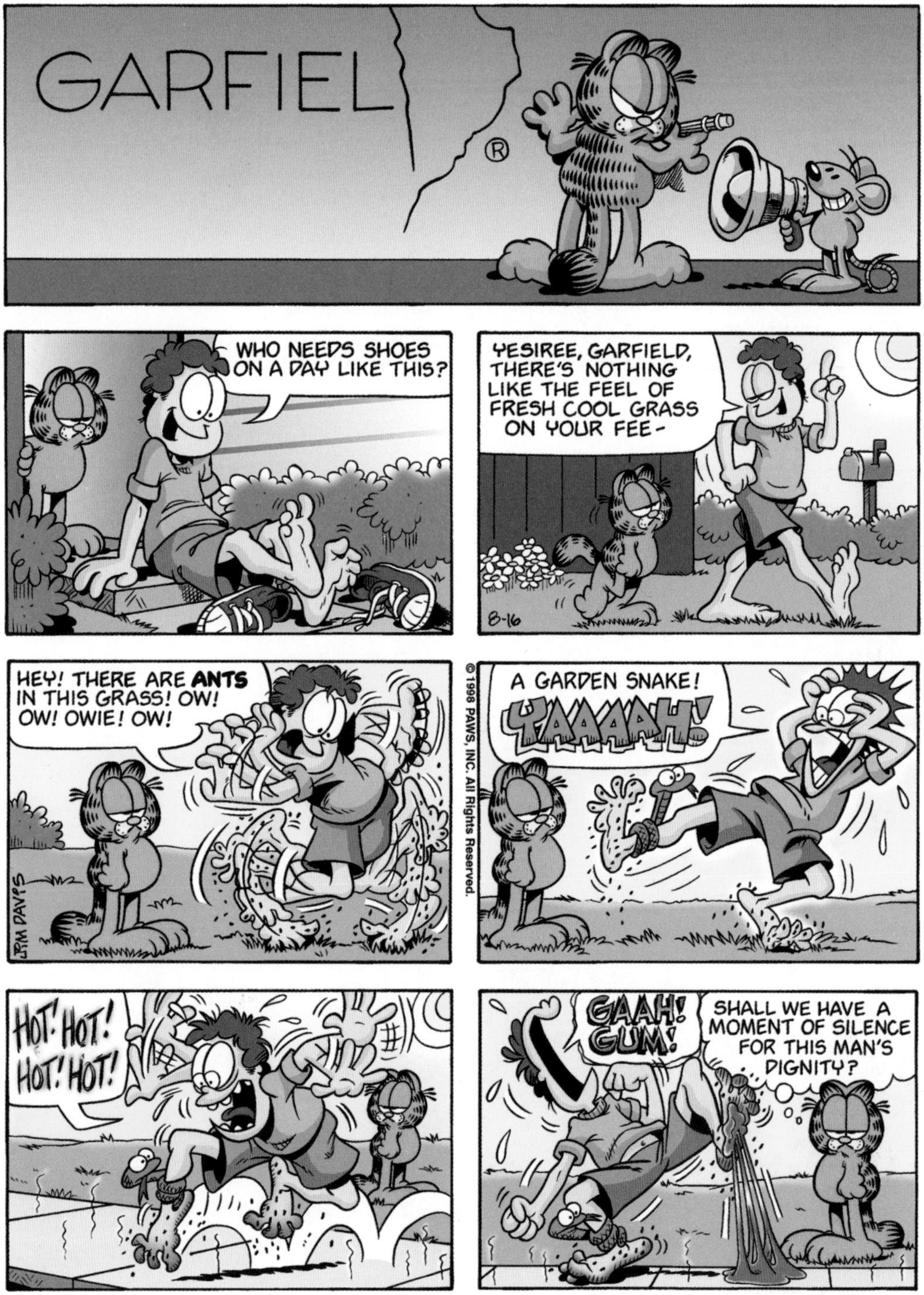
GARFIEL
WHO NEEDS SHOES ON A DAY LIKE THIS?
YESIREE, GARFIELD, THERE'S NOTHING LIKE THE FEEL OF FRESH COOL GRASS ON YOUR FEE-
8-16
HEY! THERE ARE **ANTS** IN THIS GRASS! OW! OW! OWIE! OW!
JPM DAVIS
© 1998 PAWS, INC. All Rights Reserved.
A GARDEN SNAKE!
YAAAAH!
HOT! HOT! HOT! HOT!
GAAH! GUM!
SHALL WE HAVE A MOMENT OF SILENCE FOR THIS MAN'S DIGNITY?

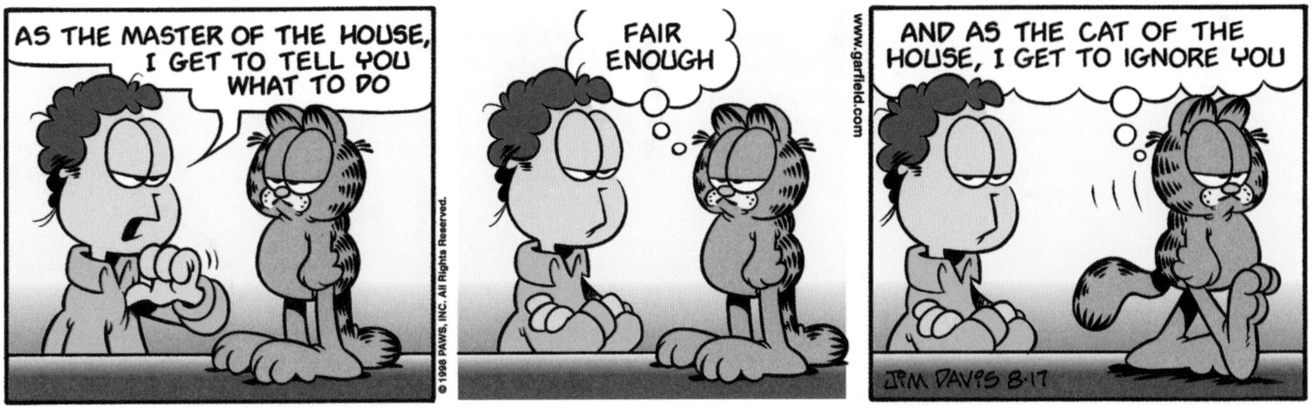
AS THE MASTER OF THE HOUSE, I GET TO TELL YOU WHAT TO DO
FAIR ENOUGH
AND AS THE CAT OF THE HOUSE, I GET TO IGNORE YOU
© 1998 PAWS, INC. All Rights Reserved.
www.garfield.com
JIM DAVIS 8-17

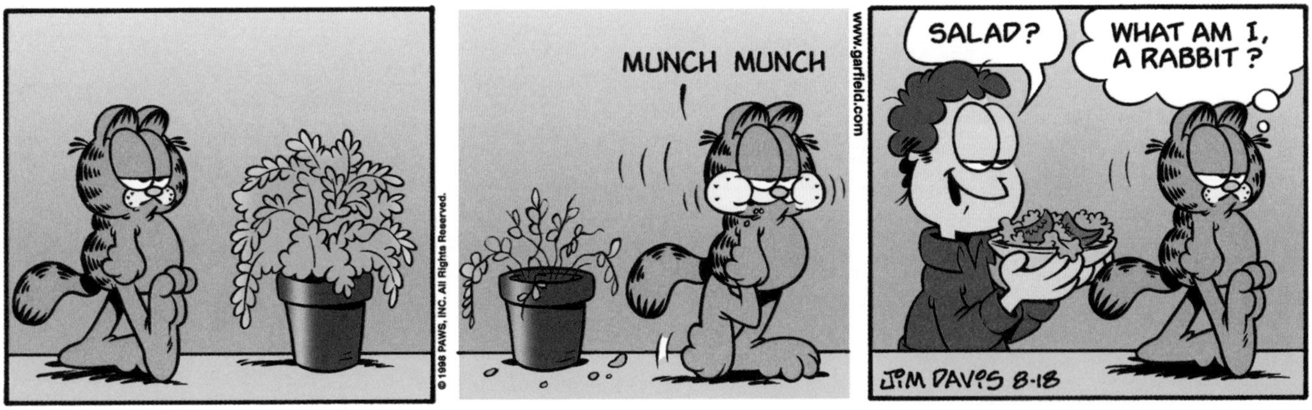
MUNCH MUNCH
SALAD?
WHAT AM I, A RABBIT?
© 1998 PAWS, INC. All Rights Reserved.
www.garfield.com
JIM DAVIS 8-18

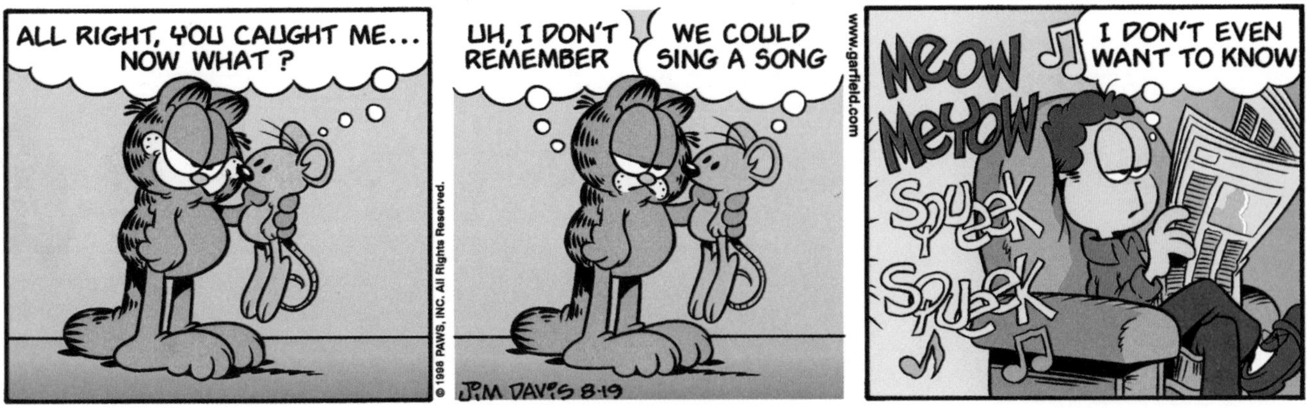
ALL RIGHT, YOU CAUGHT ME... NOW WHAT?
UH, I DON'T REMEMBER
WE COULD SING A SONG
MEOW
MEYOW
SQUEEK
SQUEEK
I DON'T EVEN WANT TO KNOW
© 1998 PAWS, INC. All Rights Reserved.
www.garfield.com
JIM DAVIS 8-19

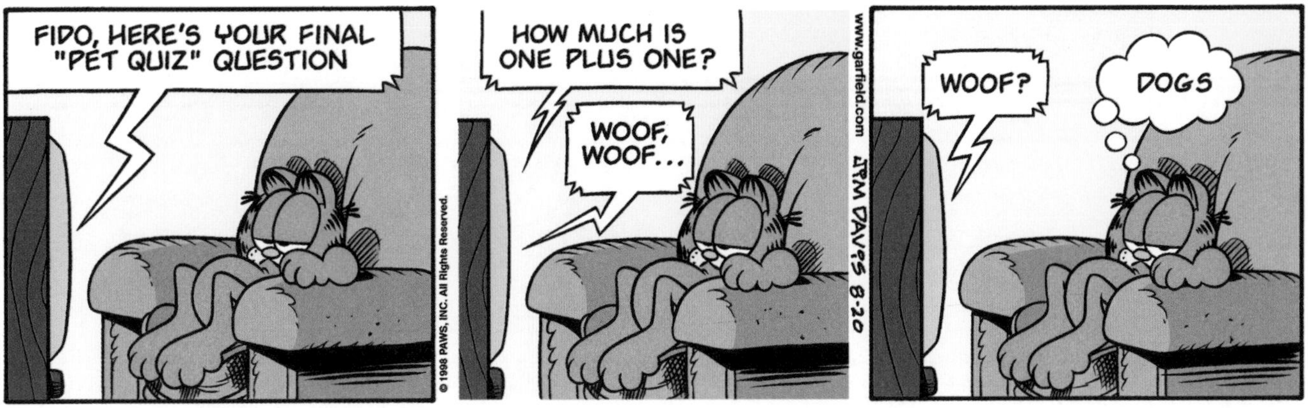
FIDO, HERE'S YOUR FINAL "PET QUIZ" QUESTION
HOW MUCH IS ONE PLUS ONE?
WOOF, WOOF...
WOOF?
DOGS
© 1998 PAWS, INC. All Rights Reserved.
www.garfield.com
JIM DAVIS 8-20

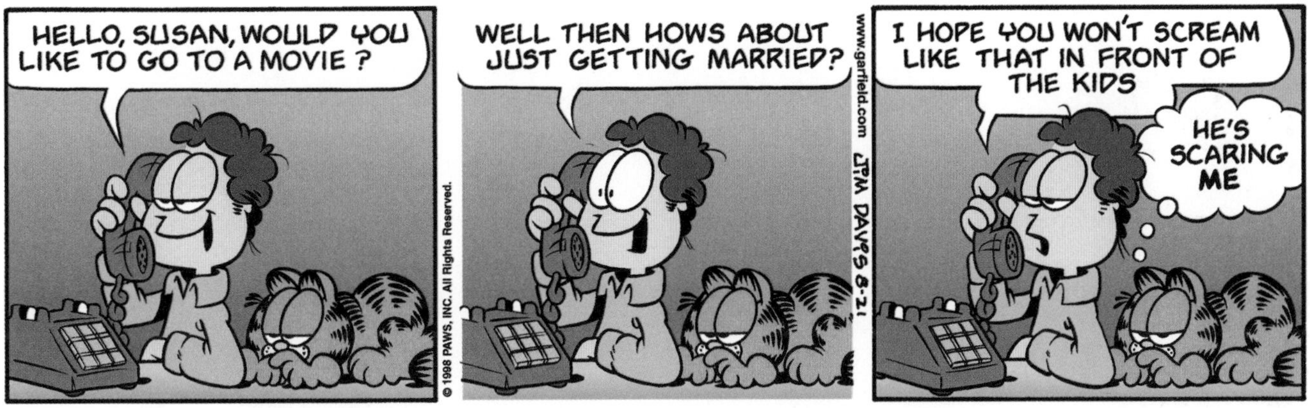
HELLO, SUSAN, WOULD YOU LIKE TO GO TO A MOVIE ?
WELL THEN HOWS ABOUT JUST GETTING MARRIED?
I HOPE YOU WON'T SCREAM LIKE THAT IN FRONT OF THE KIDS
HE'S SCARING ME
© 1998 PAWS, INC. All Rights Reserved.
www.garfield.com
JIM DAVIS 8-21

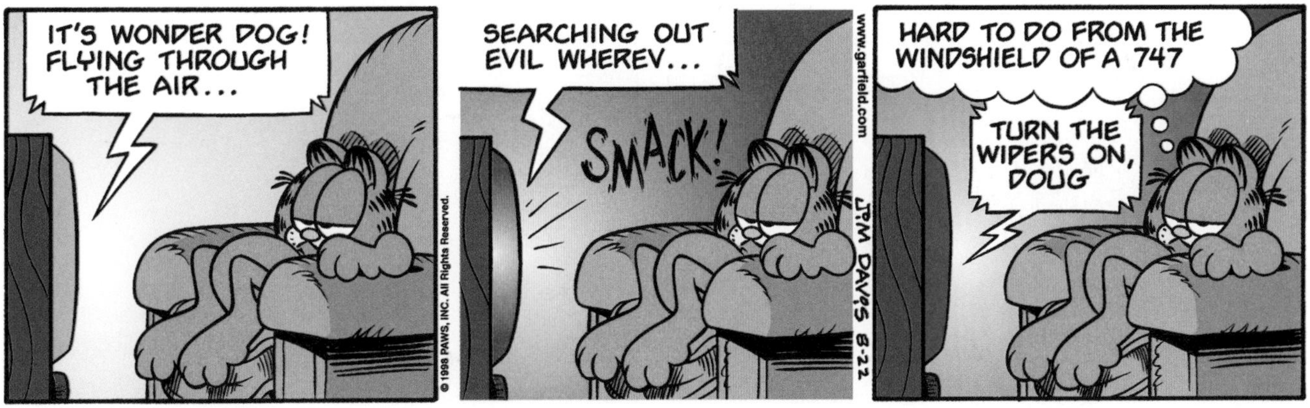
IT'S WONDER DOG! FLYING THROUGH THE AIR...
SEARCHING OUT EVIL WHEREV...
SMACK!
HARD TO DO FROM THE WINDSHIELD OF A 747
TURN THE WIPERS ON, DOUG
© 1998 PAWS, INC. All Rights Reserved.
www.garfield.com
JIM DAVIS 8-22

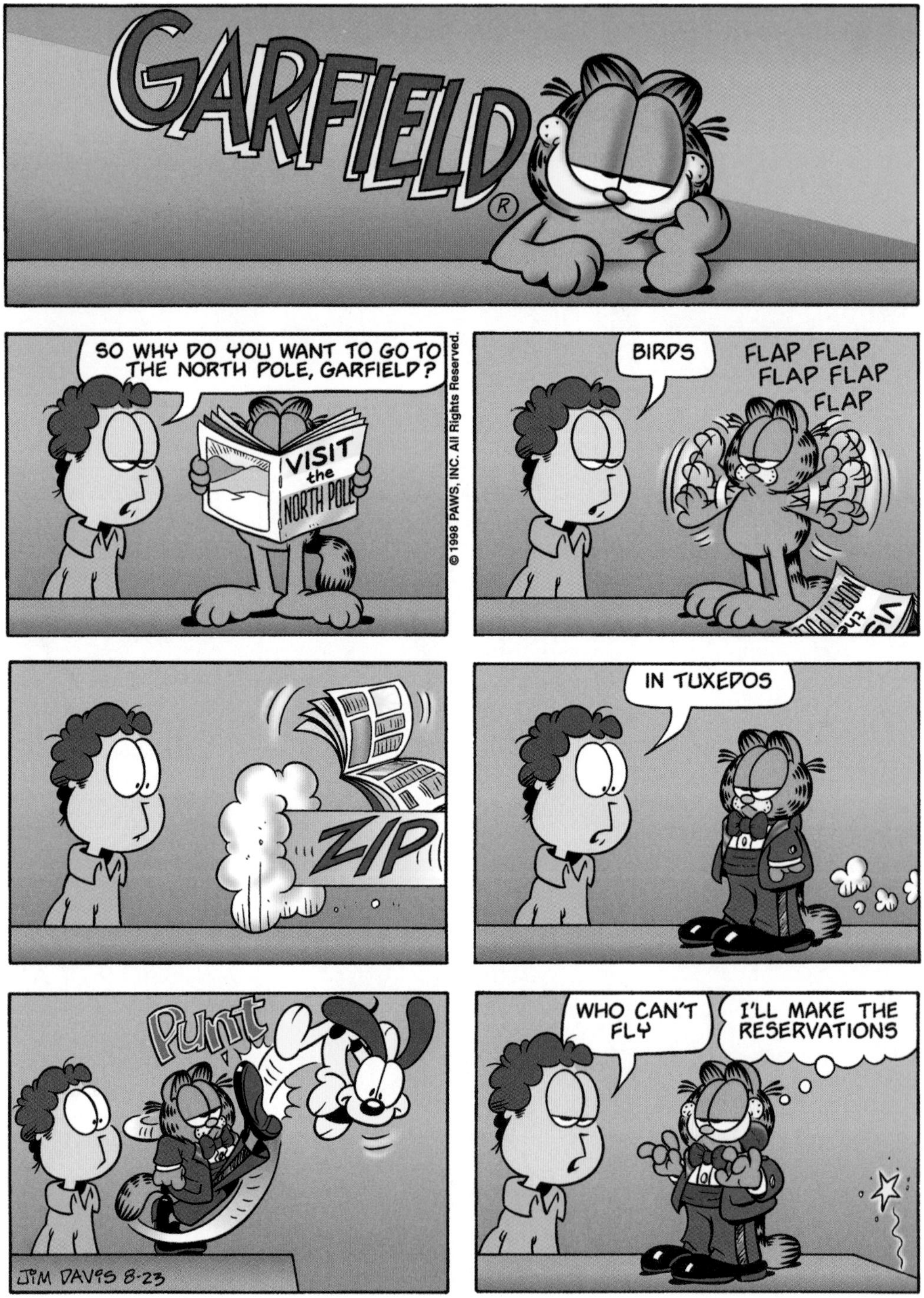
GARFIELD
SO WHY DO YOU WANT TO GO TO THE NORTH POLE, GARFIELD?
VISIT the NORTH POLE
© 1998 PAWS, INC. All Rights Reserved.
BIRDS
FLAP FLAP FLAP FLAP FLAP
ZIP
IN TUXEDOS
PUNT
JIM DAVIS 8-23
WHO CAN'T FLY
I'LL MAKE THE RESERVATIONS

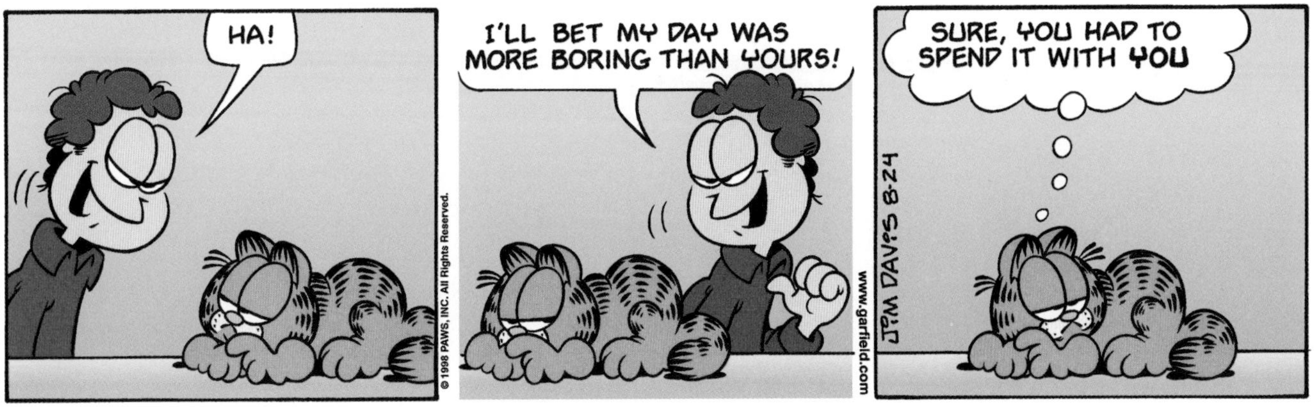
HA!
I'LL BET MY DAY WAS MORE BORING THAN YOURS!
SURE, YOU HAD TO SPEND IT WITH **YOU**
© 1998 PAWS, INC. All Rights Reserved.
www.garfield.com
JIM DAVIS 8-24

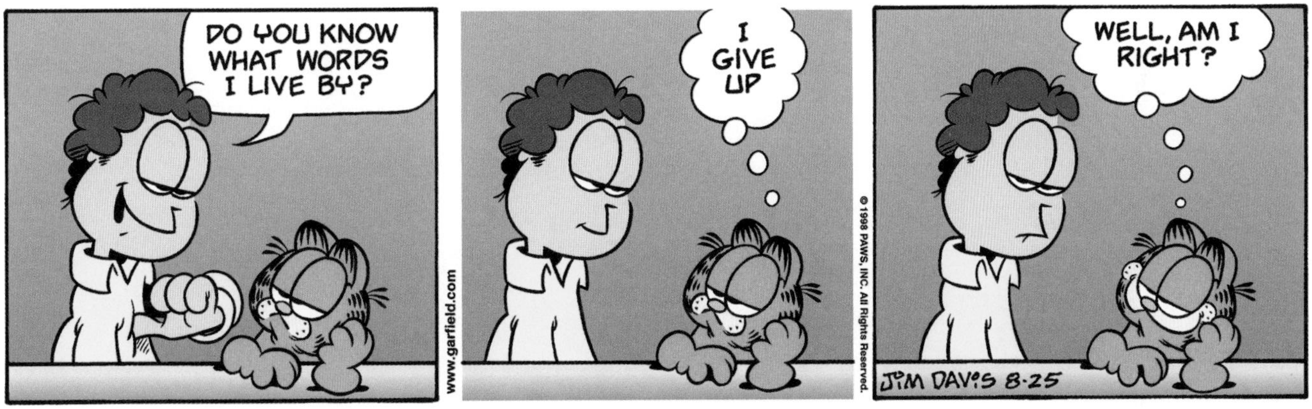
DO YOU KNOW WHAT WORDS I LIVE BY?
I GIVE UP
WELL, AM I RIGHT?
www.garfield.com
© 1998 PAWS, INC. All Rights Reserved.
JIM DAVIS 8-25

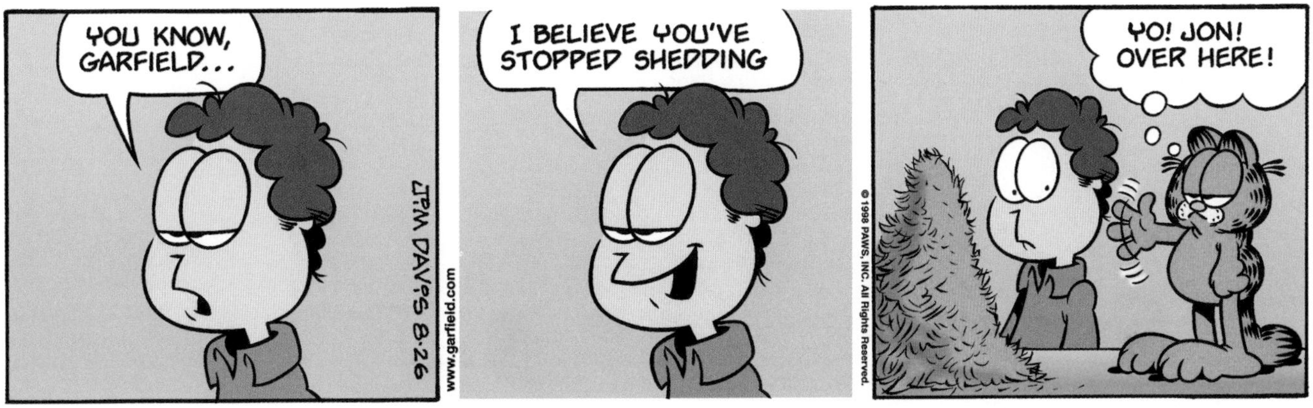
YOU KNOW, GARFIELD...
I BELIEVE YOU'VE STOPPED SHEDDING
YO! JON! OVER HERE!
JIM DAVIS 8-26
www.garfield.com
© 1998 PAWS, INC. All Rights Reserved.

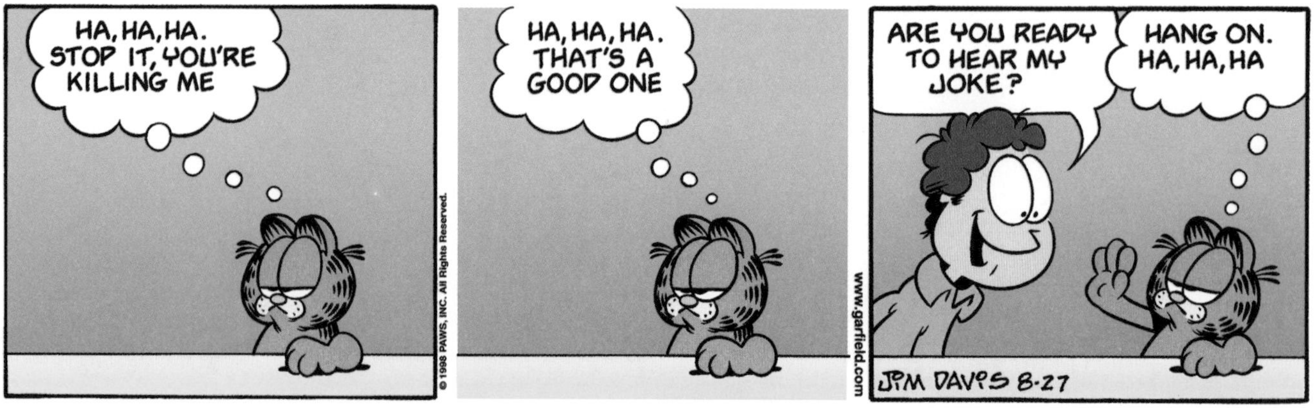
HA, HA, HA.
STOP IT, YOU'RE
KILLING ME
HA, HA, HA.
THAT'S A
GOOD ONE
ARE YOU READY
TO HEAR MY
JOKE?
HANG ON.
HA, HA, HA
© 1998 PAWS, INC. All Rights Reserved.
www.garfield.com
JIM DAVIS 8-27

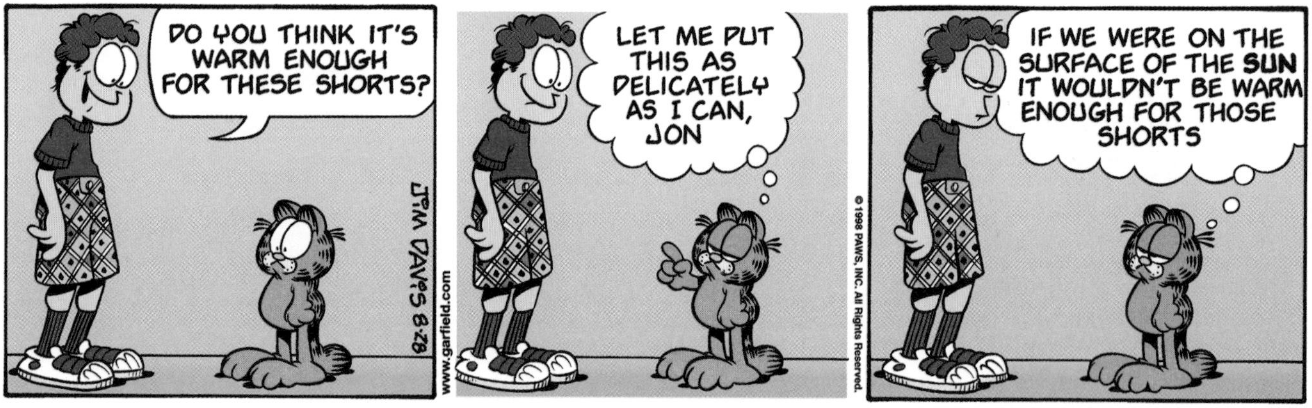
DO YOU THINK IT'S
WARM ENOUGH
FOR THESE SHORTS?
JIM DAVIS 8-28
www.garfield.com
LET ME PUT
THIS AS
DELICATELY
AS I CAN,
JON
© 1998 PAWS, INC. All Rights Reserved.
IF WE WERE ON THE
SURFACE OF THE SUN
IT WOULDN'T BE WARM
ENOUGH FOR THOSE
SHORTS

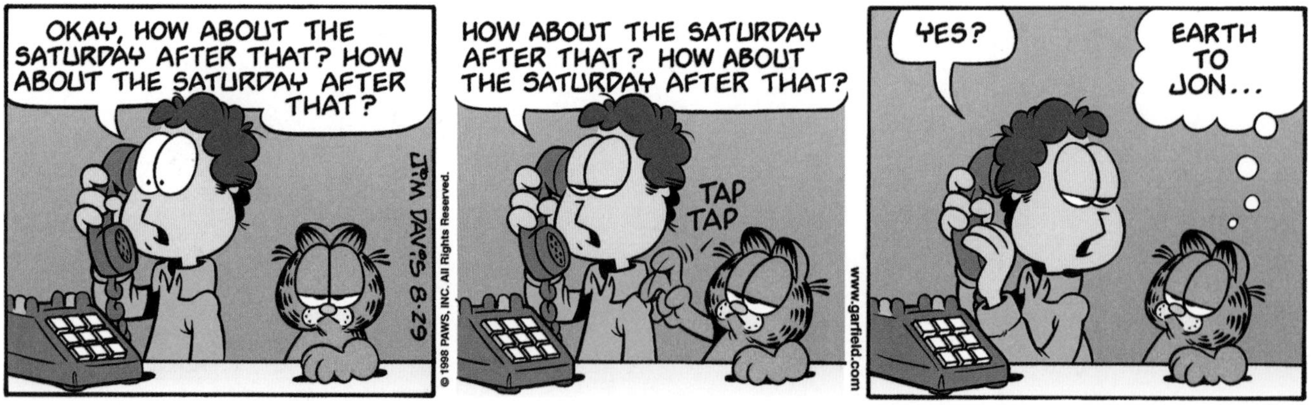
OKAY, HOW ABOUT THE
SATURDAY AFTER THAT? HOW
ABOUT THE SATURDAY AFTER
THAT?
JIM DAVIS 8-29
© 1998 PAWS, INC. All Rights Reserved.
HOW ABOUT THE SATURDAY
AFTER THAT? HOW ABOUT
THE SATURDAY AFTER THAT?
TAP
TAP
www.garfield.com
YES?
EARTH
TO
JON...

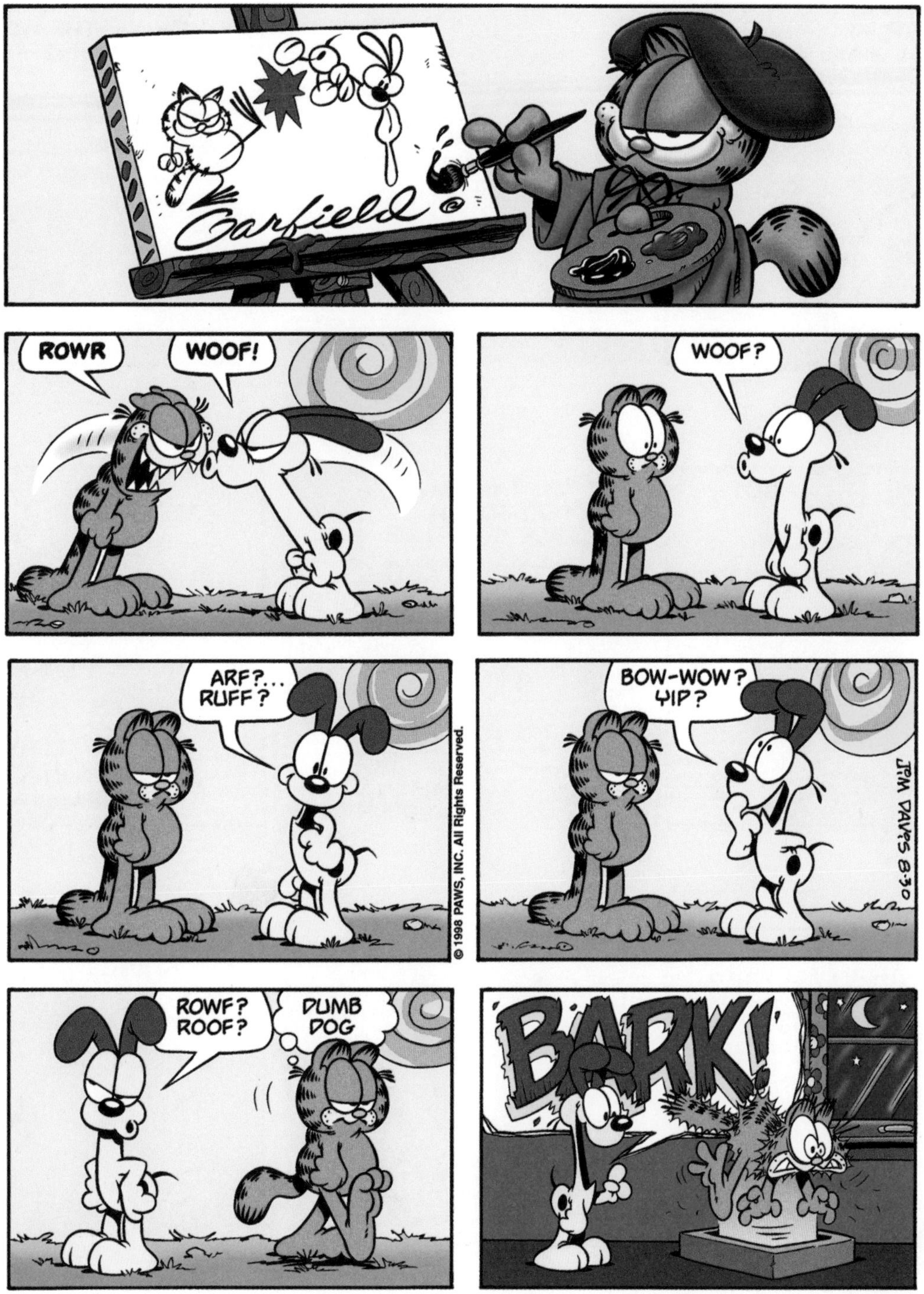
Garfield
ROWR
WOOF!
WOOF?
ARF?... RUFF?
BOW-WOW? YIP?
JIM DAVIS 8-30
ROWF? ROOF?
DUMB DOG
BARK!
© 1998 PAWS, INC. All Rights Reserved.

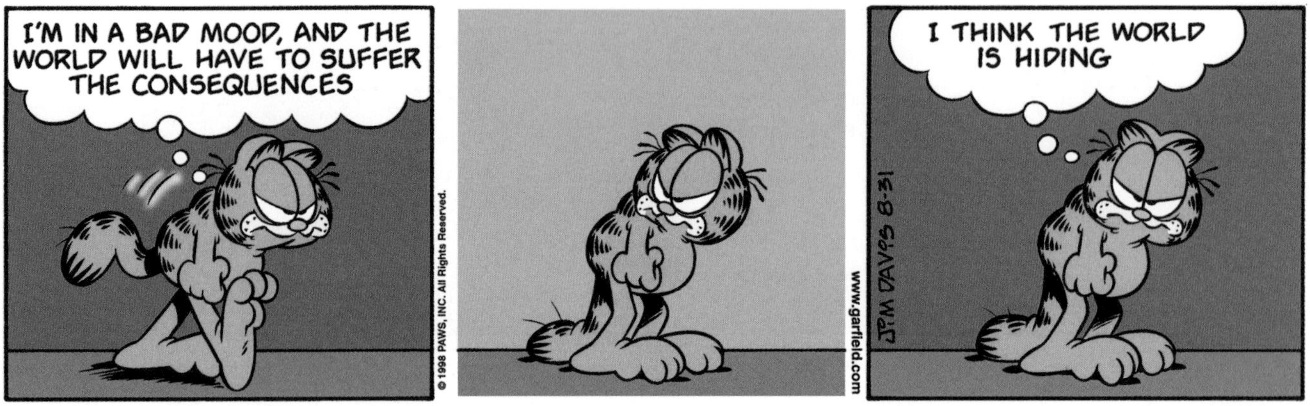
I'M IN A BAD MOOD, AND THE WORLD WILL HAVE TO SUFFER THE CONSEQUENCES
© 1998 PAWS, INC. All Rights Reserved.
www.garfield.com
JIM DAVIS 8-31
I THINK THE WORLD IS HIDING

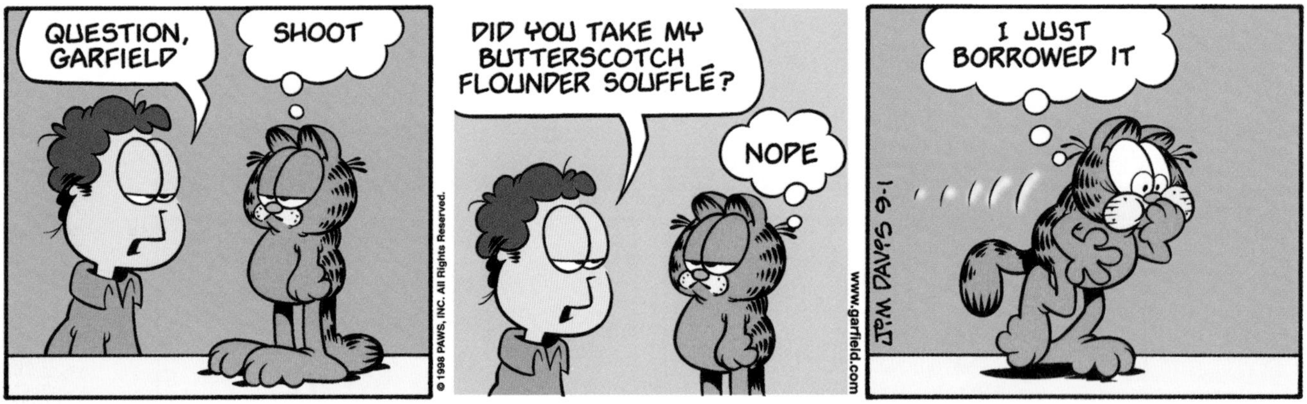
QUESTION, GARFIELD
SHOOT
© 1998 PAWS, INC. All Rights Reserved.
DID YOU TAKE MY BUTTERSCOTCH FLOUNDER SOUFFLÉ?
NOPE
www.garfield.com
JIM DAVIS 9-1
I JUST BORROWED IT

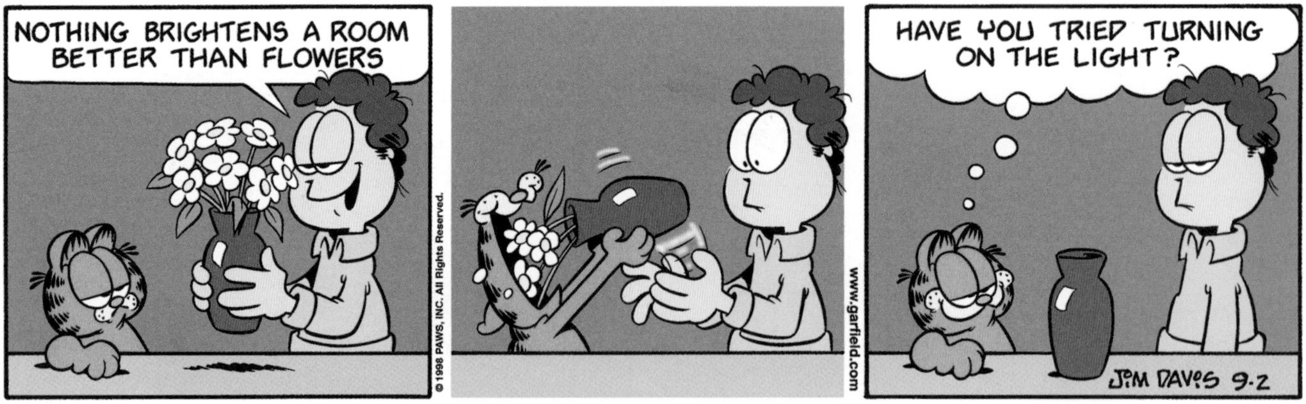
NOTHING BRIGHTENS A ROOM BETTER THAN FLOWERS
© 1998 PAWS, INC. All Rights Reserved.
www.garfield.com
HAVE YOU TRIED TURNING ON THE LIGHT?
JIM DAVIS 9-2

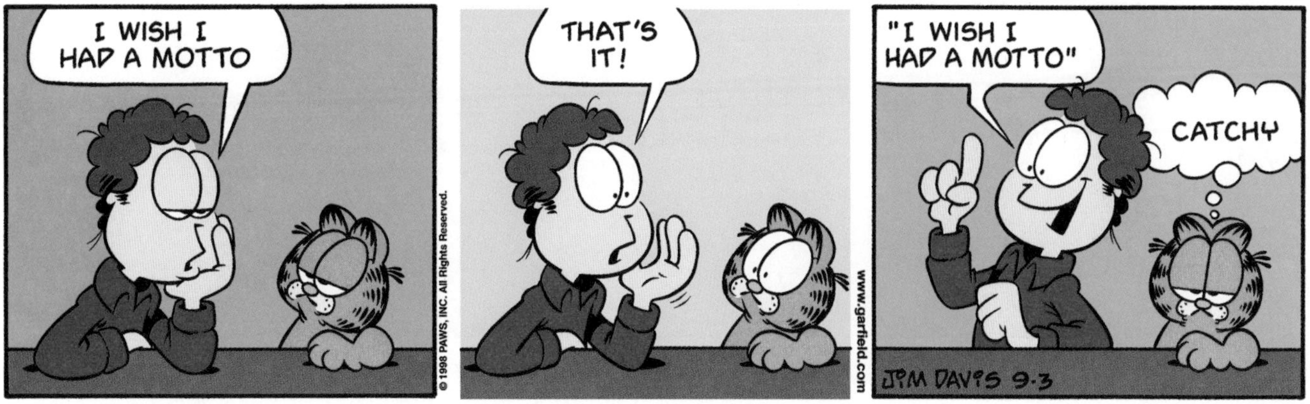
I WISH I HAD A MOTTO
THAT'S IT!
"I WISH I HAD A MOTTO"
CATCHY
© 1998 PAWS, INC. All Rights Reserved.
www.garfield.com
JIM DAVIS 9-3

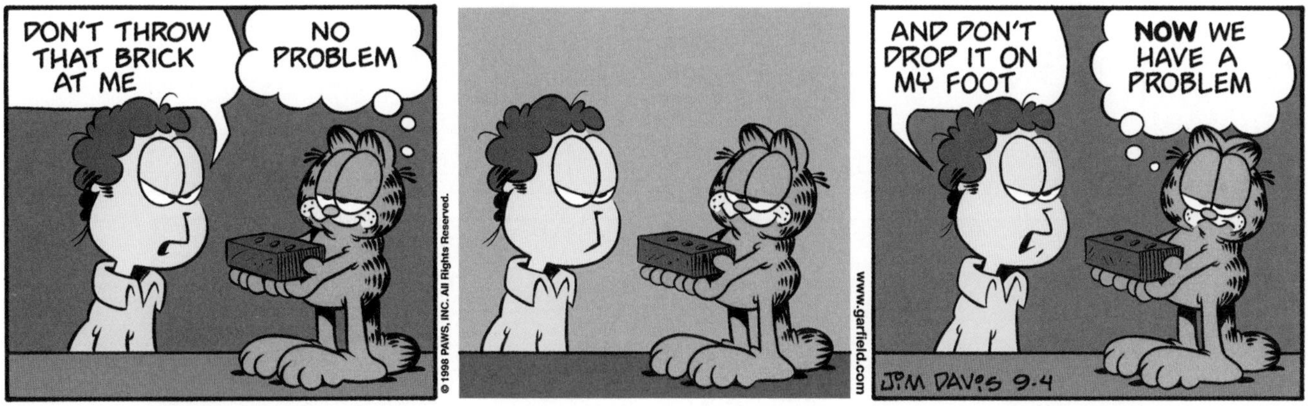
DON'T THROW THAT BRICK AT ME
NO PROBLEM
AND DON'T DROP IT ON MY FOOT
NOW WE HAVE A PROBLEM
© 1998 PAWS, INC. All Rights Reserved.
www.garfield.com
JIM DAVIS 9-4

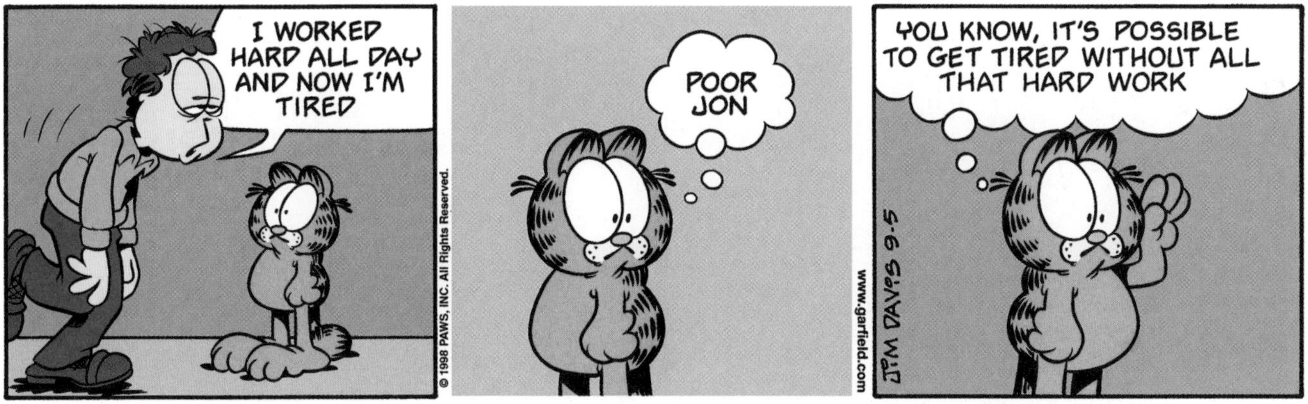
I WORKED HARD ALL DAY AND NOW I'M TIRED
POOR JON
YOU KNOW, IT'S POSSIBLE TO GET TIRED WITHOUT ALL THAT HARD WORK
© 1998 PAWS, INC. All Rights Reserved.
www.garfield.com
JIM DAVIS 9-5

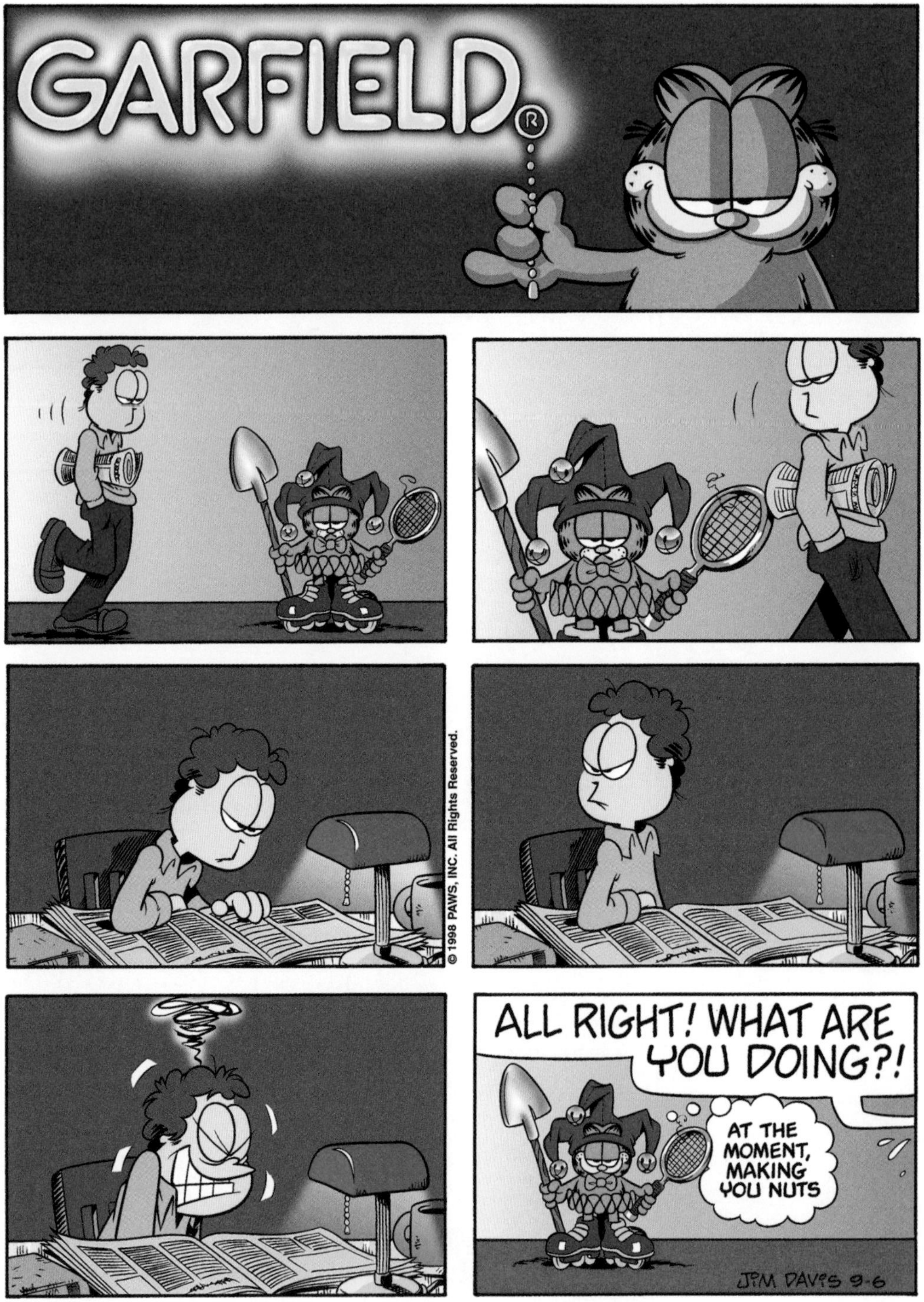
GARFIELD®
© 1998 PAWS, INC. All Rights Reserved.
ALL RIGHT! WHAT ARE YOU DOING?!
AT THE MOMENT, MAKING YOU NUTS
JIM DAVIS 9-6

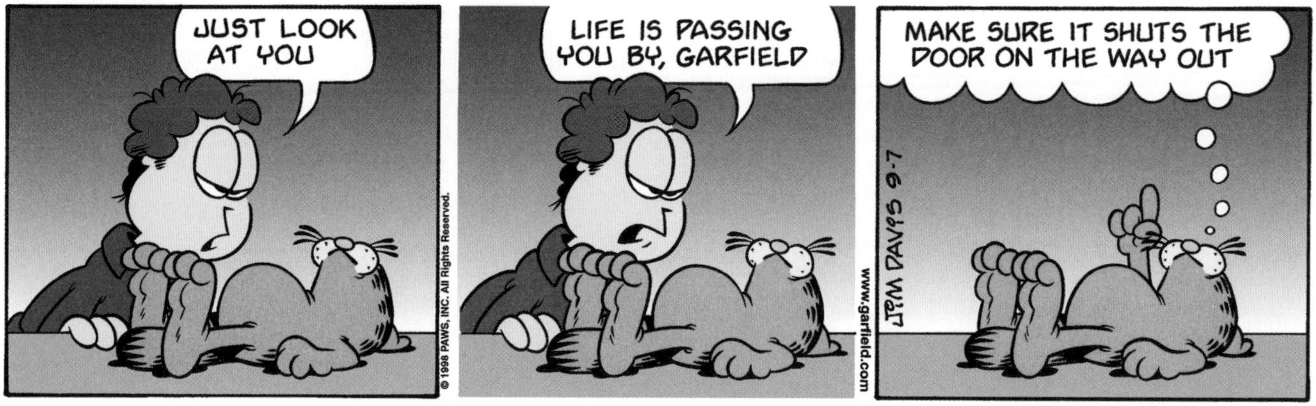
JUST LOOK AT YOU
© 1998 PAWS, INC. All Rights Reserved.
LIFE IS PASSING YOU BY, GARFIELD
www.garfield.com
JIM DAVIS 9-7
MAKE SURE IT SHUTS THE DOOR ON THE WAY OUT

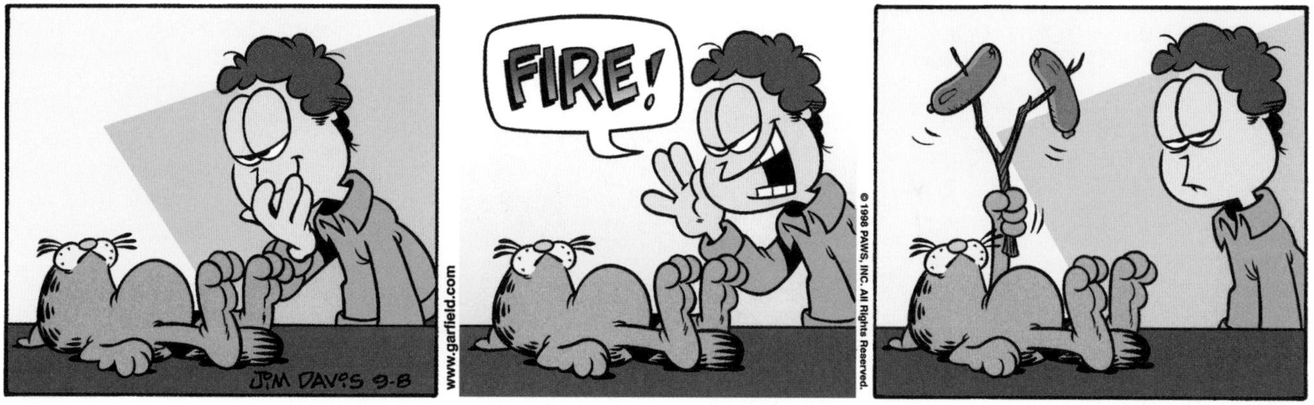
JIM DAVIS 9-8
www.garfield.com
FIRE!
© 1998 PAWS, INC. All Rights Reserved.

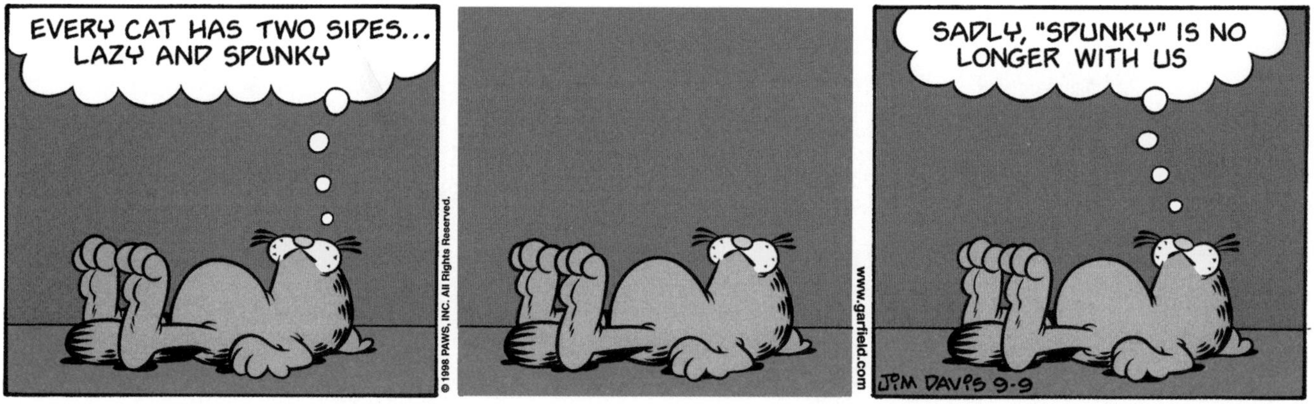
EVERY CAT HAS TWO SIDES... LAZY AND SPUNKY
© 1998 PAWS, INC. All Rights Reserved.
www.garfield.com
SADLY, "SPUNKY" IS NO LONGER WITH US
JIM DAVIS 9-9

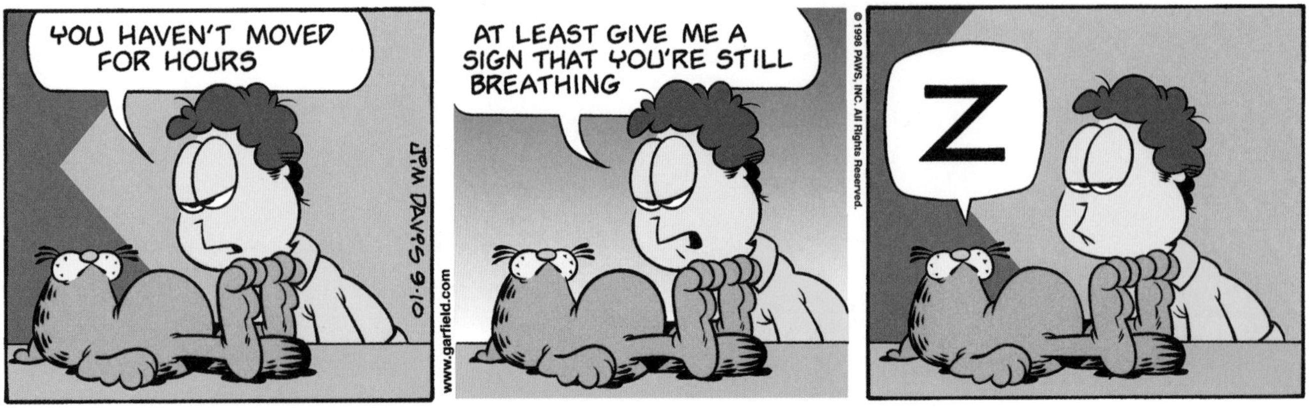
YOU HAVEN'T MOVED FOR HOURS
JIM DAVIS 9-10
www.garfield.com
AT LEAST GIVE ME A SIGN THAT YOU'RE STILL BREATHING
© 1998 PAWS, INC. All Rights Reserved.
Z

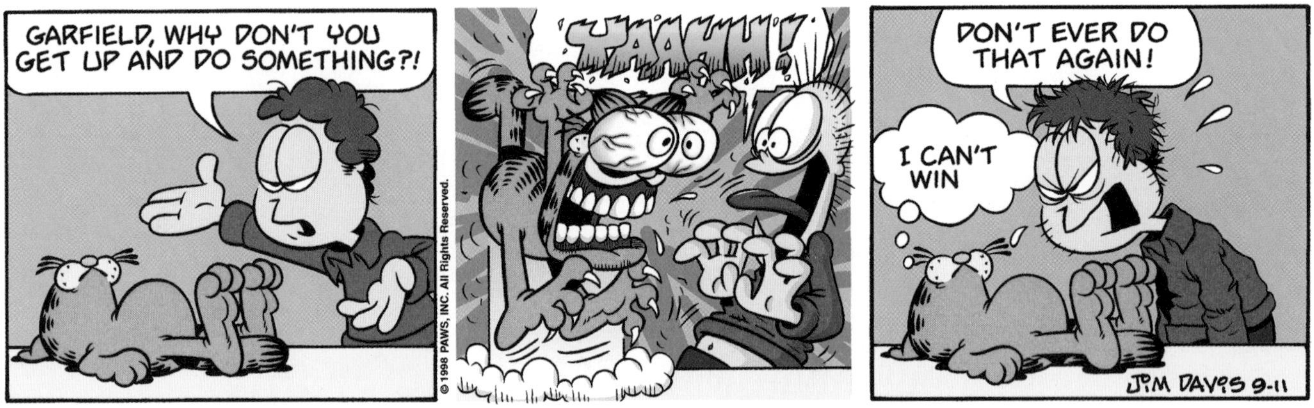
GARFIELD, WHY DON'T YOU GET UP AND DO SOMETHING?!
© 1998 PAWS, INC. All Rights Reserved.
YAAHH!
DON'T EVER DO THAT AGAIN!
I CAN'T WIN
JIM DAVIS 9-11

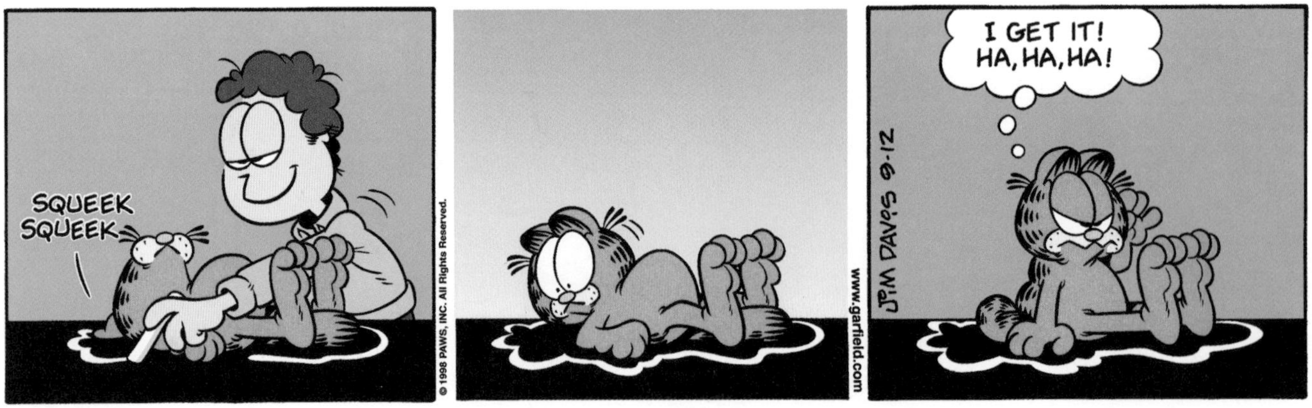
SQUEEK SQUEEK
© 1998 PAWS, INC. All Rights Reserved.
www.garfield.com
JIM DAVIS 9-12
I GET IT! HA, HA, HA!

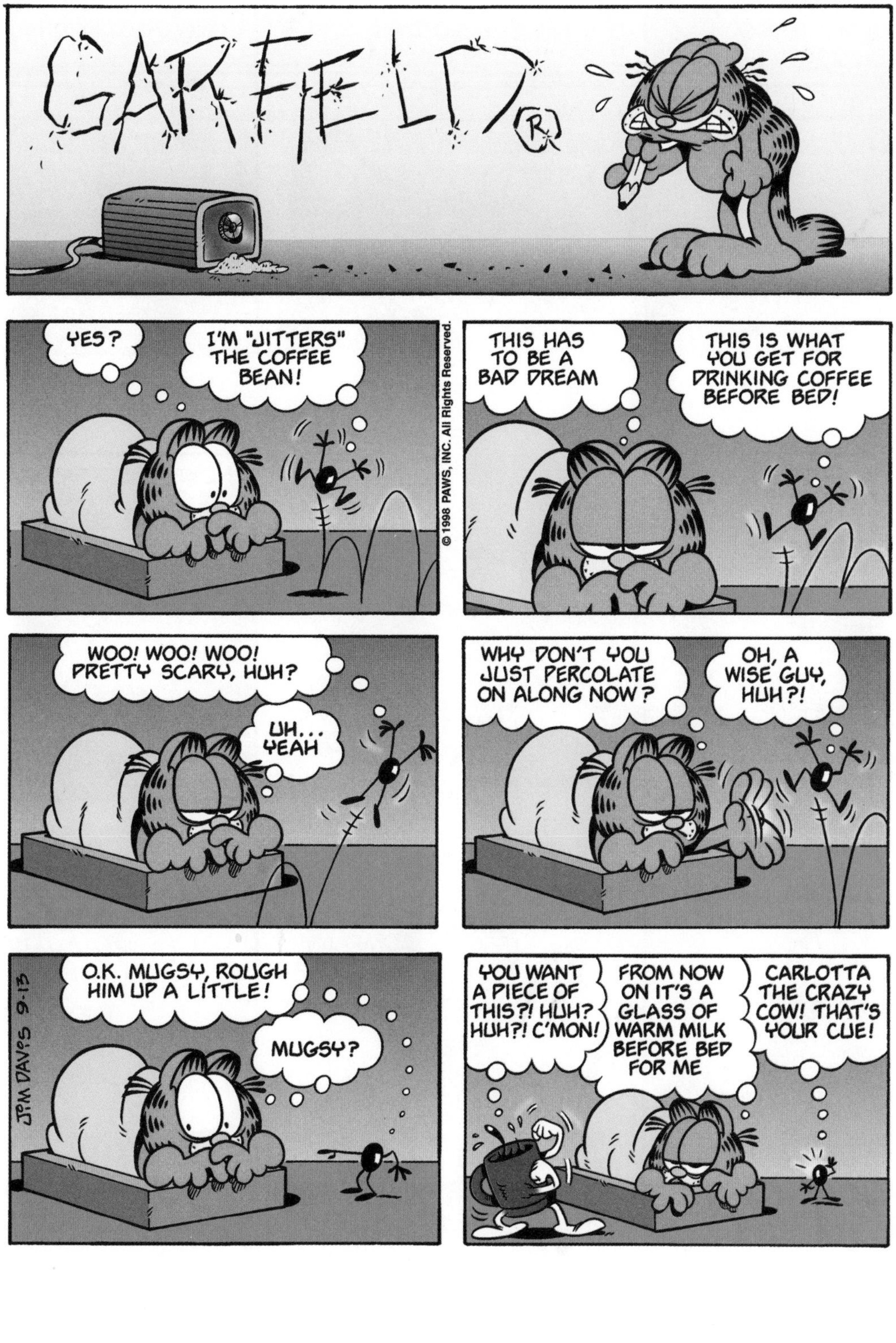
GARFIELD®
© 1998 PAWS, INC. All Rights Reserved.
YES?
I'M "JITTERS" THE COFFEE BEAN!
THIS HAS TO BE A BAD DREAM
THIS IS WHAT YOU GET FOR DRINKING COFFEE BEFORE BED!
WOO! WOO! WOO! PRETTY SCARY, HUH?
UH... YEAH
WHY DON'T YOU JUST PERCOLATE ON ALONG NOW?
OH, A WISE GUY, HUH?!
JIM DAVIS 9-13
O.K. MUGSY, ROUGH HIM UP A LITTLE!
MUGSY?
YOU WANT A PIECE OF THIS?! HUH? HUH?! C'MON!
FROM NOW ON IT'S A GLASS OF WARM MILK BEFORE BED FOR ME
CARLOTTA THE CRAZY COW! THAT'S YOUR CUE!

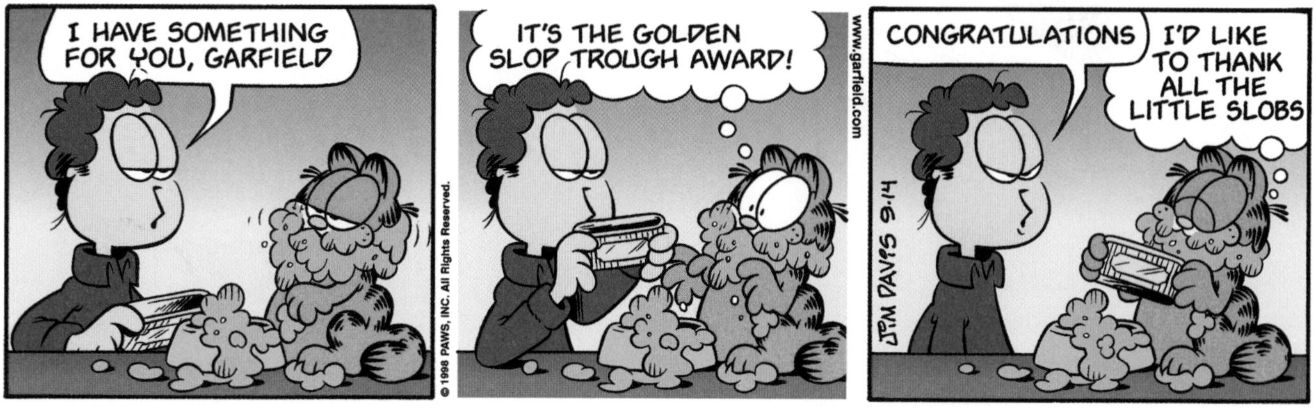
I HAVE SOMETHING FOR YOU, GARFIELD
© 1998 PAWS, INC. All Rights Reserved.
IT'S THE GOLDEN SLOP TROUGH AWARD!
www.garfield.com
JIM DAVIS 9-14
CONGRATULATIONS
I'D LIKE TO THANK ALL THE LITTLE SLOBS

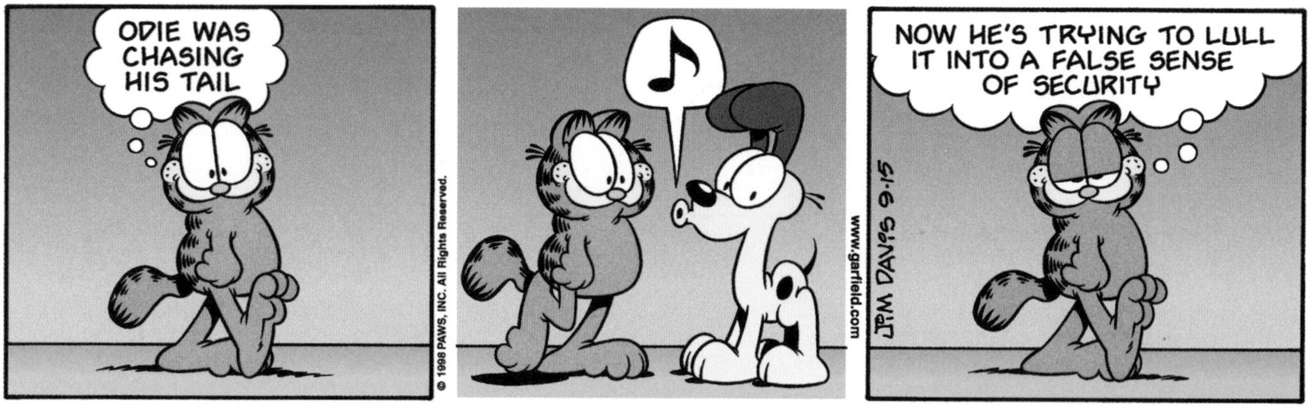
ODIE WAS CHASING HIS TAIL
© 1998 PAWS, INC. All Rights Reserved.
♪
www.garfield.com
JIM DAVIS 9-15
NOW HE'S TRYING TO LULL IT INTO A FALSE SENSE OF SECURITY

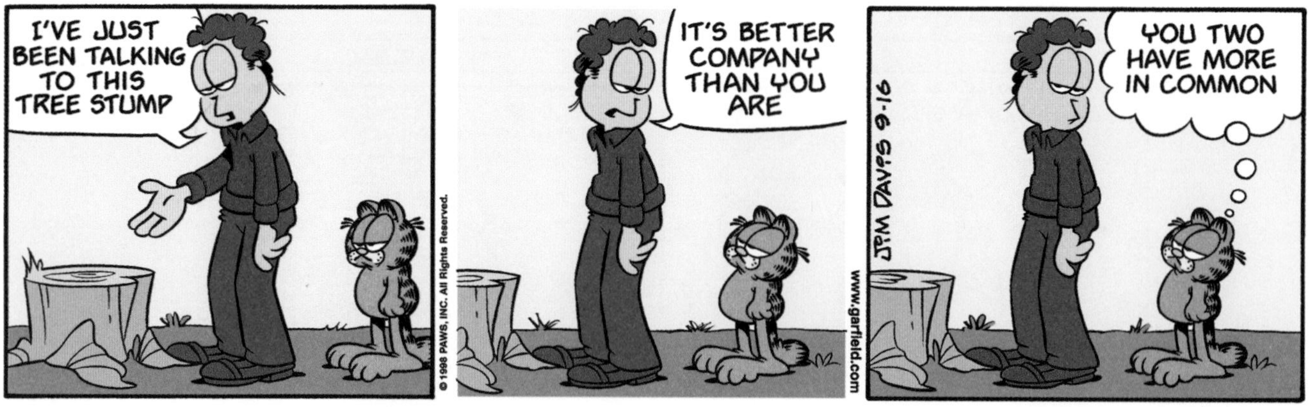
I'VE JUST BEEN TALKING TO THIS TREE STUMP
© 1998 PAWS, INC. All Rights Reserved.
IT'S BETTER COMPANY THAN YOU ARE
www.garfield.com
JIM DAVIS 9-16
YOU TWO HAVE MORE IN COMMON

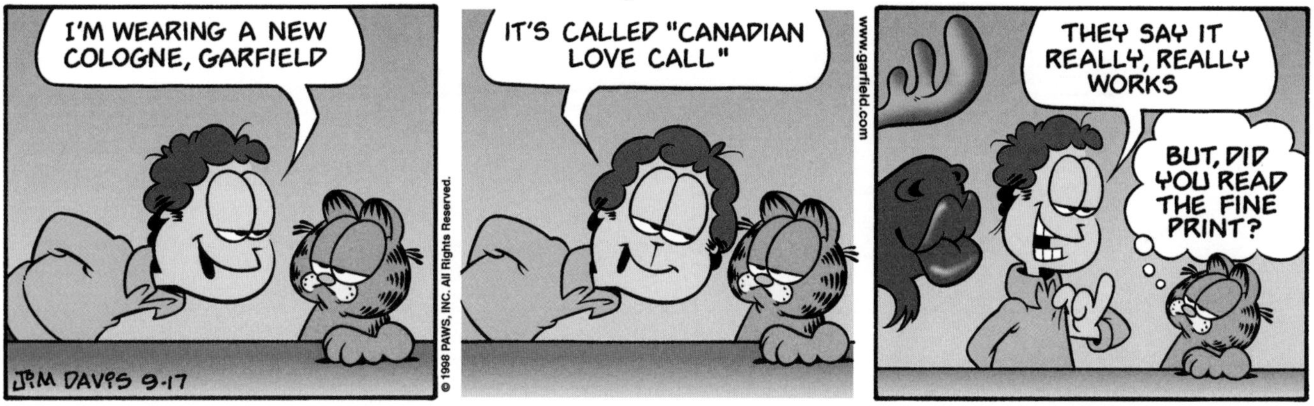
I'M WEARING A NEW COLOGNE, GARFIELD
JIM DAVIS 9-17
© 1998 PAWS, INC. All Rights Reserved.
IT'S CALLED "CANADIAN LOVE CALL"
www.garfield.com
THEY SAY IT REALLY, REALLY WORKS
BUT, DID YOU READ THE FINE PRINT?

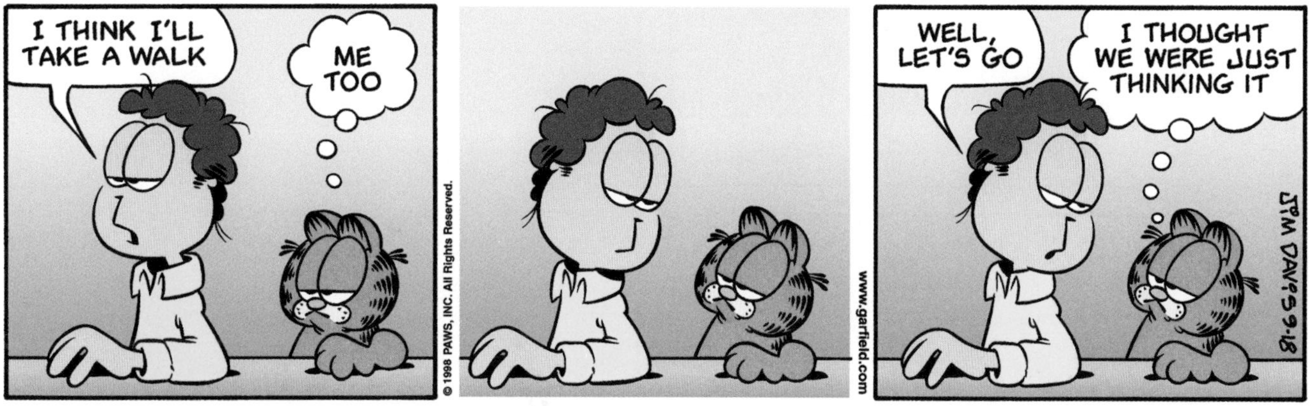
I THINK I'LL TAKE A WALK
ME TOO
© 1998 PAWS, INC. All Rights Reserved.
www.garfield.com
WELL, LET'S GO
I THOUGHT WE WERE JUST THINKING IT
JIM DAVIS 9-18

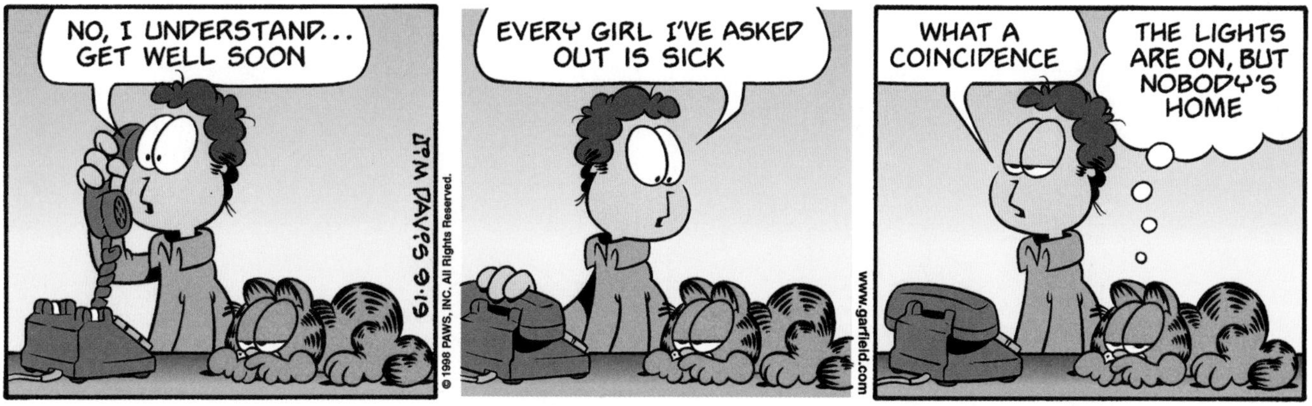
NO, I UNDERSTAND... GET WELL SOON
JIM DAVIS 9-19
© 1998 PAWS, INC. All Rights Reserved.
EVERY GIRL I'VE ASKED OUT IS SICK
www.garfield.com
WHAT A COINCIDENCE
THE LIGHTS ARE ON, BUT NOBODY'S HOME

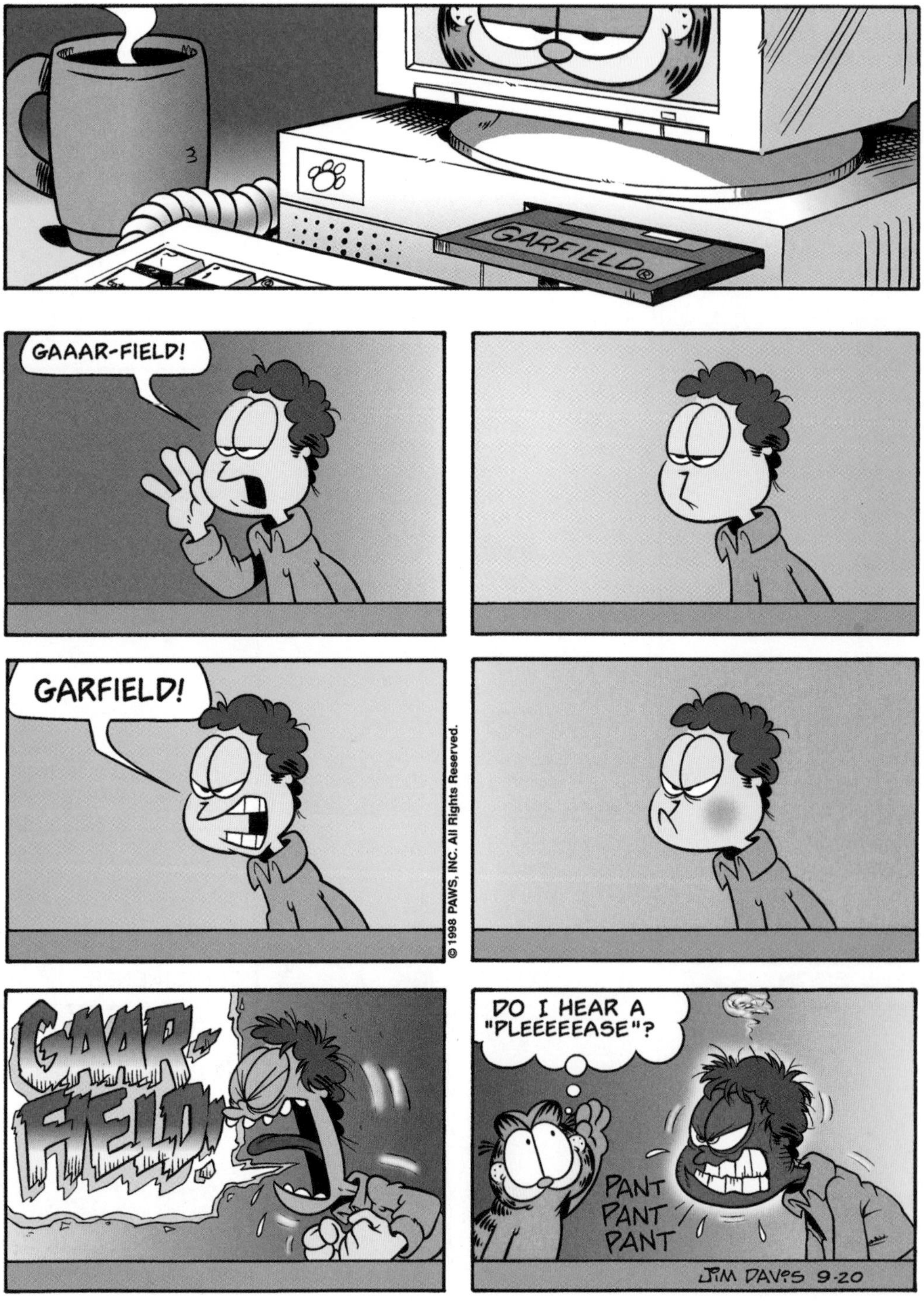
GARFIELD®
GAAAR-FIELD!
GARFIELD!
GAAR-FIELD!
DO I HEAR A "PLEEEEEASE"?
PANT PANT PANT
JIM DAVIS 9-20

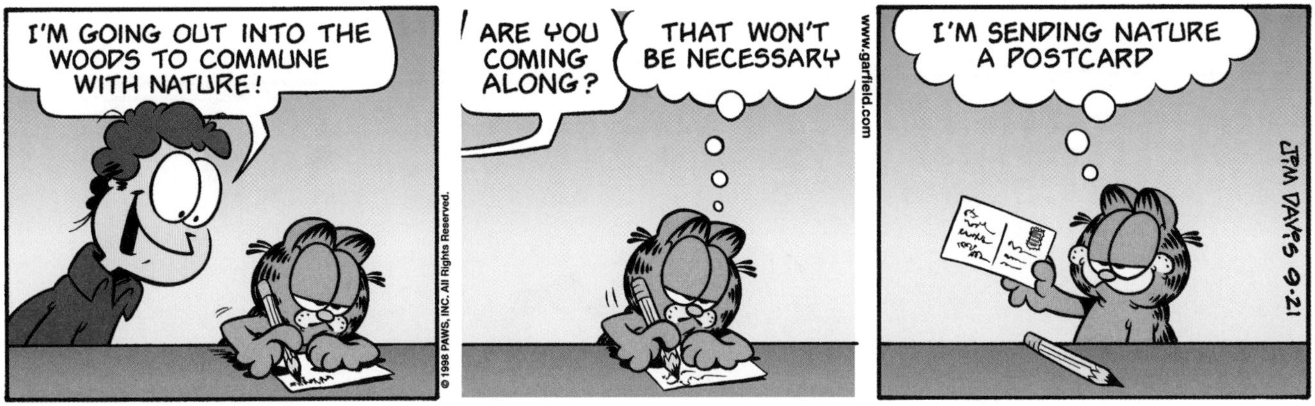
I'M GOING OUT INTO THE WOODS TO COMMUNE WITH NATURE!
© 1998 PAWS, INC. All Rights Reserved.
ARE YOU COMING ALONG?
THAT WON'T BE NECESSARY
www.garfield.com
I'M SENDING NATURE A POSTCARD
JIM DAVIS 9-21

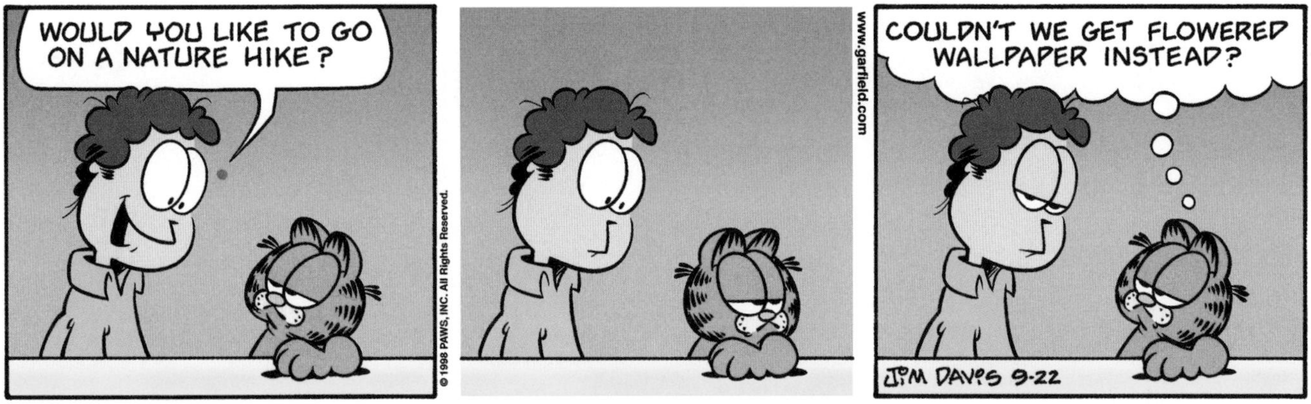
WOULD YOU LIKE TO GO ON A NATURE HIKE?
© 1998 PAWS, INC. All Rights Reserved.
www.garfield.com
COULDN'T WE GET FLOWERED WALLPAPER INSTEAD?
JIM DAVIS 9-22

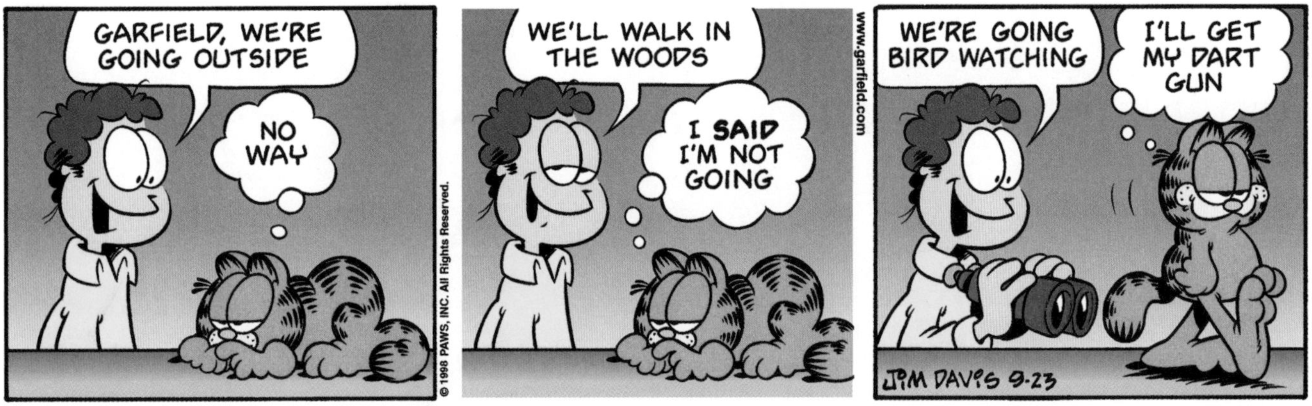
GARFIELD, WE'RE GOING OUTSIDE
NO WAY
© 1998 PAWS, INC. All Rights Reserved.
WE'LL WALK IN THE WOODS
I **SAID** I'M NOT GOING
www.garfield.com
WE'RE GOING BIRD WATCHING
I'LL GET MY DART GUN
JIM DAVIS 9-23

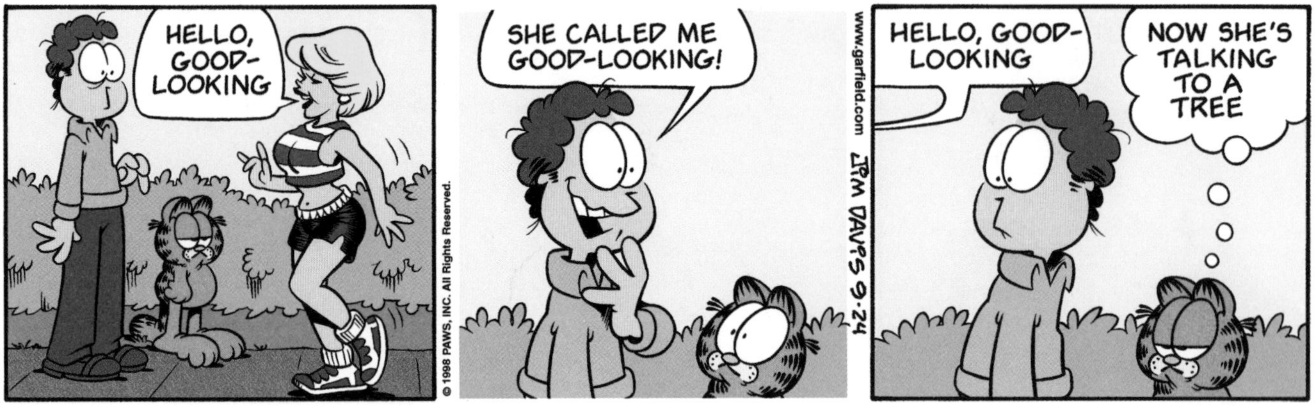
HELLO, GOOD-LOOKING
© 1998 PAWS, INC. All Rights Reserved.
SHE CALLED ME GOOD-LOOKING!
www.garfield.com
JIM DAVIS 9-24
HELLO, GOOD-LOOKING
NOW SHE'S TALKING TO A TREE

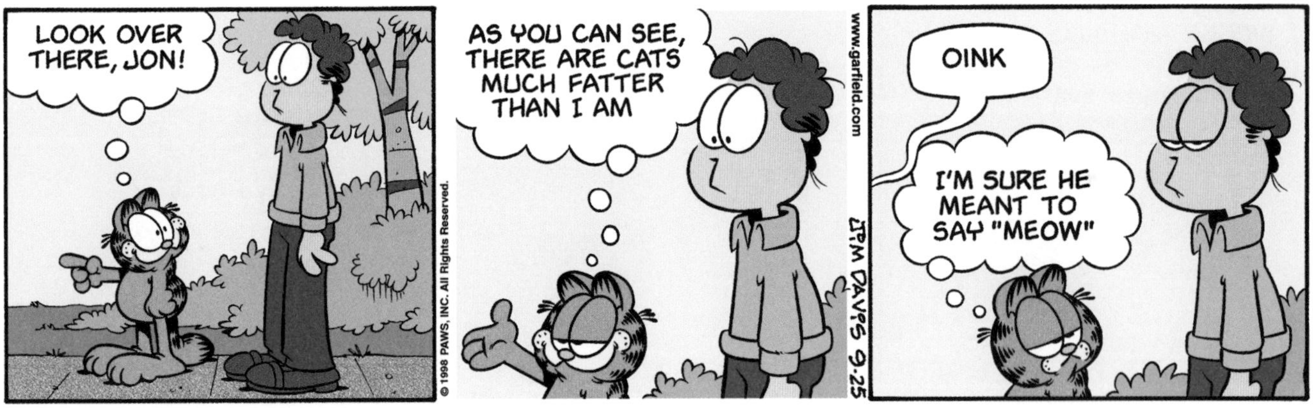
LOOK OVER THERE, JON!
© 1998 PAWS, INC. All Rights Reserved.
AS YOU CAN SEE, THERE ARE CATS MUCH FATTER THAN I AM
www.garfield.com
JIM DAVIS 9-25
OINK
I'M SURE HE MEANT TO SAY "MEOW"

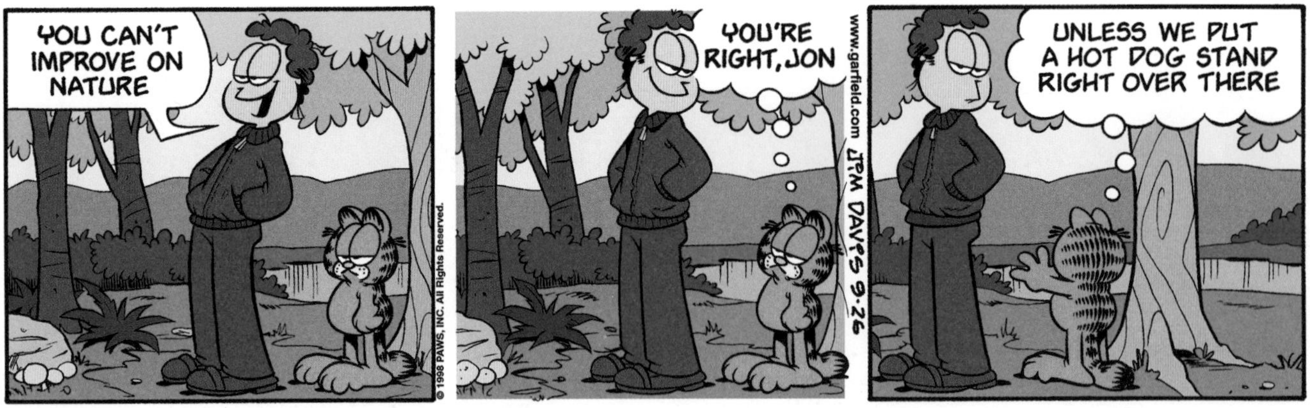
YOU CAN'T IMPROVE ON NATURE
© 1998 PAWS, INC. All Rights Reserved.
YOU'RE RIGHT, JON
www.garfield.com
JIM DAVIS 9-26
UNLESS WE PUT A HOT DOG STAND RIGHT OVER THERE

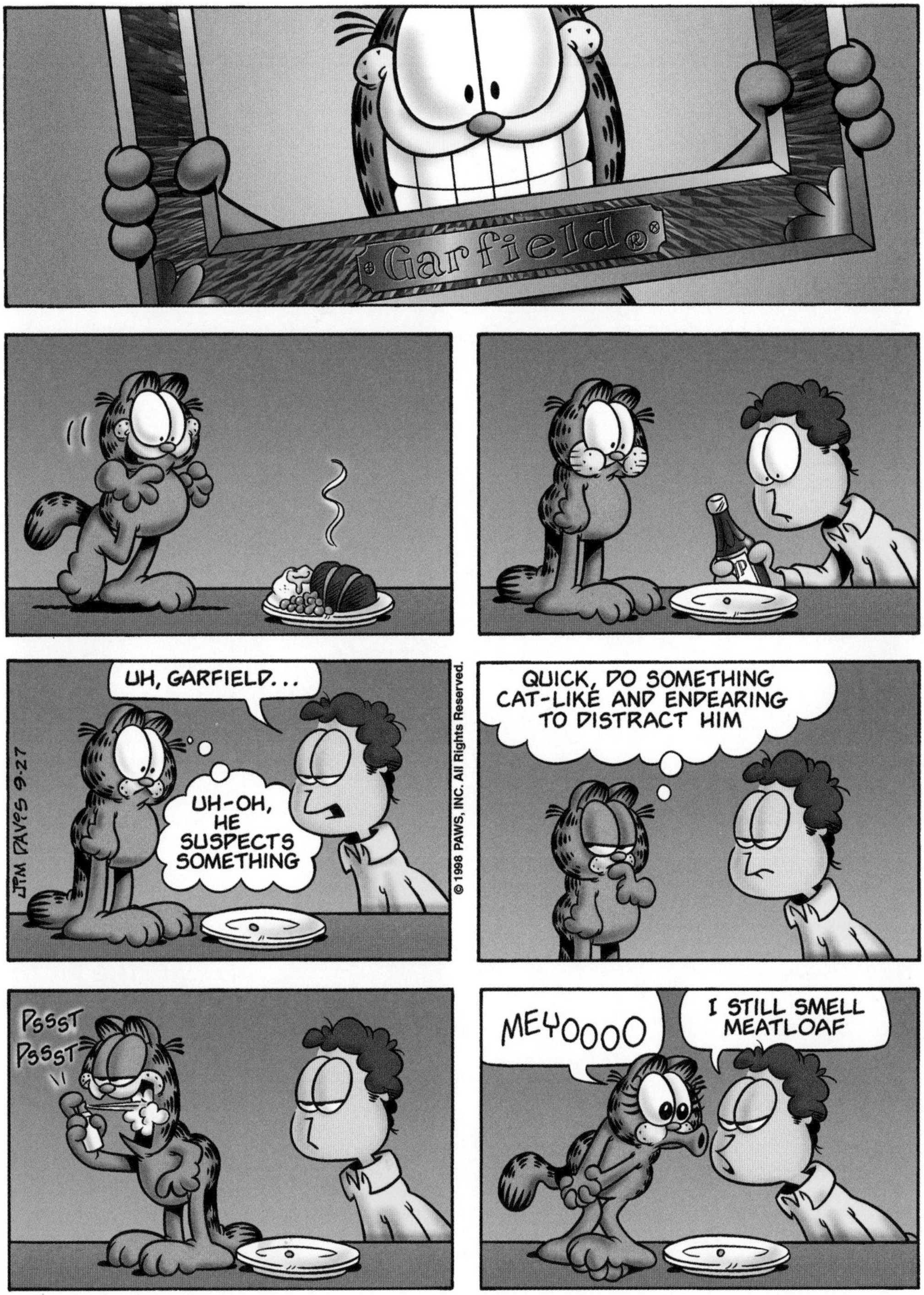

Garfield®
UH, GARFIELD...
UH-OH, HE SUSPECTS SOMETHING
JPM DAVPS 9-27
© 1998 PAWS, INC. All Rights Reserved.
QUICK, DO SOMETHING CAT-LIKE AND ENDEARING TO DISTRACT HIM
PSSST PSSST
MEYOOOO
I STILL SMELL MEATLOAF

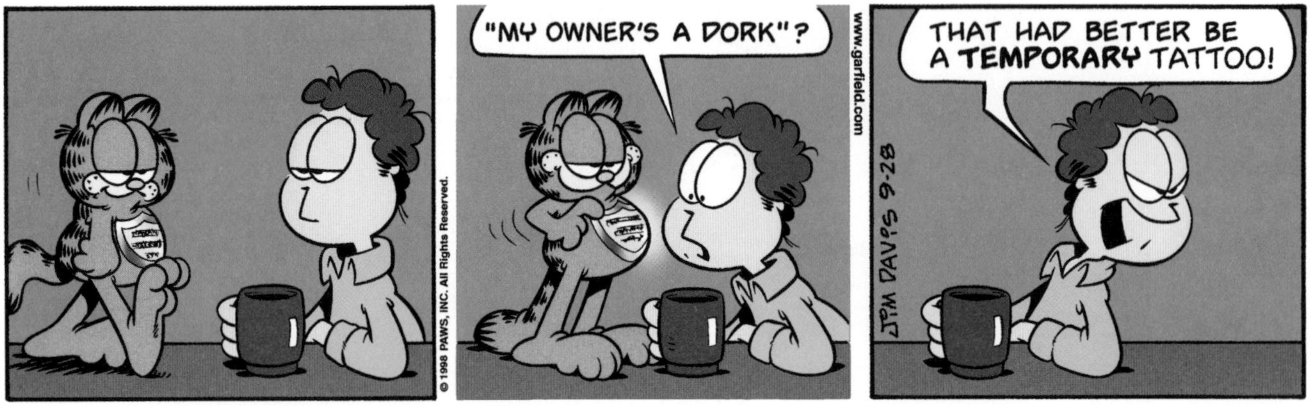
"MY OWNER'S A DORK"?
THAT HAD BETTER BE A **TEMPORARY** TATTOO!
JIM DAVIS 9-28
© 1998 PAWS, INC. All Rights Reserved.
www.garfield.com

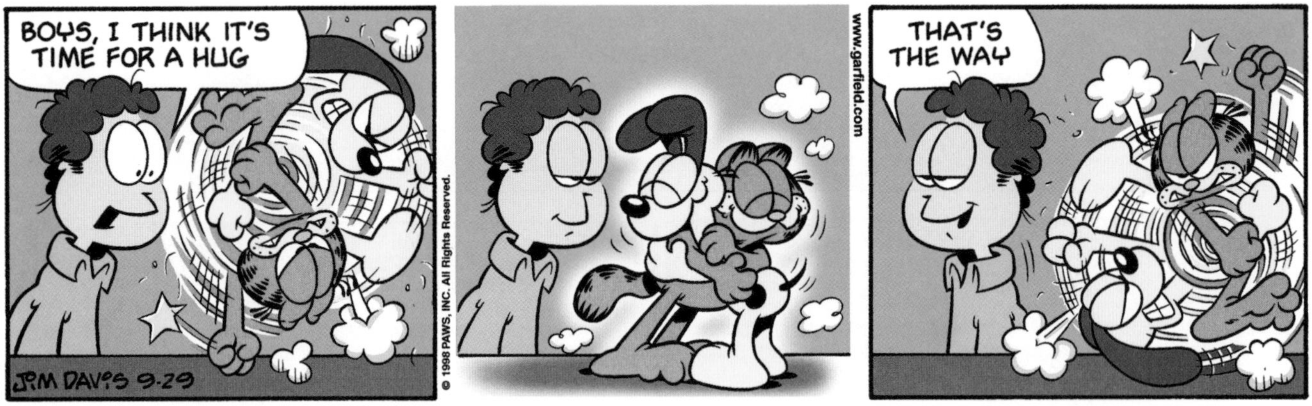
BOYS, I THINK IT'S TIME FOR A HUG
THAT'S THE WAY
JIM DAVIS 9-29
© 1998 PAWS, INC. All Rights Reserved.
www.garfield.com

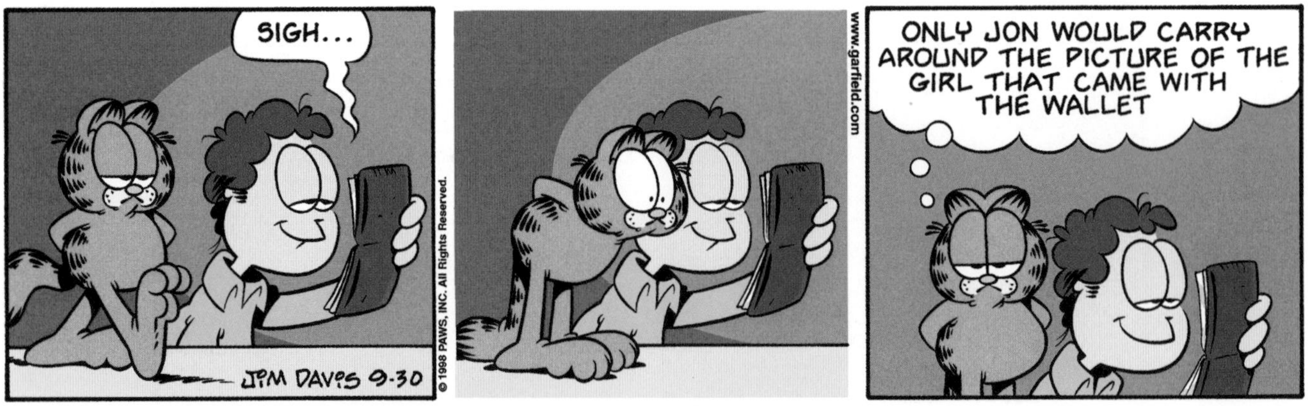
SIGH...
ONLY JON WOULD CARRY AROUND THE PICTURE OF THE GIRL THAT CAME WITH THE WALLET
JIM DAVIS 9-30
© 1998 PAWS, INC. All Rights Reserved.
www.garfield.com

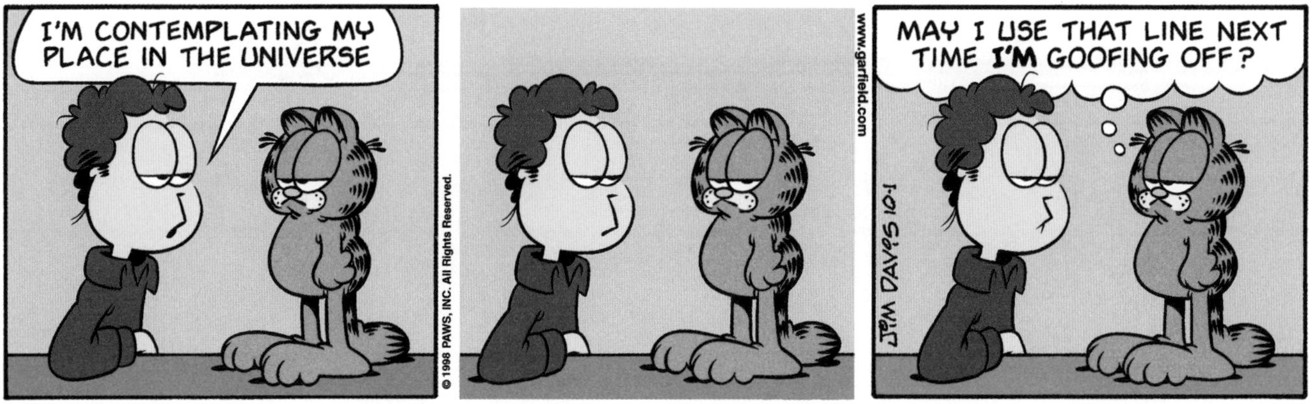
I'M CONTEMPLATING MY PLACE IN THE UNIVERSE
MAY I USE THAT LINE NEXT TIME I'M GOOFING OFF?
JIM DAVIS 10-1
© 1998 PAWS, INC. All Rights Reserved.
www.garfield.com

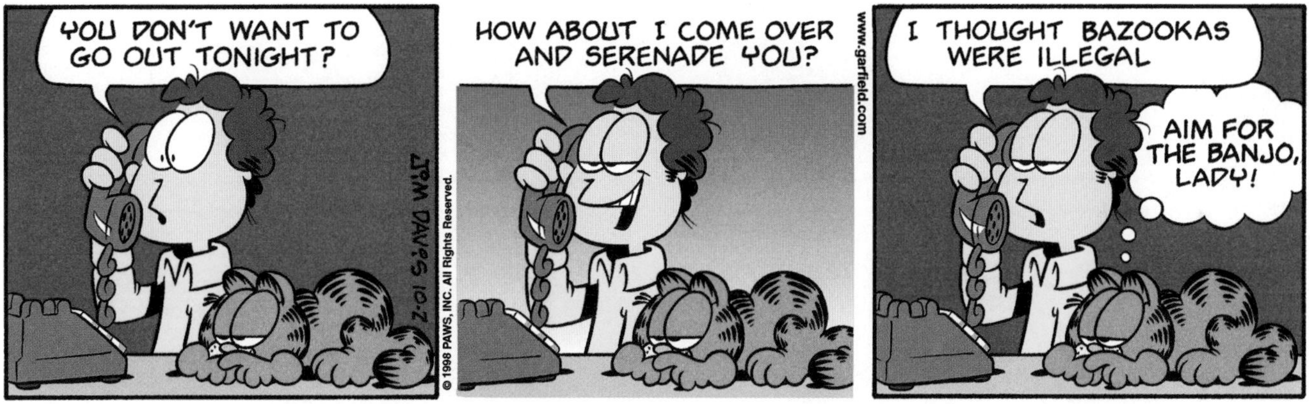
YOU DON'T WANT TO GO OUT TONIGHT?
HOW ABOUT I COME OVER AND SERENADE YOU?
I THOUGHT BAZOOKAS WERE ILLEGAL
AIM FOR THE BANJO, LADY!
JIM DAVIS 10-2
© 1998 PAWS, INC. All Rights Reserved.
www.garfield.com

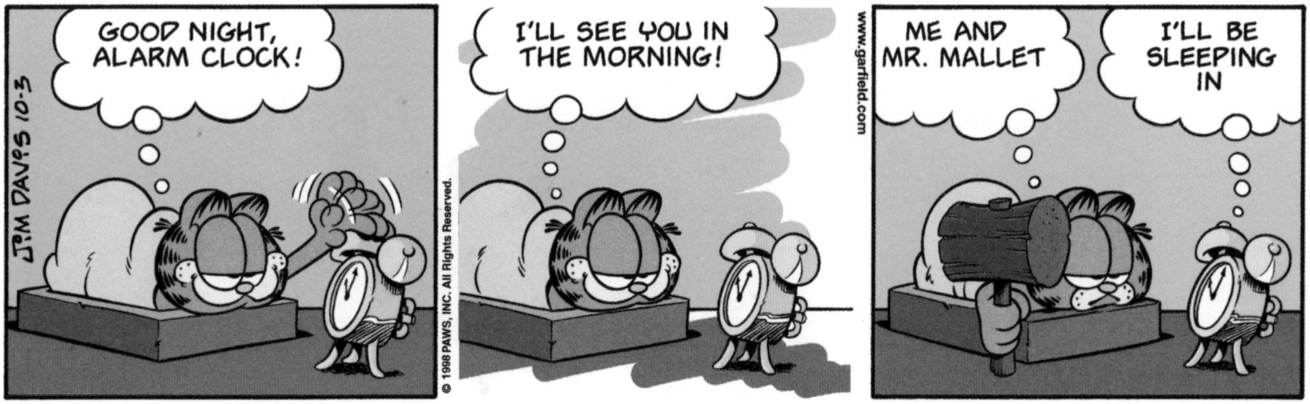
GOOD NIGHT, ALARM CLOCK!
I'LL SEE YOU IN THE MORNING!
ME AND MR. MALLET
I'LL BE SLEEPING IN
JIM DAVIS 10-3
© 1998 PAWS, INC. All Rights Reserved.
www.garfield.com

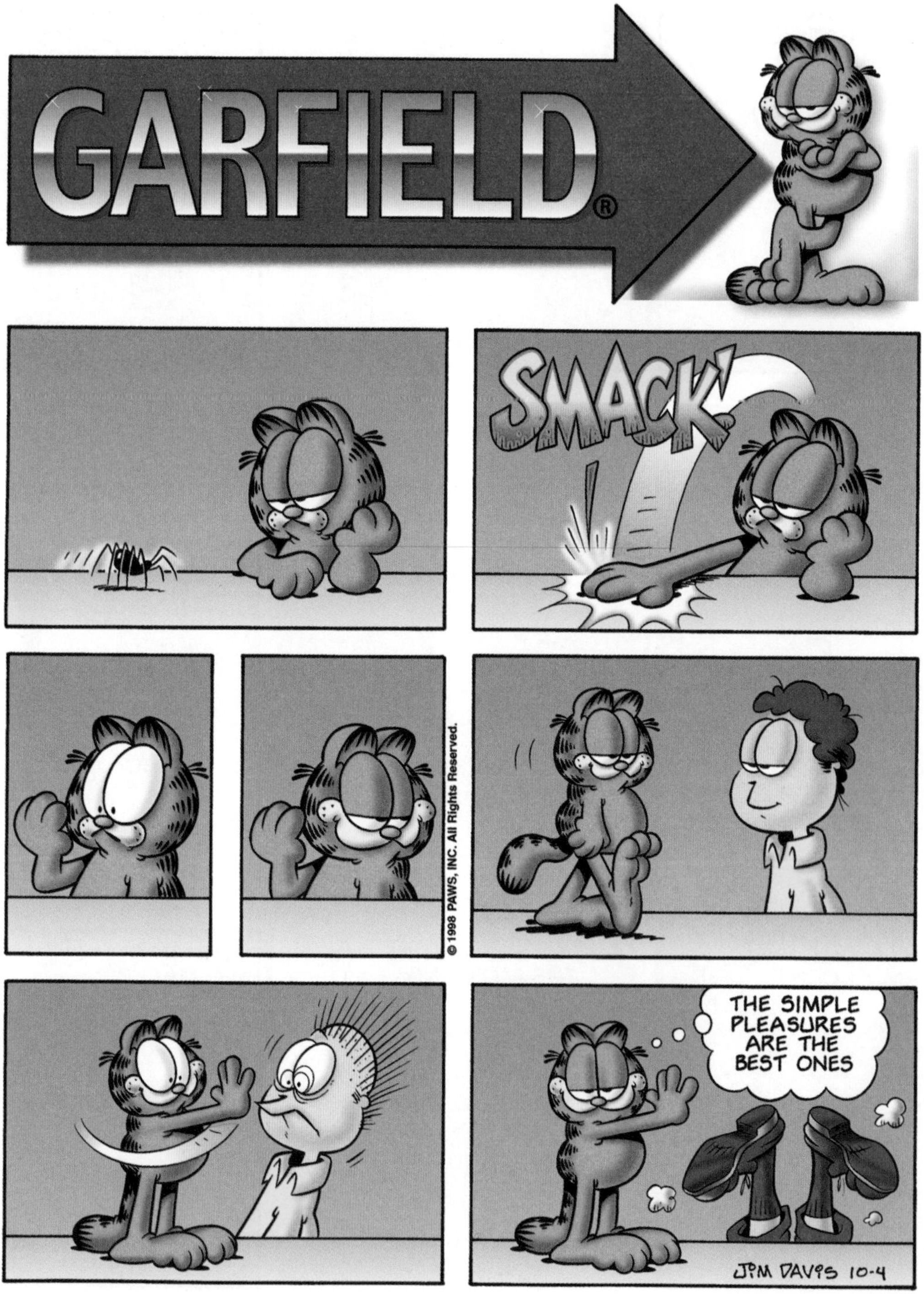
GARFIELD®
SMACK!
THE SIMPLE PLEASURES ARE THE BEST ONES
JIM DAVIS 10-4

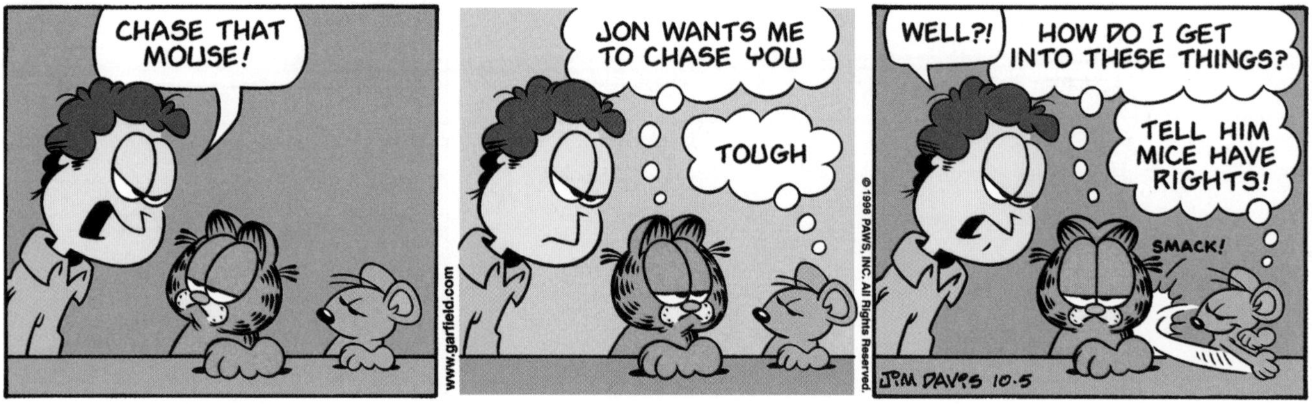
CHASE THAT MOUSE!
www.garfield.com
JON WANTS ME TO CHASE YOU
TOUGH
© 1998 PAWS, INC. All Rights Reserved.
WELL?!
HOW DO I GET INTO THESE THINGS?
TELL HIM MICE HAVE RIGHTS!
SMACK!
JIM DAVIS 10-5

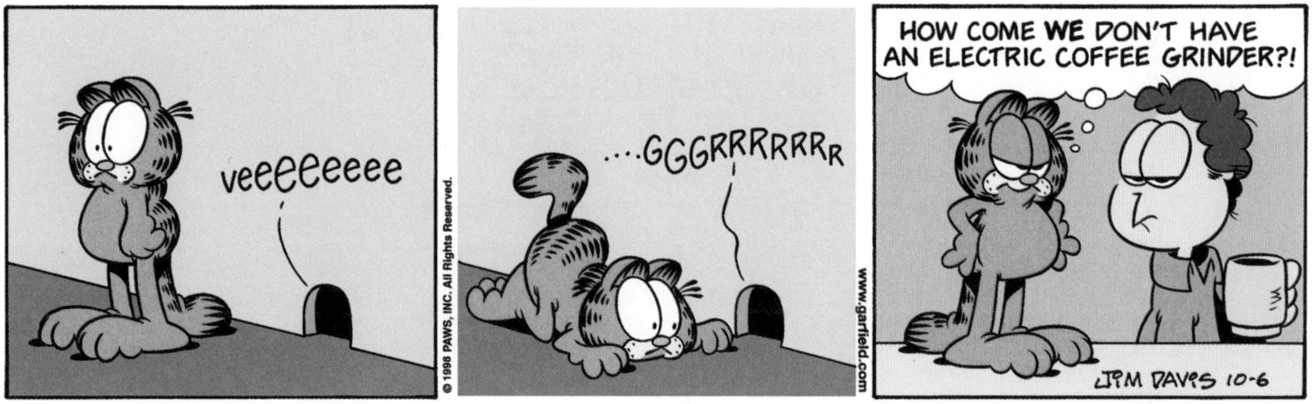
veeEEeeee
© 1998 PAWS, INC. All Rights Reserved.
....GGGRRRRRRR
www.garfield.com
HOW COME WE DON'T HAVE AN ELECTRIC COFFEE GRINDER?!
JIM DAVIS 10-6

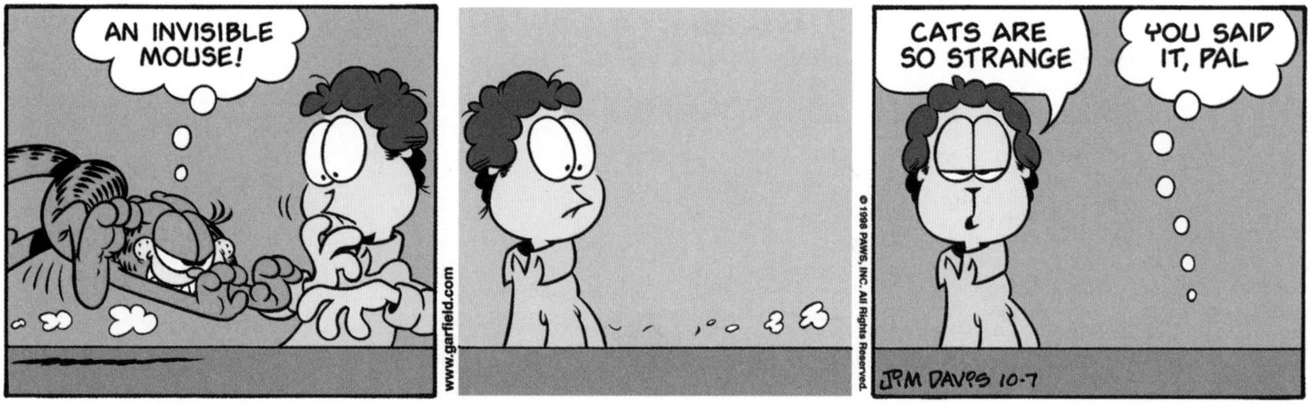
AN INVISIBLE MOUSE!
www.garfield.com
© 1998 PAWS, INC. All Rights Reserved.
CATS ARE SO STRANGE
YOU SAID IT, PAL
JIM DAVIS 10-7

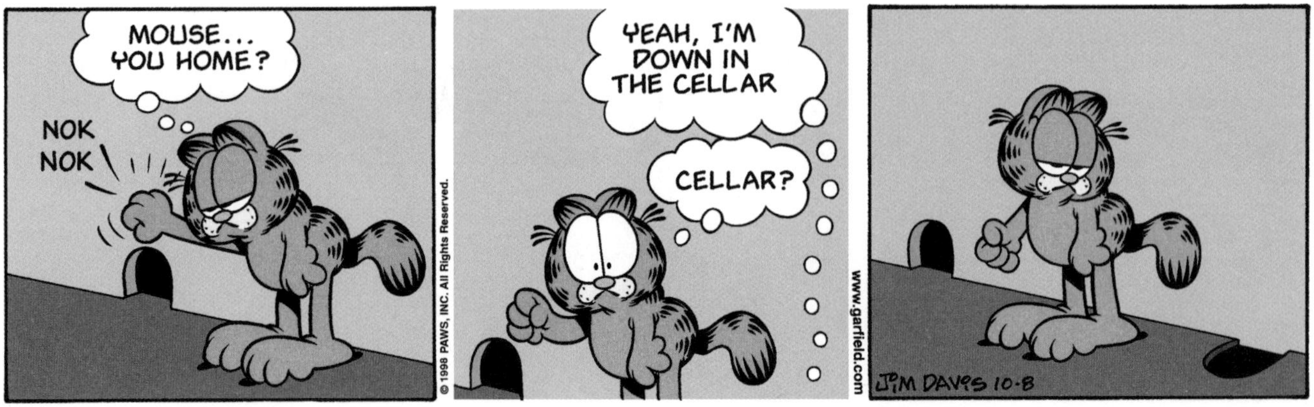
MOUSE... YOU HOME?
NOK NOK
YEAH, I'M DOWN IN THE CELLAR
CELLAR?
© 1998 PAWS, INC. All Rights Reserved.
www.garfield.com
JIM DAVIS 10-8

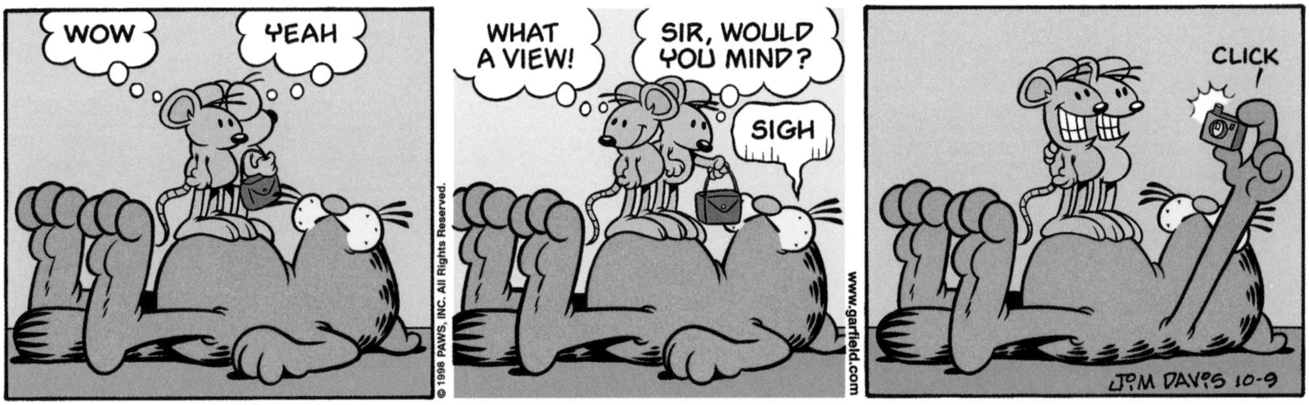
WOW
YEAH
WHAT A VIEW!
SIR, WOULD YOU MIND?
SIGH
CLICK
© 1998 PAWS, INC. All Rights Reserved.
www.garfield.com
JIM DAVIS 10-9

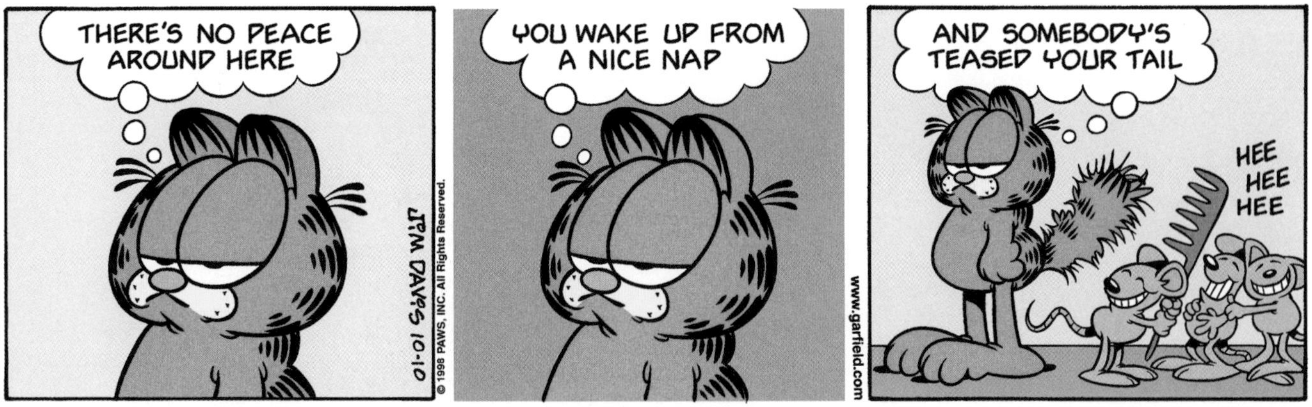
THERE'S NO PEACE AROUND HERE
JIM DAVIS 10-10
YOU WAKE UP FROM A NICE NAP
AND SOMEBODY'S TEASED YOUR TAIL
HEE HEE HEE
© 1998 PAWS, INC. All Rights Reserved.
www.garfield.com

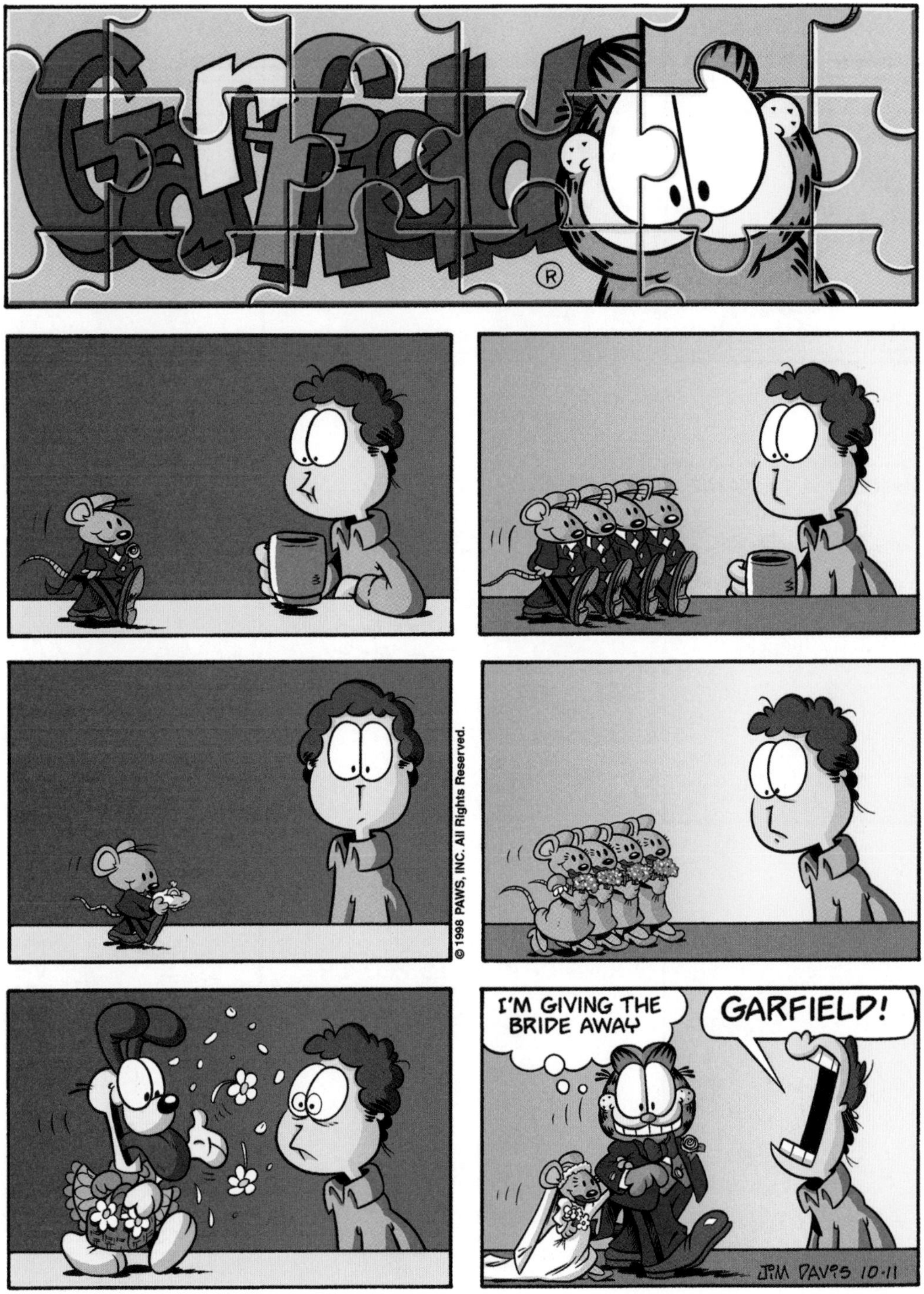
Garfield®
I'M GIVING THE BRIDE AWAY
GARFIELD!
JIM DAVIS 10-11

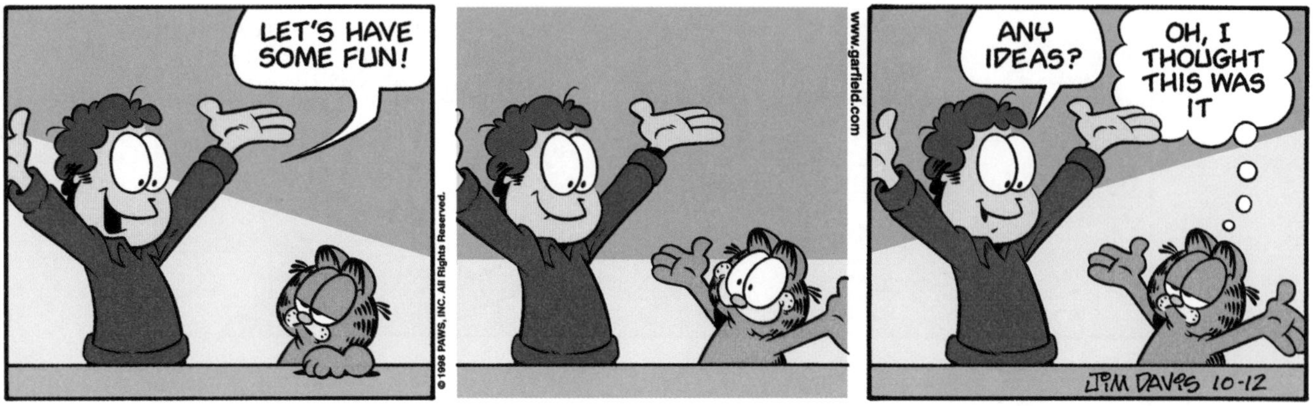
LET'S HAVE SOME FUN!
© 1998 PAWS, INC. All Rights Reserved.
www.garfield.com
ANY IDEAS?
OH, I THOUGHT THIS WAS IT
JIM DAVIS 10-12

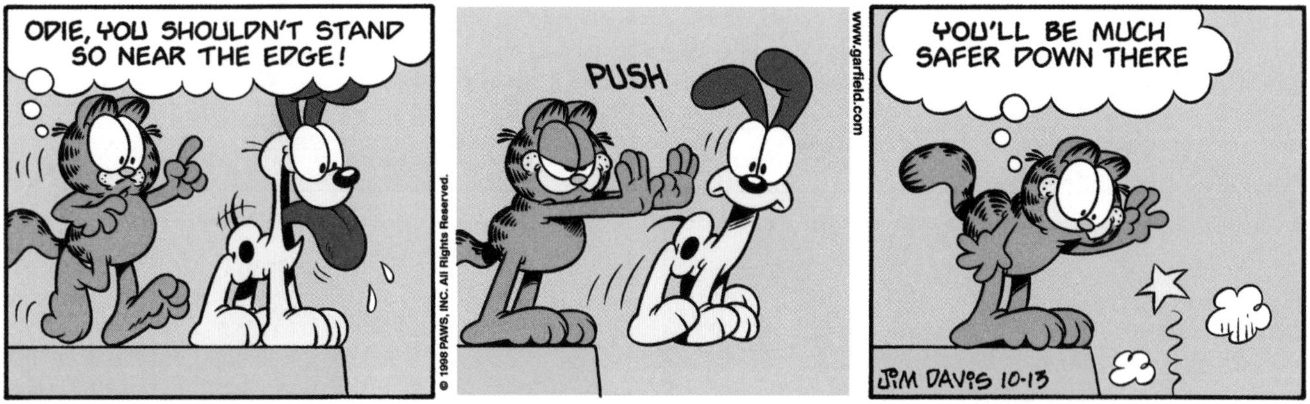
ODIE, YOU SHOULDN'T STAND SO NEAR THE EDGE!
© 1998 PAWS, INC. All Rights Reserved.
PUSH
www.garfield.com
YOU'LL BE MUCH SAFER DOWN THERE
JIM DAVIS 10-13

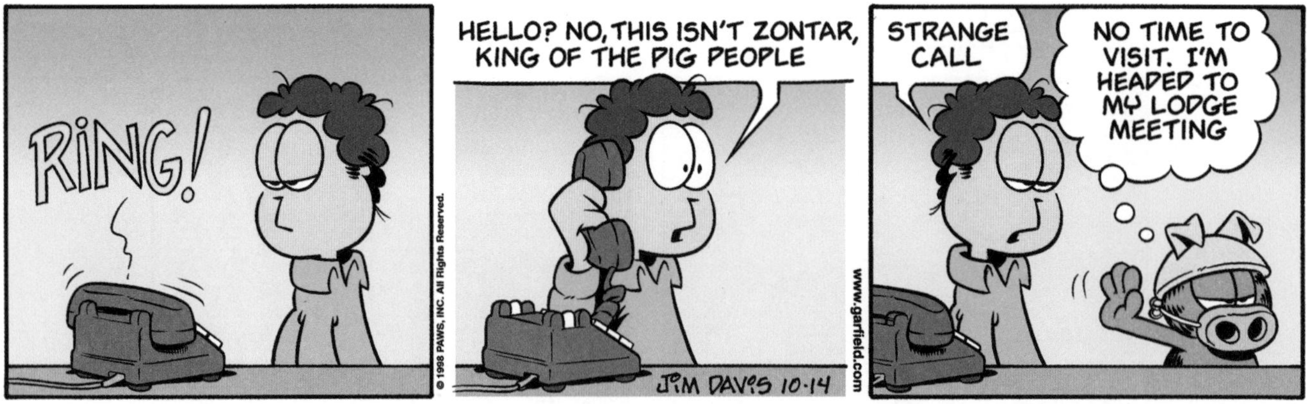
RING!
© 1998 PAWS, INC. All Rights Reserved.
HELLO? NO, THIS ISN'T ZONTAR, KING OF THE PIG PEOPLE
JIM DAVIS 10-14
www.garfield.com
STRANGE CALL
NO TIME TO VISIT. I'M HEADED TO MY LODGE MEETING

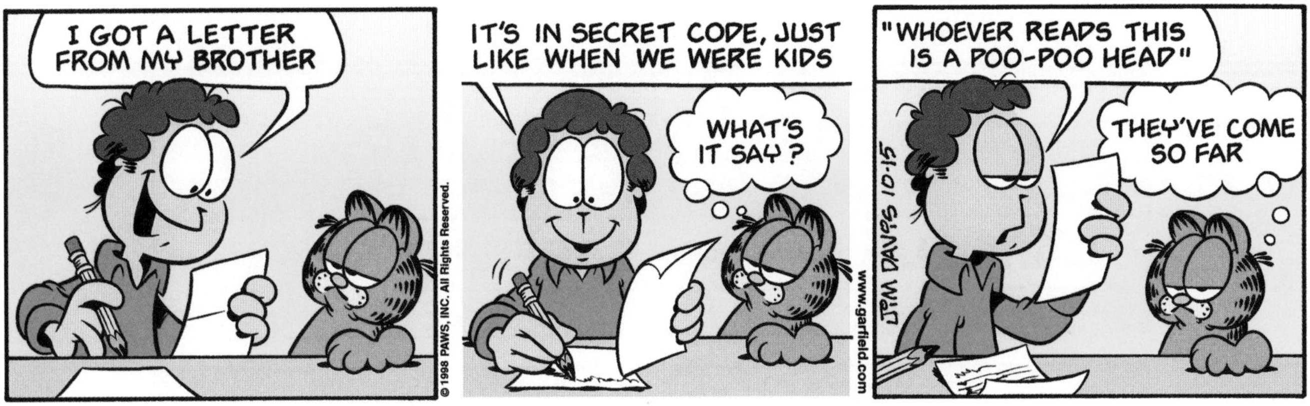
I GOT A LETTER FROM MY BROTHER
© 1998 PAWS, INC. All Rights Reserved.
IT'S IN SECRET CODE, JUST LIKE WHEN WE WERE KIDS
WHAT'S IT SAY?
www.garfield.com
"WHOEVER READS THIS IS A POO-POO HEAD"
THEY'VE COME SO FAR
JIM DAVIS 10-15

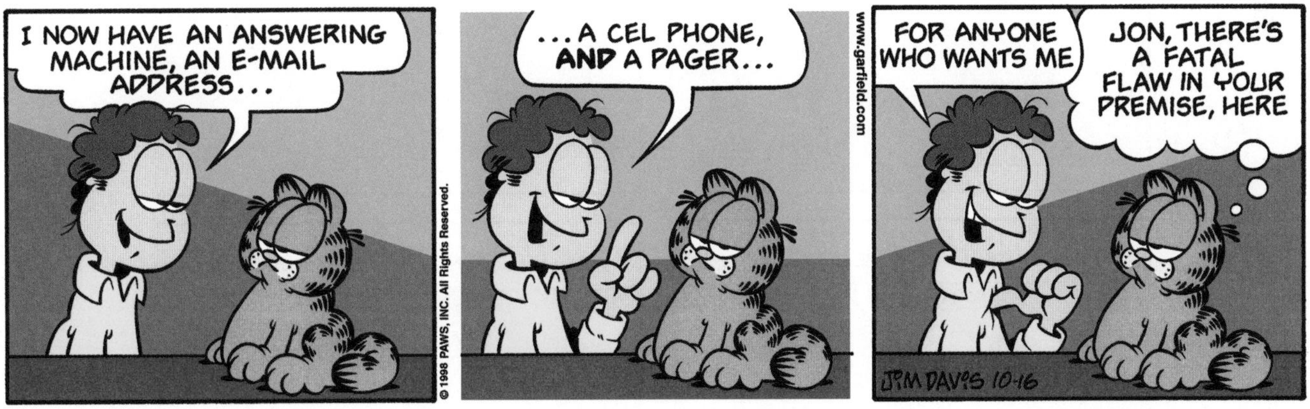
I NOW HAVE AN ANSWERING MACHINE, AN E-MAIL ADDRESS...
© 1998 PAWS, INC. All Rights Reserved.
...A CEL PHONE, AND A PAGER...
www.garfield.com
FOR ANYONE WHO WANTS ME
JON, THERE'S A FATAL FLAW IN YOUR PREMISE, HERE
JIM DAVIS 10-16

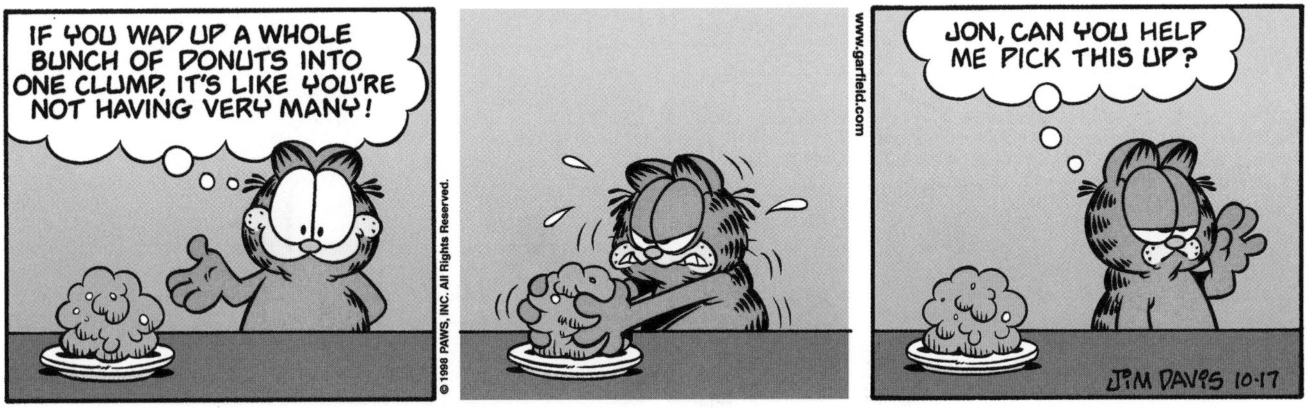
IF YOU WAD UP A WHOLE BUNCH OF DONUTS INTO ONE CLUMP, IT'S LIKE YOU'RE NOT HAVING VERY MANY!
© 1998 PAWS, INC. All Rights Reserved.
www.garfield.com
JON, CAN YOU HELP ME PICK THIS UP?
JIM DAVIS 10-17

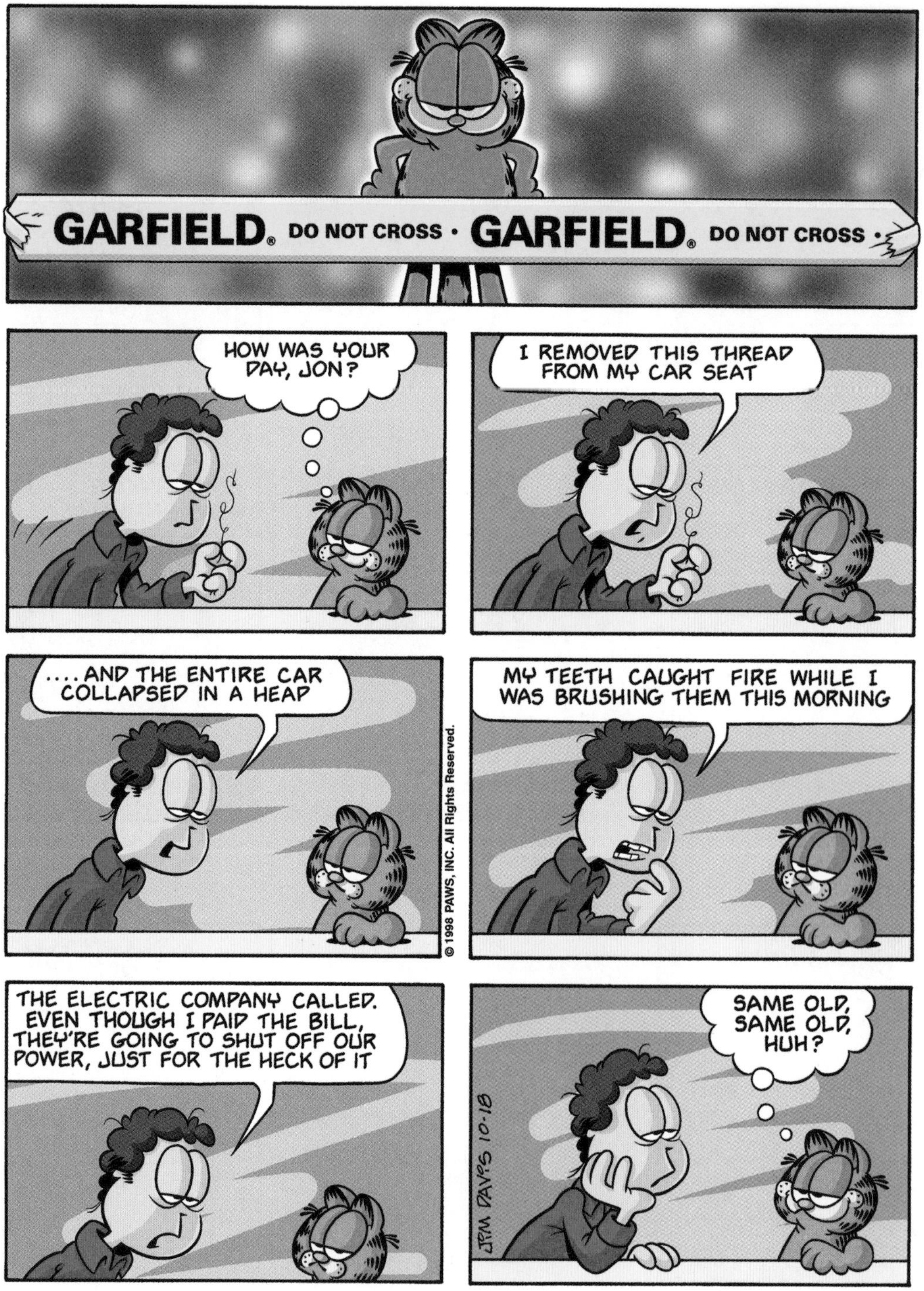
GARFIELD® DO NOT CROSS • GARFIELD® DO NOT CROSS •
HOW WAS YOUR DAY, JON?
I REMOVED THIS THREAD FROM MY CAR SEAT
....AND THE ENTIRE CAR COLLAPSED IN A HEAP
MY TEETH CAUGHT FIRE WHILE I WAS BRUSHING THEM THIS MORNING
THE ELECTRIC COMPANY CALLED. EVEN THOUGH I PAID THE BILL, THEY'RE GOING TO SHUT OFF OUR POWER, JUST FOR THE HECK OF IT
SAME OLD, SAME OLD, HUH?

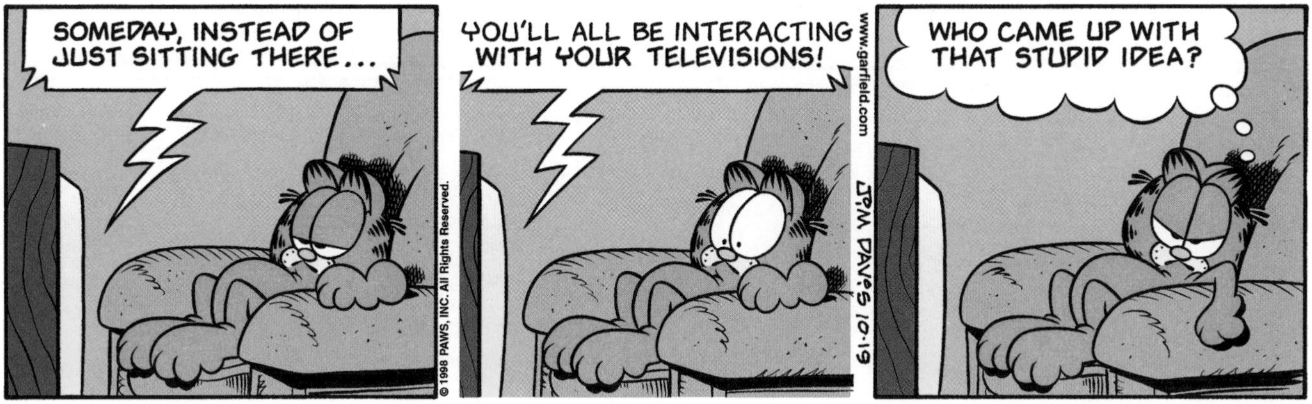
SOMEDAY, INSTEAD OF JUST SITTING THERE...
© 1998 PAWS, INC. All Rights Reserved.
YOU'LL ALL BE INTERACTING WITH YOUR TELEVISIONS!
www.garfield.com
JIM DAVIS 10-19
WHO CAME UP WITH THAT STUPID IDEA?

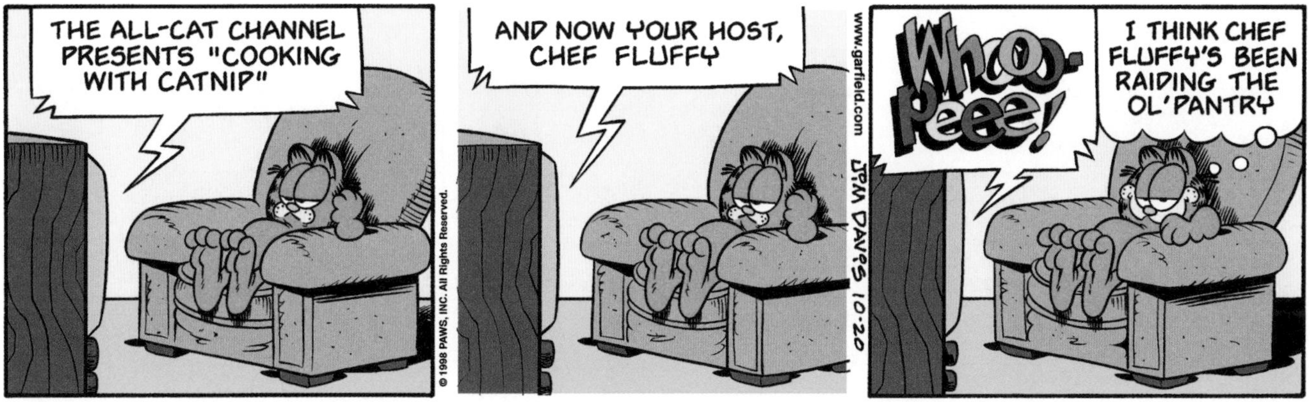
THE ALL-CAT CHANNEL PRESENTS "COOKING WITH CATNIP"
© 1998 PAWS, INC. All Rights Reserved.
AND NOW YOUR HOST, CHEF FLUFFY
www.garfield.com
JIM DAVIS 10-20
Whoo-Peee!
I THINK CHEF FLUFFY'S BEEN RAIDING THE OL' PANTRY

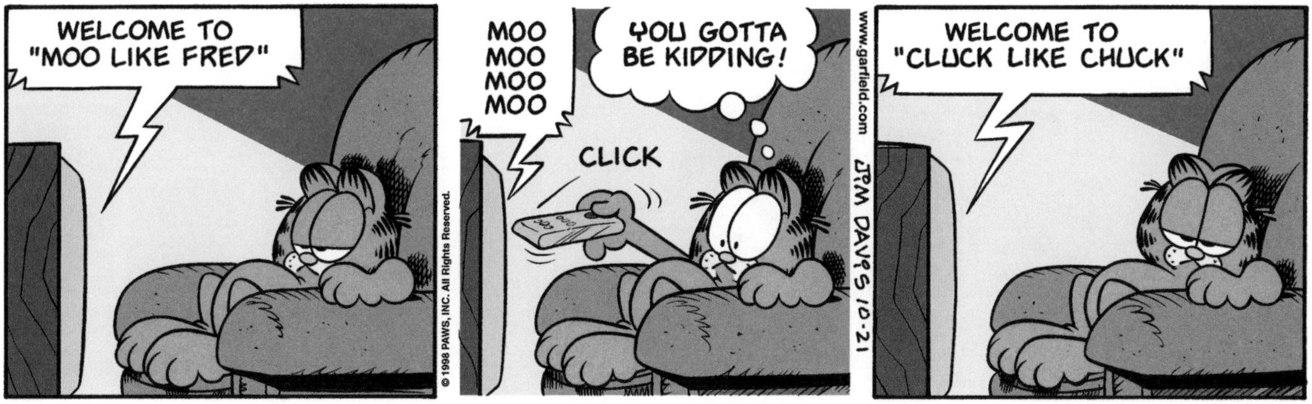
WELCOME TO "MOO LIKE FRED"
© 1998 PAWS, INC. All Rights Reserved.
MOO MOO MOO MOO
YOU GOTTA BE KIDDING!
CLICK
www.garfield.com
JIM DAVIS 10-21
WELCOME TO "CLUCK LIKE CHUCK"

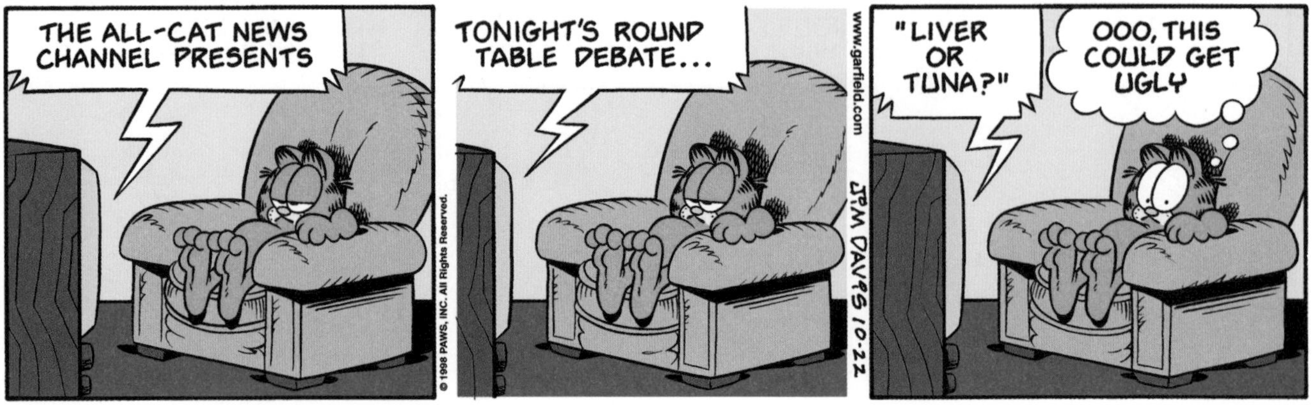
THE ALL-CAT NEWS CHANNEL PRESENTS
© 1998 PAWS, INC. All Rights Reserved.
TONIGHT'S ROUND TABLE DEBATE...
www.garfield.com
JIM DAVIS 10-22
"LIVER OR TUNA?"
OOO, THIS COULD GET UGLY

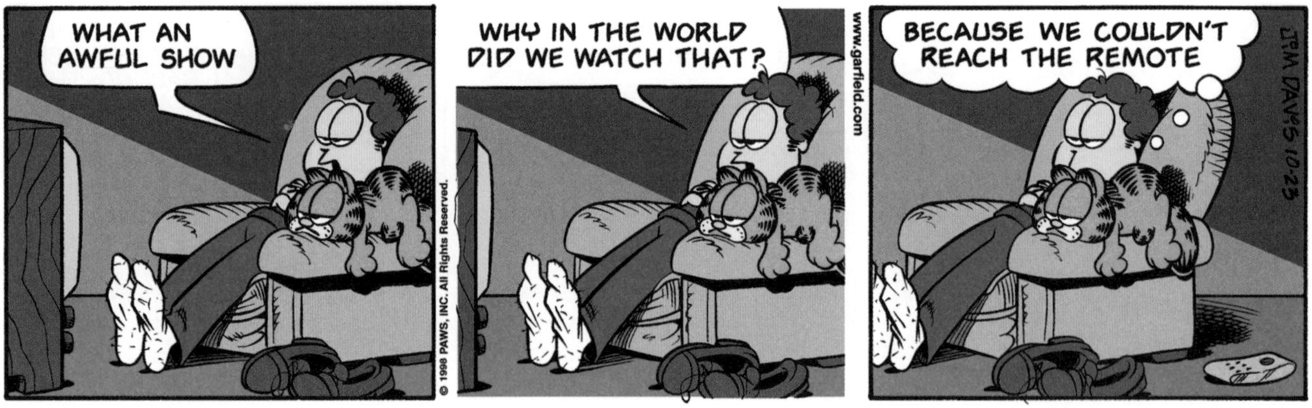
WHAT AN AWFUL SHOW
© 1998 PAWS, INC. All Rights Reserved.
WHY IN THE WORLD DID WE WATCH THAT?
www.garfield.com
BECAUSE WE COULDN'T REACH THE REMOTE
JIM DAVIS 10-23

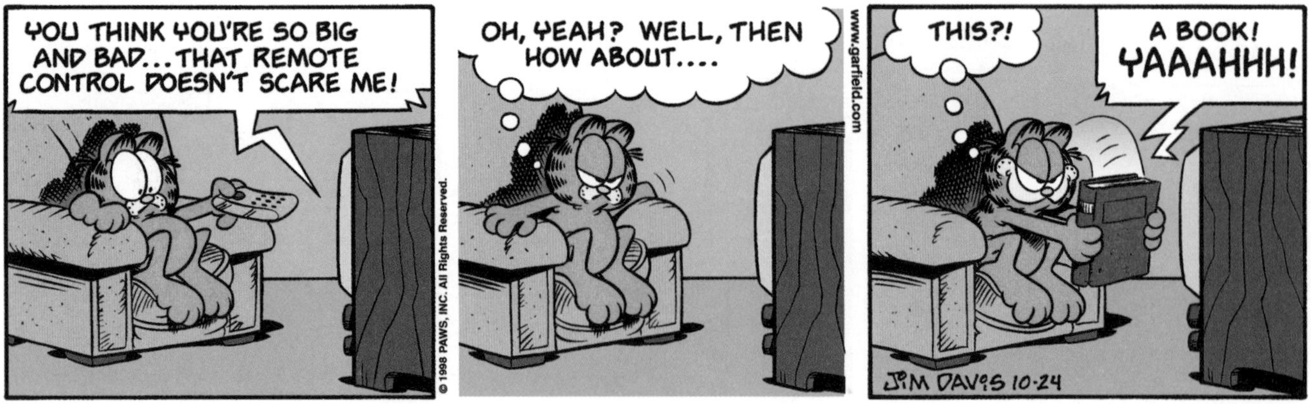
YOU THINK YOU'RE SO BIG AND BAD... THAT REMOTE CONTROL DOESN'T SCARE ME!
© 1998 PAWS, INC. All Rights Reserved.
OH, YEAH? WELL, THEN HOW ABOUT....
www.garfield.com
THIS?!
A BOOK! YAAAHHH!
JIM DAVIS 10-24

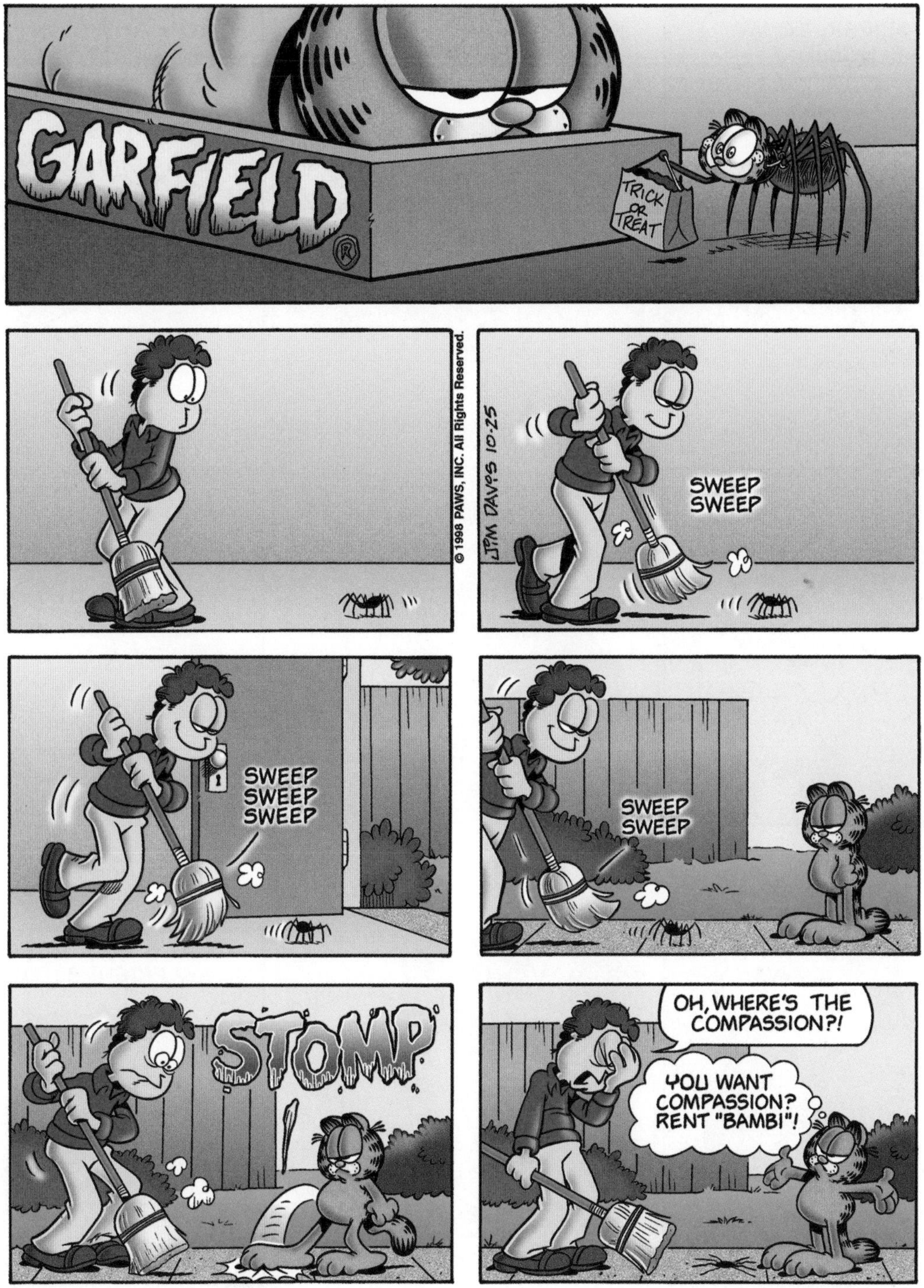
GARFIELD
TRICK OR TREAT
© 1998 PAWS, INC. All Rights Reserved.
JIM DAVIS 10-25
SWEEP SWEEP
SWEEP SWEEP SWEEP
SWEEP SWEEP
STOMP
OH, WHERE'S THE COMPASSION?!
YOU WANT COMPASSION? RENT "BAMBI"!

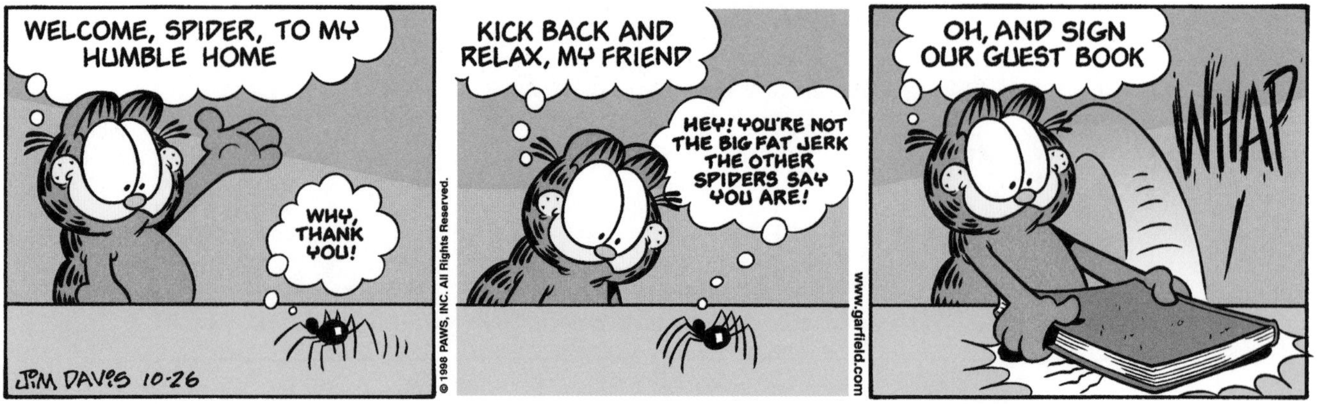
WELCOME, SPIDER, TO MY HUMBLE HOME
WHY, THANK YOU!
JIM DAVIS 10-26
© 1998 PAWS, INC. All Rights Reserved.
KICK BACK AND RELAX, MY FRIEND
HEY! YOU'RE NOT THE BIG FAT JERK THE OTHER SPIDERS SAY YOU ARE!
www.garfield.com
OH, AND SIGN OUR GUEST BOOK
WHAP

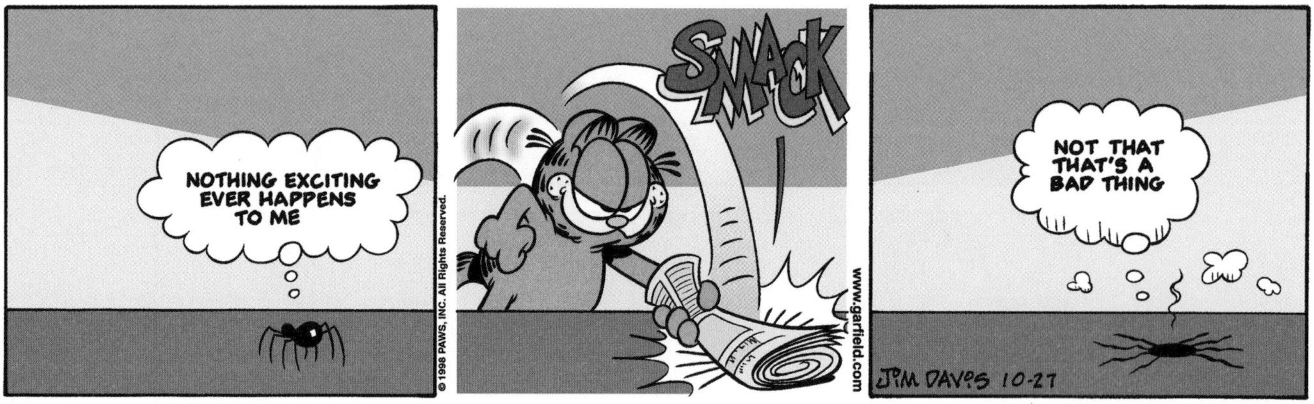
NOTHING EXCITING EVER HAPPENS TO ME
© 1998 PAWS, INC. All Rights Reserved.
SMACK
www.garfield.com
NOT THAT THAT'S A BAD THING
JIM DAVIS 10-27

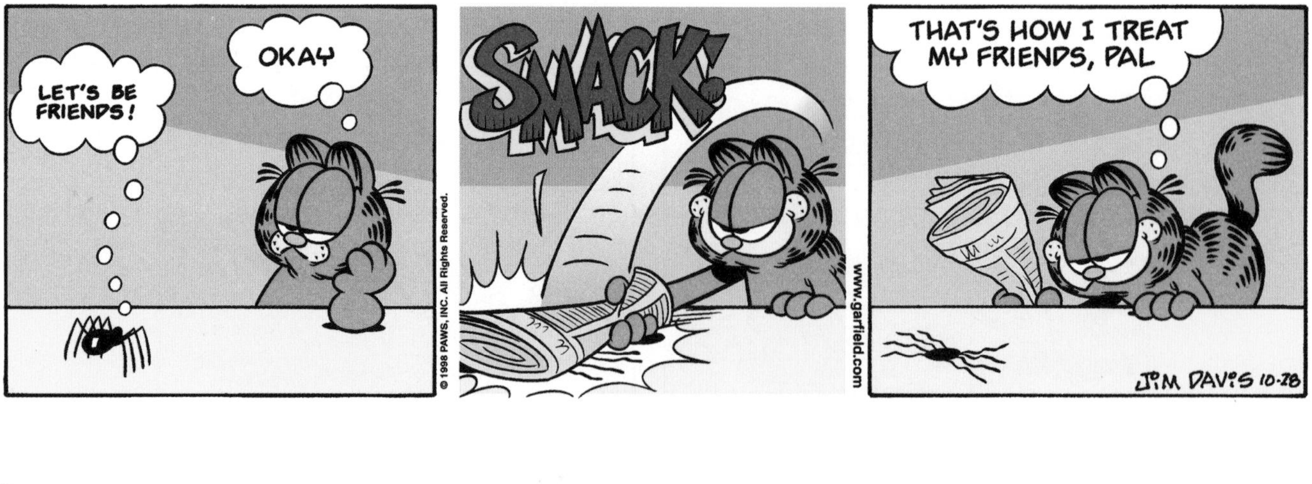
LET'S BE FRIENDS!
OKAY
© 1998 PAWS, INC. All Rights Reserved.
SMACK!
www.garfield.com
THAT'S HOW I TREAT MY FRIENDS, PAL
JIM DAVIS 10-28

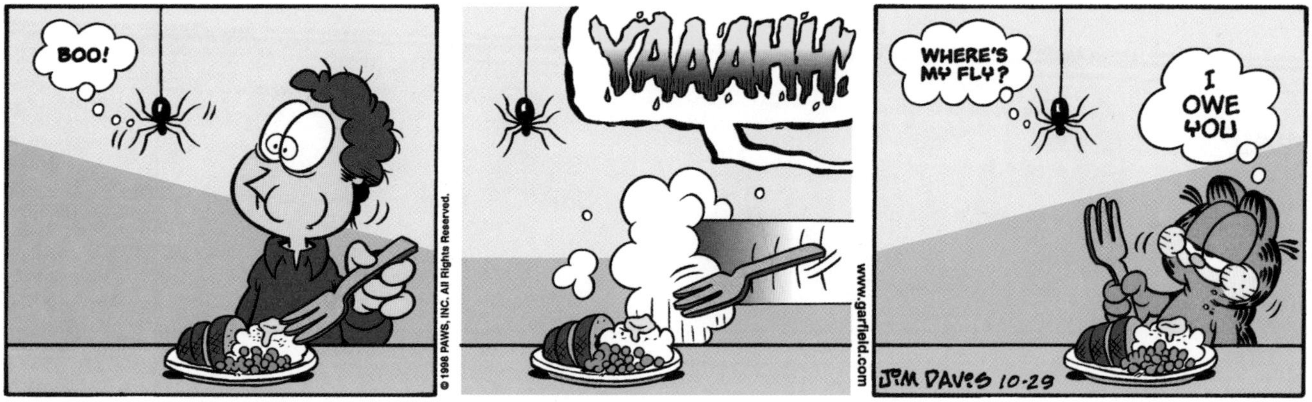
BOO!
YAAAHH!
WHERE'S MY FLY?
I OWE YOU
© 1998 PAWS, INC. All Rights Reserved.
www.garfield.com
JIM DAVIS 10-29

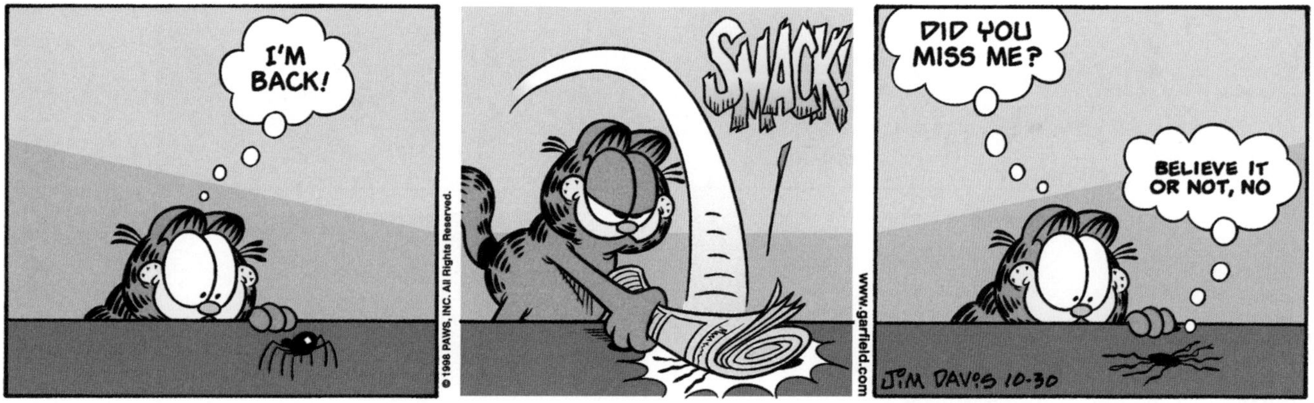
I'M BACK!
SMACK!
DID YOU MISS ME?
BELIEVE IT OR NOT, NO
© 1998 PAWS, INC. All Rights Reserved.
www.garfield.com
JIM DAVIS 10-30

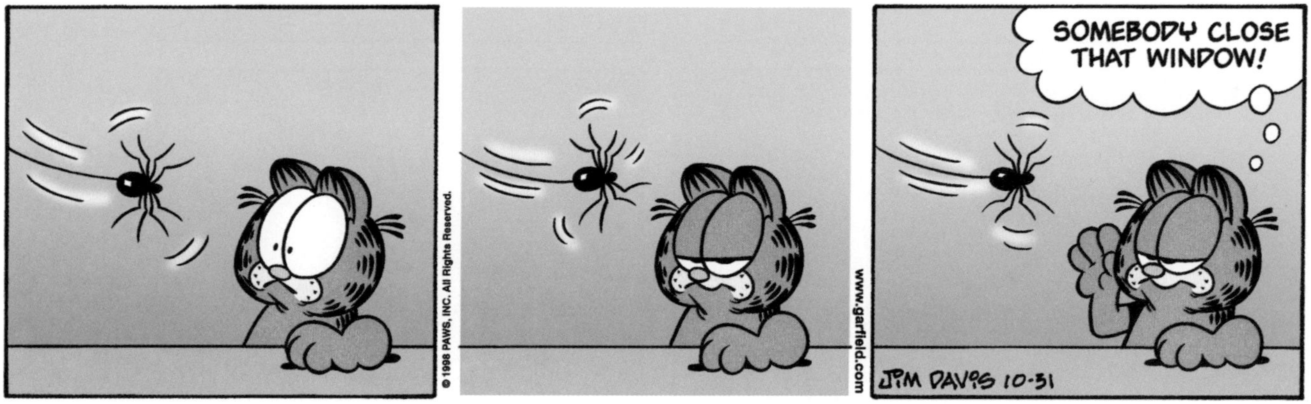
SOMEBODY CLOSE THAT WINDOW!
© 1998 PAWS, INC. All Rights Reserved.
www.garfield.com
JIM DAVIS 10-31

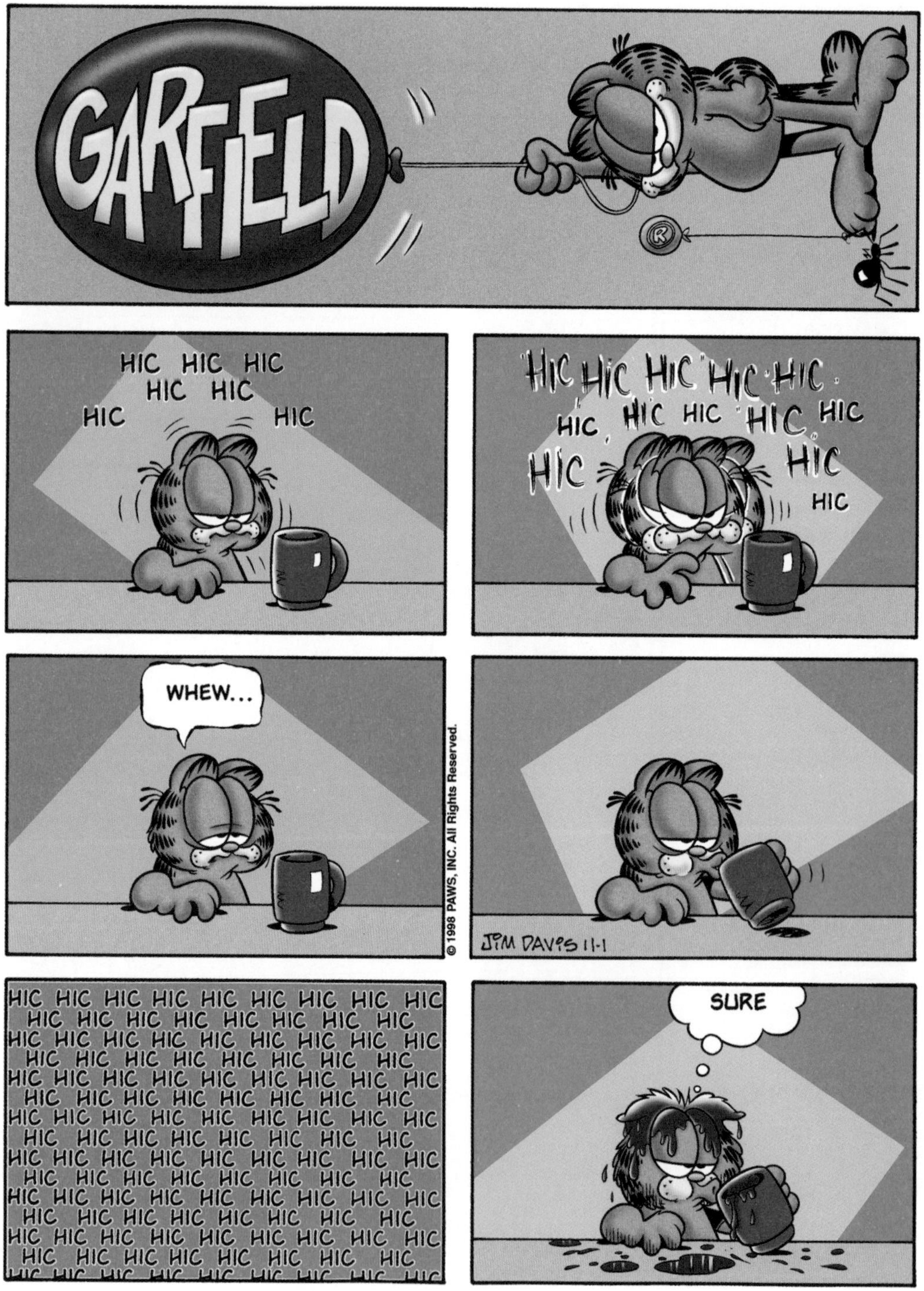
GARFIELD
HIC HIC HIC
HIC HIC
HIC
HIC
HIC HIC HIC HIC HIC
HIC HIC HIC HIC HIC
HIC
HIC
HIC
WHEW...
© 1998 PAWS, INC. All Rights Reserved.
JIM DAVIS 11-1
HIC HIC HIC HIC HIC HIC HIC HIC HIC
HIC HIC HIC HIC HIC HIC HIC HIC
HIC HIC HIC HIC HIC HIC HIC HIC HIC
HIC HIC HIC HIC HIC HIC HIC HIC
HIC HIC HIC HIC HIC HIC HIC HIC HIC
HIC HIC HIC HIC HIC HIC HIC HIC
HIC HIC HIC HIC HIC HIC HIC HIC HIC
HIC HIC HIC HIC HIC HIC HIC HIC
HIC HIC HIC HIC HIC HIC HIC HIC HIC
HIC HIC HIC HIC HIC HIC HIC HIC
HIC HIC HIC HIC HIC HIC HIC HIC HIC
HIC HIC HIC HIC HIC HIC HIC HIC
HIC HIC HIC HIC HIC HIC HIC HIC HIC
HIC HIC HIC HIC HIC HIC HIC HIC
SURE

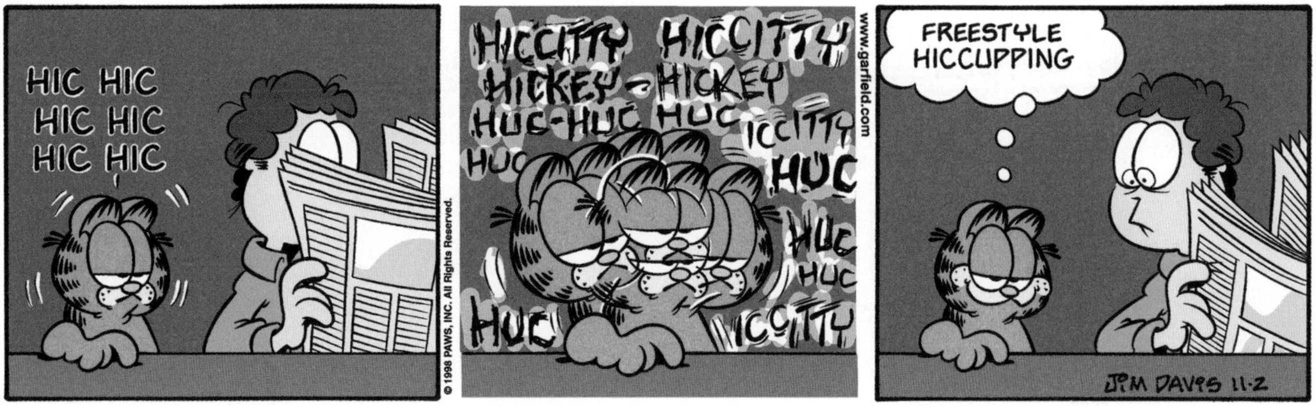
HIC HIC HIC HIC HIC HIC
HICCITTY HICCITTY HICKEY-HICKEY HUC-HUC HUC ICCITTY HUC HUC HUC HUC HUC ICCITTY
FREESTYLE HICCUPPING
© 1998 PAWS, INC. All Rights Reserved.
www.garfield.com
JIM DAVIS 11-2

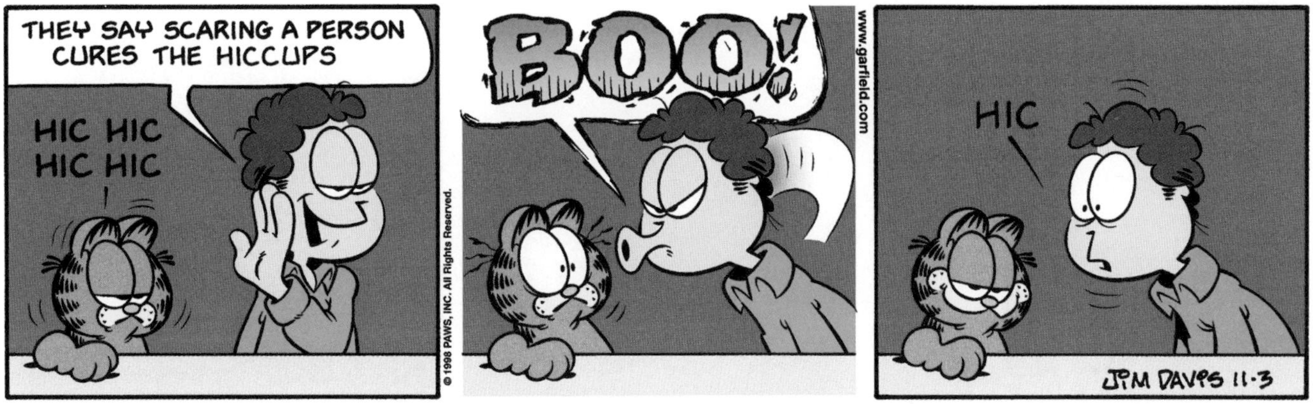
THEY SAY SCARING A PERSON CURES THE HICCUPS
HIC HIC HIC HIC
BOO!
HIC
© 1998 PAWS, INC. All Rights Reserved.
www.garfield.com
JIM DAVIS 11-3

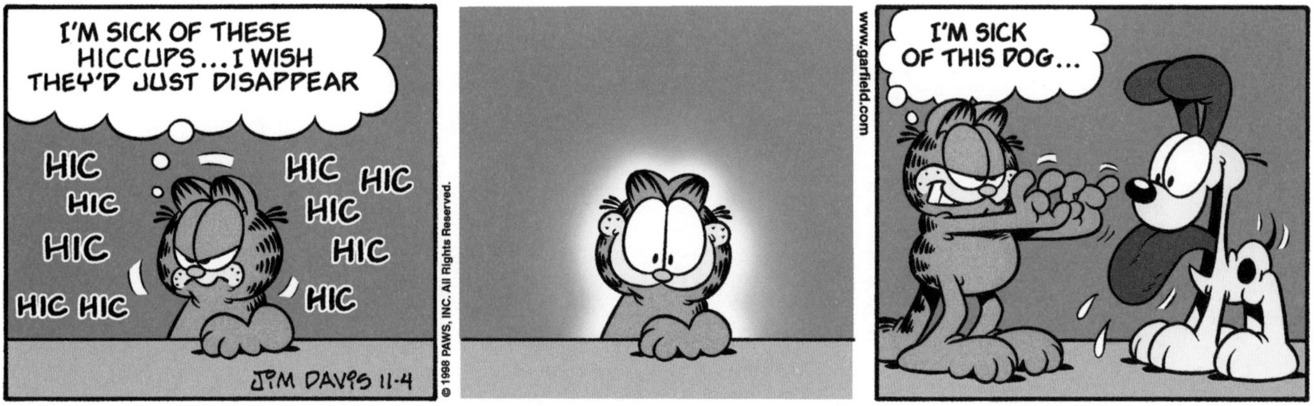
I'M SICK OF THESE HICCUPS... I WISH THEY'D JUST DISAPPEAR
HIC HIC HIC HIC HIC HIC HIC HIC HIC HIC HIC
I'M SICK OF THIS DOG...
© 1998 PAWS, INC. All Rights Reserved.
www.garfield.com
JIM DAVIS 11-4

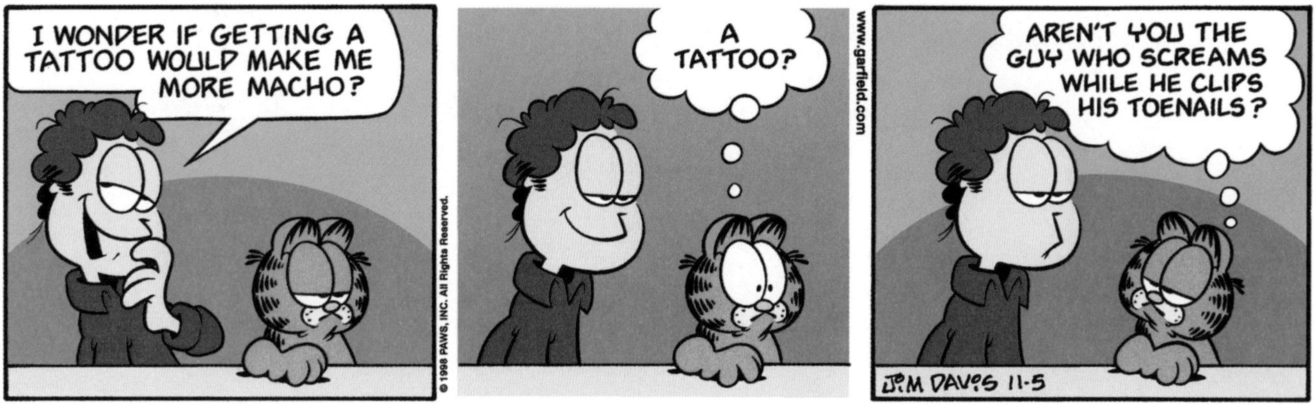
I WONDER IF GETTING A TATTOO WOULD MAKE ME MORE MACHO?
© 1998 PAWS, INC. All Rights Reserved.
A TATTOO?
www.garfield.com
AREN'T YOU THE GUY WHO SCREAMS WHILE HE CLIPS HIS TOENAILS?
JIM DAVIS 11-5

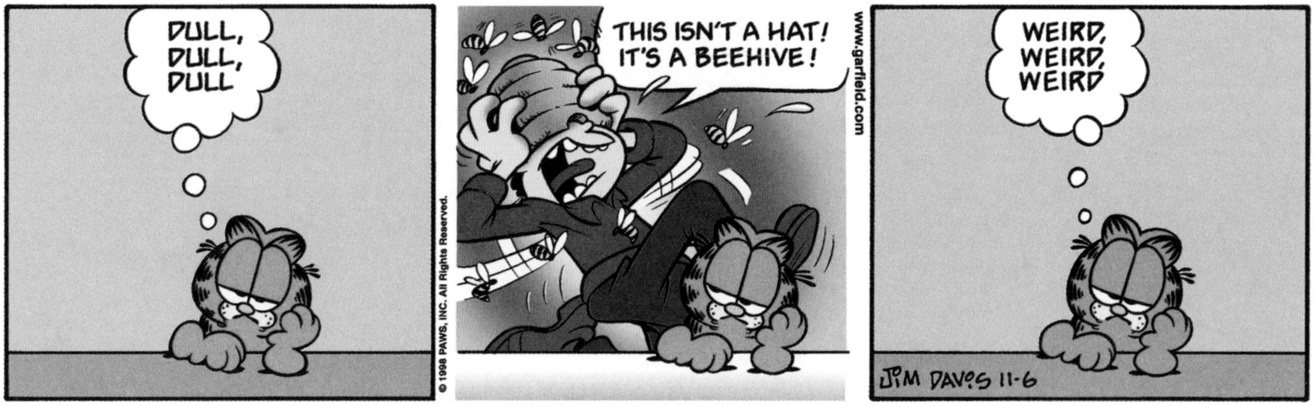
DULL, DULL, DULL
© 1998 PAWS, INC. All Rights Reserved.
THIS ISN'T A HAT! IT'S A BEEHIVE!
www.garfield.com
WEIRD, WEIRD, WEIRD
JIM DAVIS 11-6

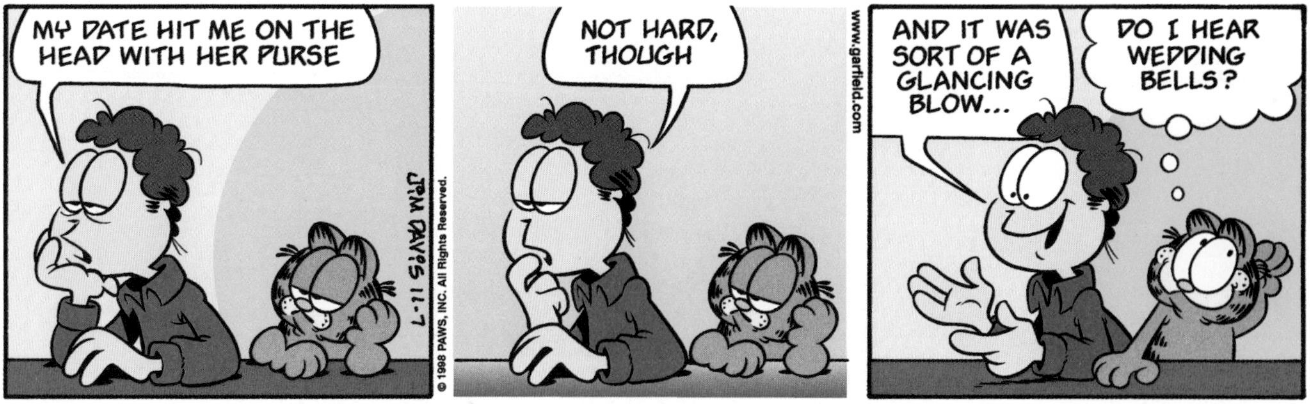
MY DATE HIT ME ON THE HEAD WITH HER PURSE
JIM DAVIS 11-7
© 1998 PAWS, INC. All Rights Reserved.
NOT HARD, THOUGH
www.garfield.com
AND IT WAS SORT OF A GLANCING BLOW...
DO I HEAR WEDDING BELLS?

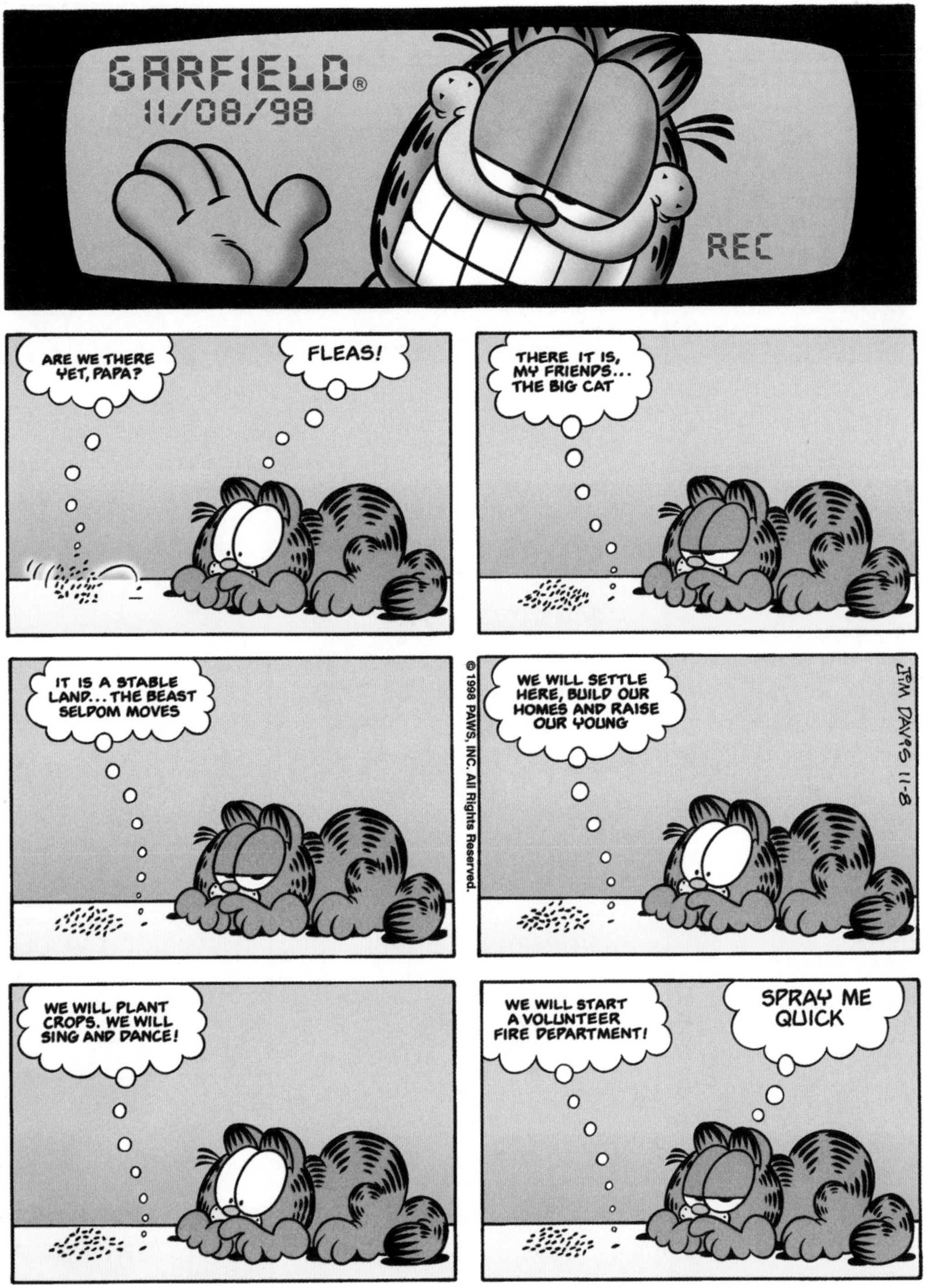

GARFIELD®
11/08/98
REC
ARE WE THERE YET, PAPA?
FLEAS!
THERE IT IS, MY FRIENDS... THE BIG CAT
IT IS A STABLE LAND... THE BEAST SELDOM MOVES
© 1998 PAWS, INC. All Rights Reserved.
WE WILL SETTLE HERE, BUILD OUR HOMES AND RAISE OUR YOUNG
JIM DAVIS 11-8
WE WILL PLANT CROPS. WE WILL SING AND DANCE!
WE WILL START A VOLUNTEER FIRE DEPARTMENT!
SPRAY ME QUICK

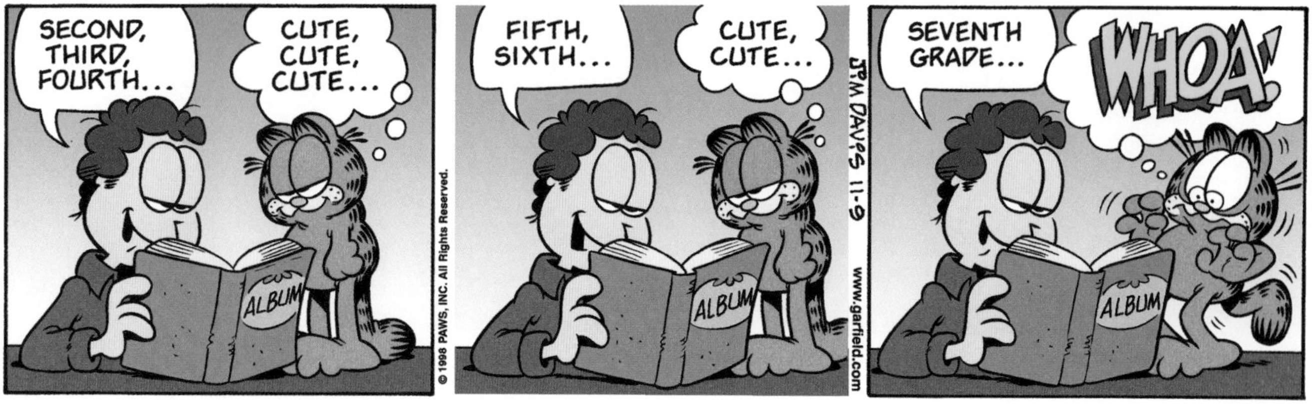
SECOND, THIRD, FOURTH...
CUTE, CUTE, CUTE...
© 1998 PAWS, INC. All Rights Reserved.
FIFTH, SIXTH...
CUTE, CUTE...
JIM DAVIS 11-9
www.garfield.com
SEVENTH GRADE...
WHOA!

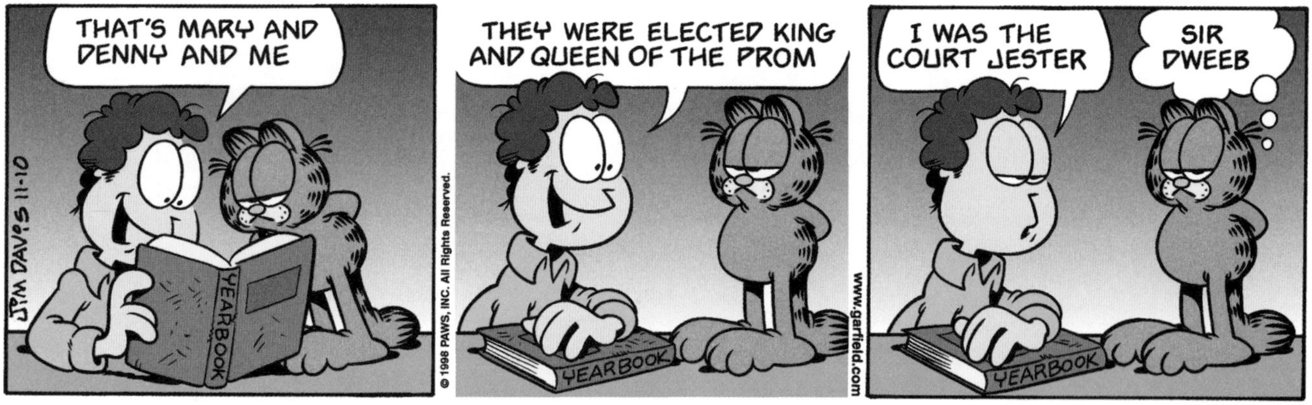
THAT'S MARY AND DENNY AND ME
JIM DAVIS 11-10
© 1998 PAWS, INC. All Rights Reserved.
THEY WERE ELECTED KING AND QUEEN OF THE PROM
www.garfield.com
I WAS THE COURT JESTER
SIR DWEEB

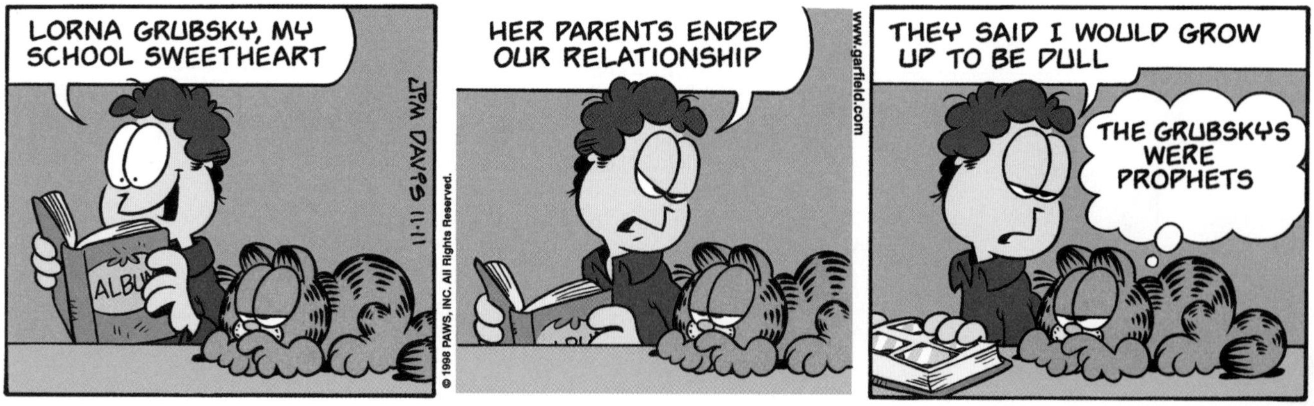
LORNA GRUBSKY, MY SCHOOL SWEETHEART
JIM DAVIS 11-11
© 1998 PAWS, INC. All Rights Reserved.
HER PARENTS ENDED OUR RELATIONSHIP
www.garfield.com
THEY SAID I WOULD GROW UP TO BE DULL
THE GRUBSKYS WERE PROPHETS

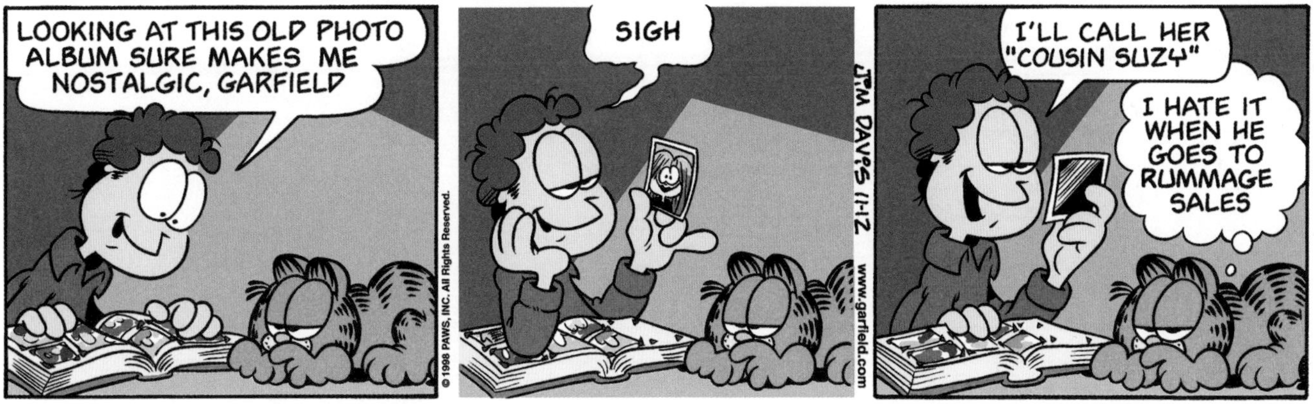
LOOKING AT THIS OLD PHOTO ALBUM SURE MAKES ME NOSTALGIC, GARFIELD
© 1998 PAWS, INC. All Rights Reserved.
SIGH
JIM DAVIS 11-12
www.garfield.com
I'LL CALL HER "COUSIN SUZY"
I HATE IT WHEN HE GOES TO RUMMAGE SALES

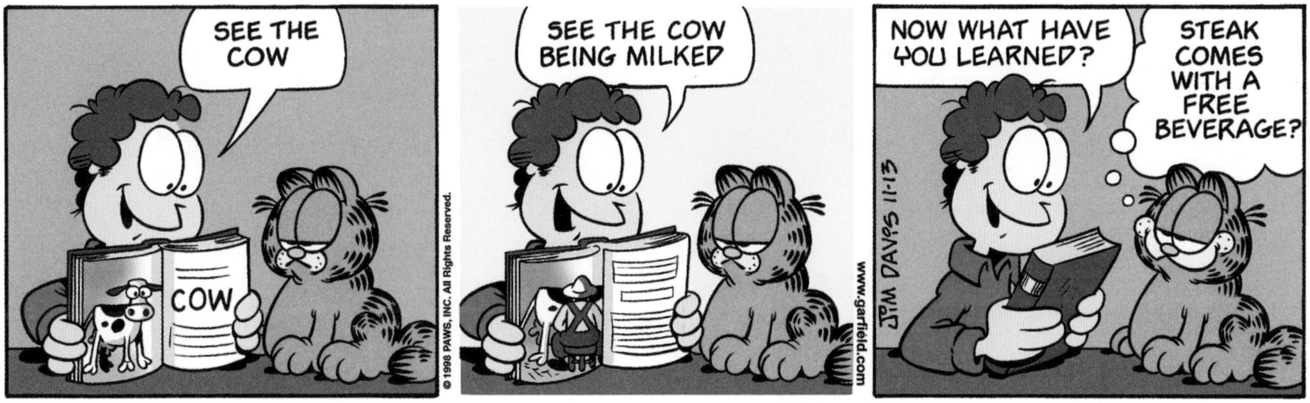
SEE THE COW
COW
© 1998 PAWS, INC. All Rights Reserved.
SEE THE COW BEING MILKED
www.garfield.com
JIM DAVIS 11-13
NOW WHAT HAVE YOU LEARNED?
STEAK COMES WITH A FREE BEVERAGE?

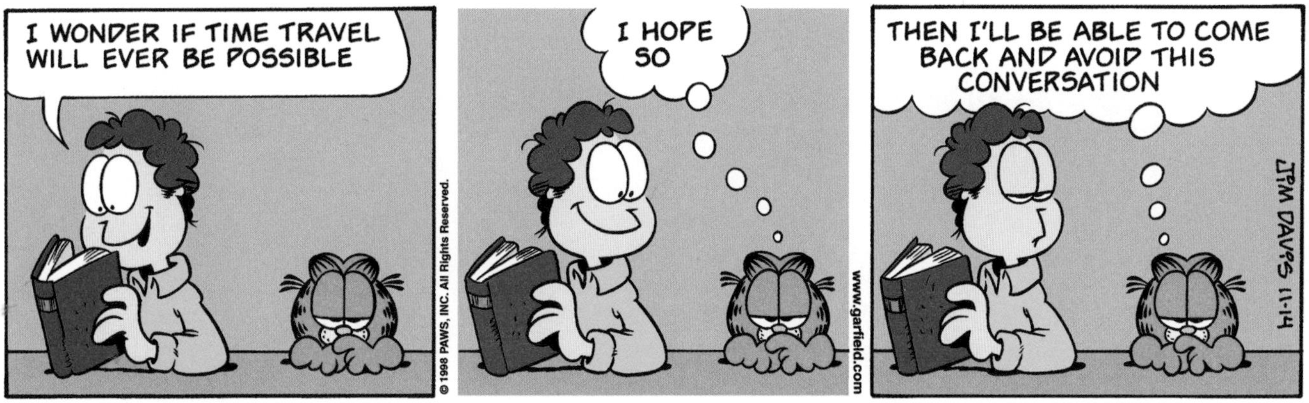
I WONDER IF TIME TRAVEL WILL EVER BE POSSIBLE
© 1998 PAWS, INC. All Rights Reserved.
I HOPE SO
www.garfield.com
THEN I'LL BE ABLE TO COME BACK AND AVOID THIS CONVERSATION
JIM DAVIS 11-14

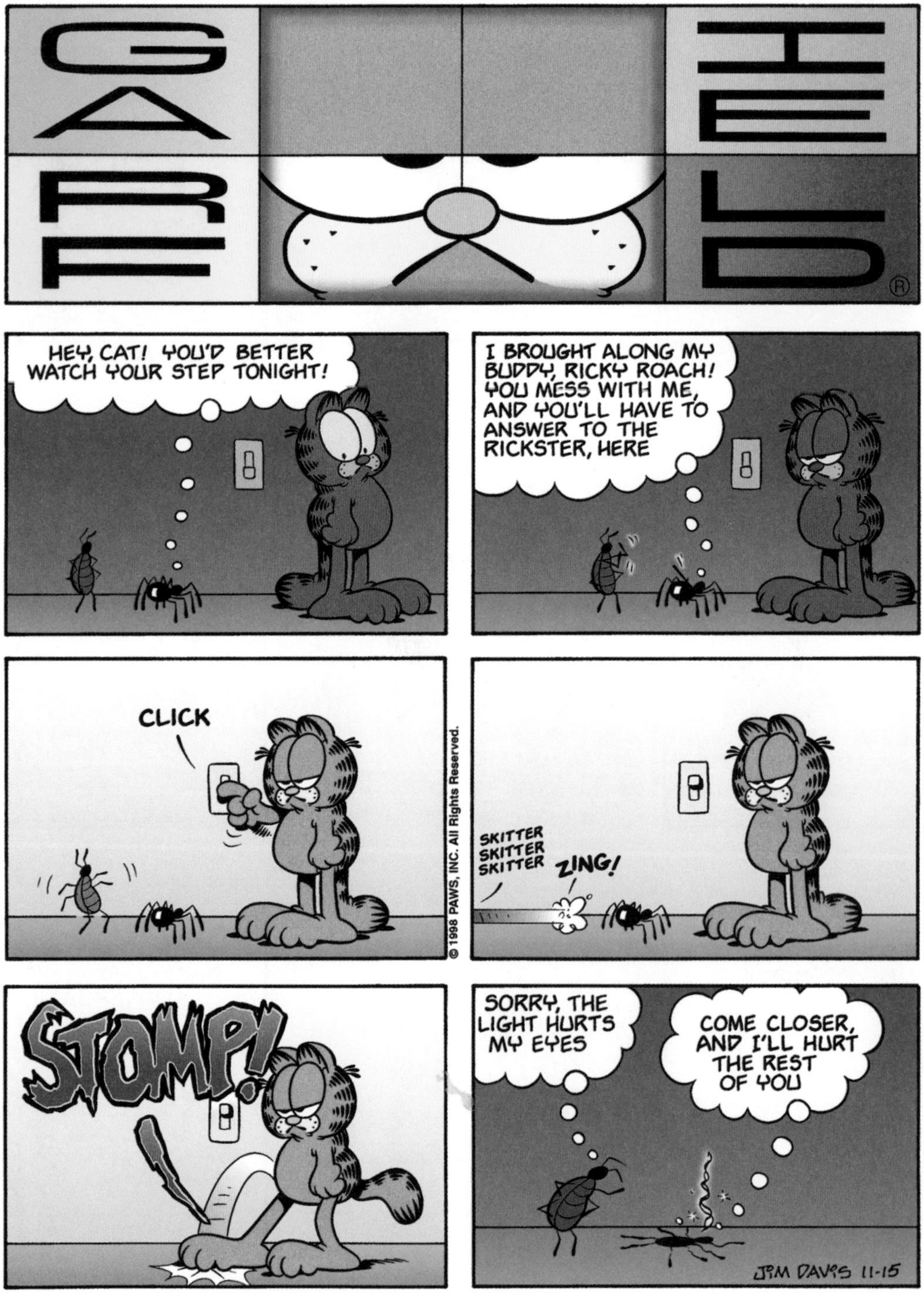
GARFIELD®
HEY, CAT! YOU'D BETTER WATCH YOUR STEP TONIGHT!
I BROUGHT ALONG MY BUDDY, RICKY ROACH! YOU MESS WITH ME, AND YOU'LL HAVE TO ANSWER TO THE RICKSTER, HERE
CLICK
SKITTER SKITTER SKITTER
ZING!
STOMP!
SORRY, THE LIGHT HURTS MY EYES
COME CLOSER, AND I'LL HURT THE REST OF YOU
JIM DAVIS 11-15
© 1998 PAWS, INC. All Rights Reserved.

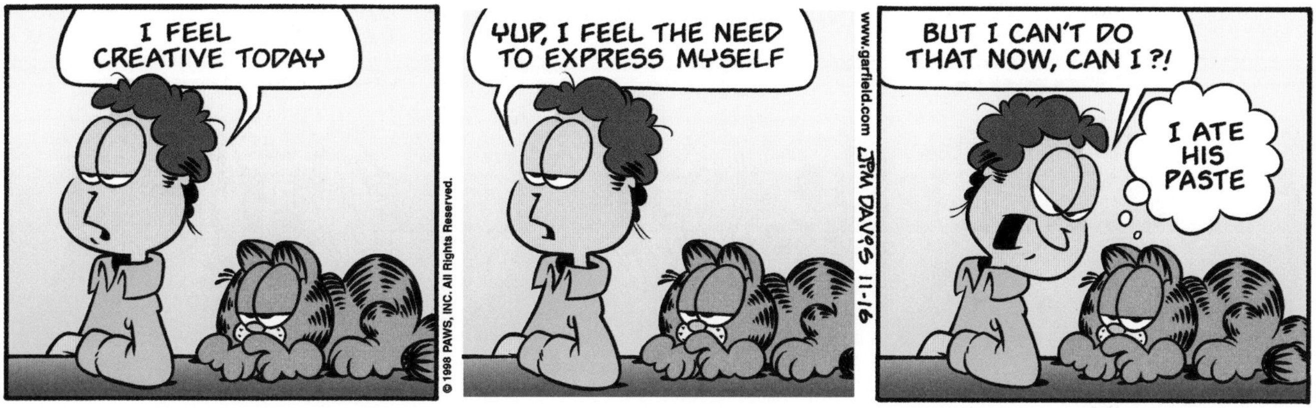
I FEEL CREATIVE TODAY
YUP, I FEEL THE NEED TO EXPRESS MYSELF
BUT I CAN'T DO THAT NOW, CAN I ?!
I ATE HIS PASTE
© 1998 PAWS, INC. All Rights Reserved.
www.garfield.com
JIM DAVIS 11-16

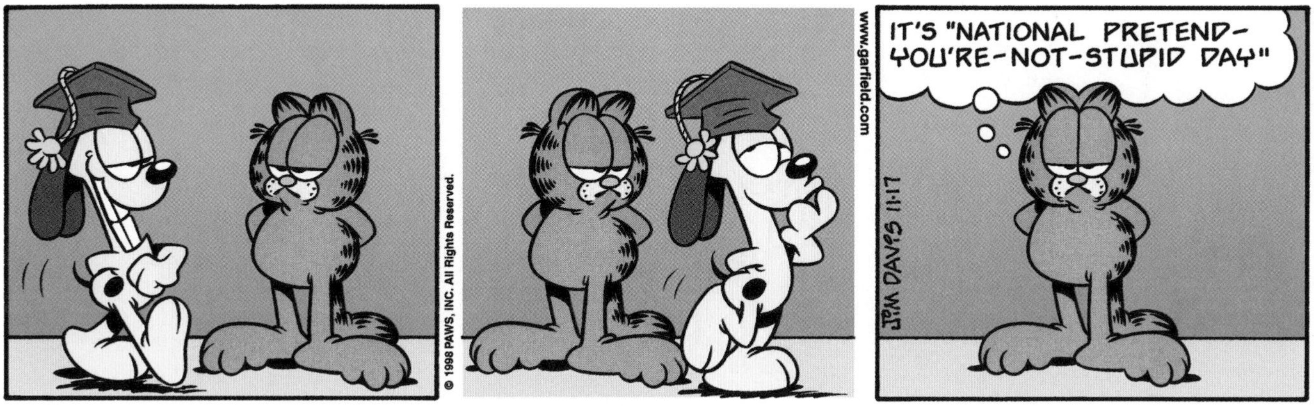
IT'S "NATIONAL PRETEND-YOU'RE-NOT-STUPID DAY"
© 1998 PAWS, INC. All Rights Reserved.
www.garfield.com
JIM DAVIS 11-17

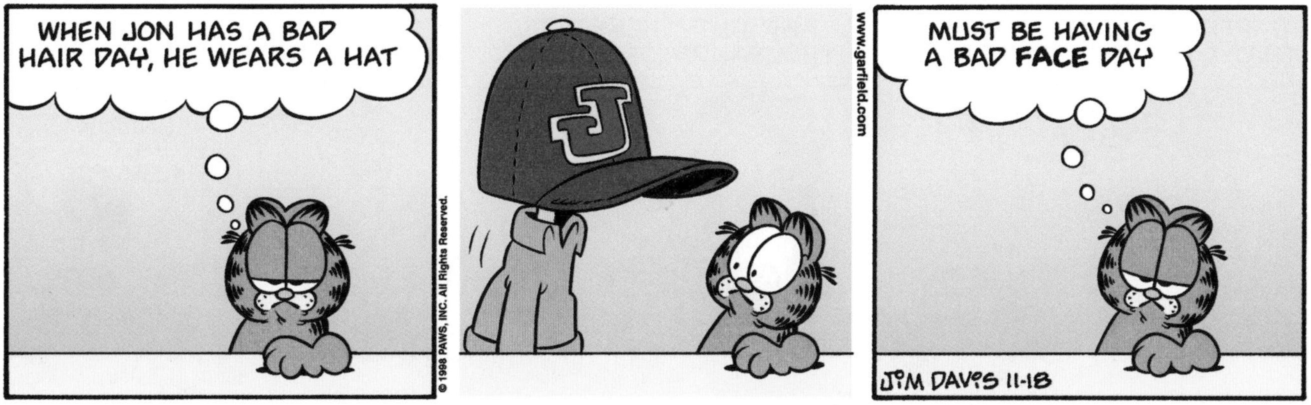
WHEN JON HAS A BAD HAIR DAY, HE WEARS A HAT
J
MUST BE HAVING A BAD FACE DAY
© 1998 PAWS, INC. All Rights Reserved.
www.garfield.com
JIM DAVIS 11-18

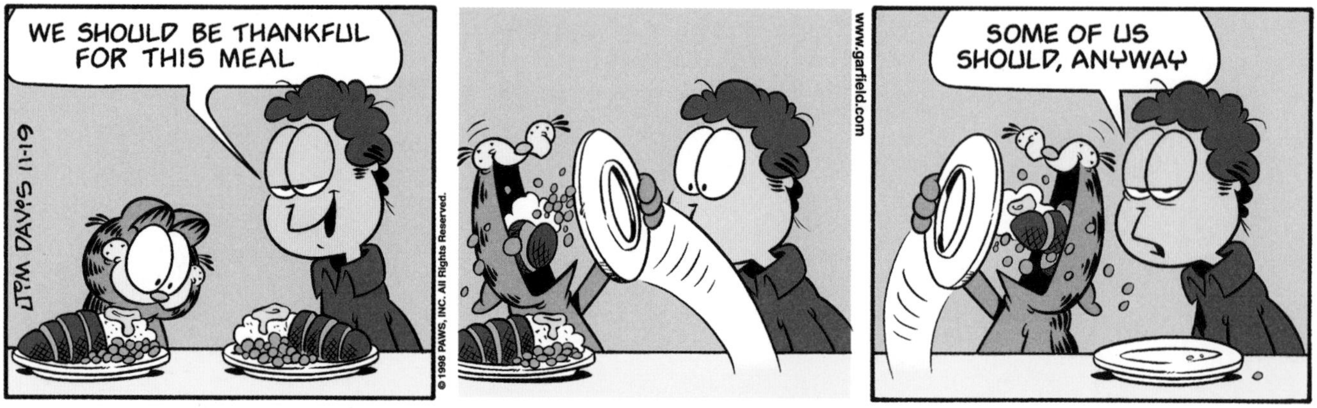
WE SHOULD BE THANKFUL FOR THIS MEAL
JIM DAVIS 11-19
© 1998 PAWS, INC. All Rights Reserved.
www.garfield.com
SOME OF US SHOULD, ANYWAY

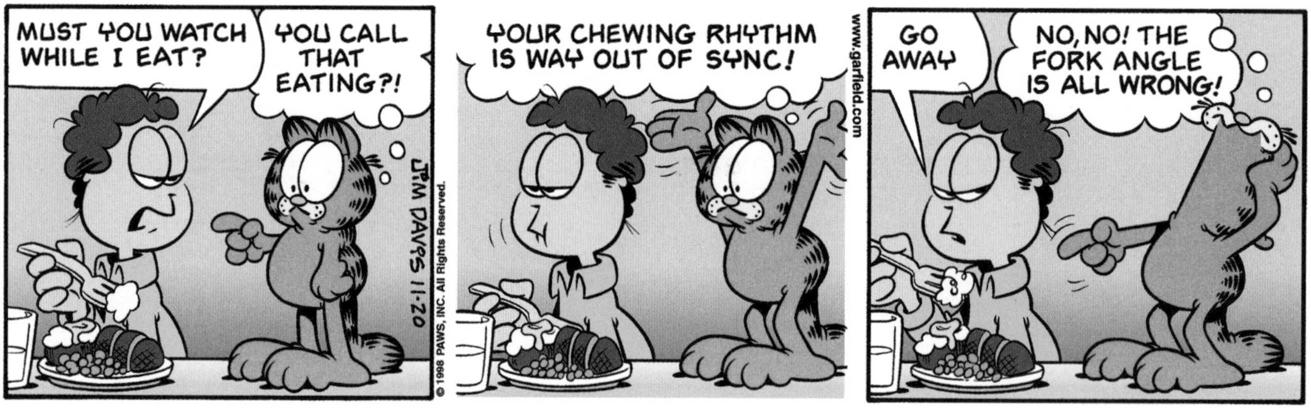
MUST YOU WATCH WHILE I EAT?
YOU CALL THAT EATING?!
JIM DAVIS 11-20
© 1998 PAWS, INC. All Rights Reserved.
YOUR CHEWING RHYTHM IS WAY OUT OF SYNC!
www.garfield.com
GO AWAY
NO, NO! THE FORK ANGLE IS ALL WRONG!

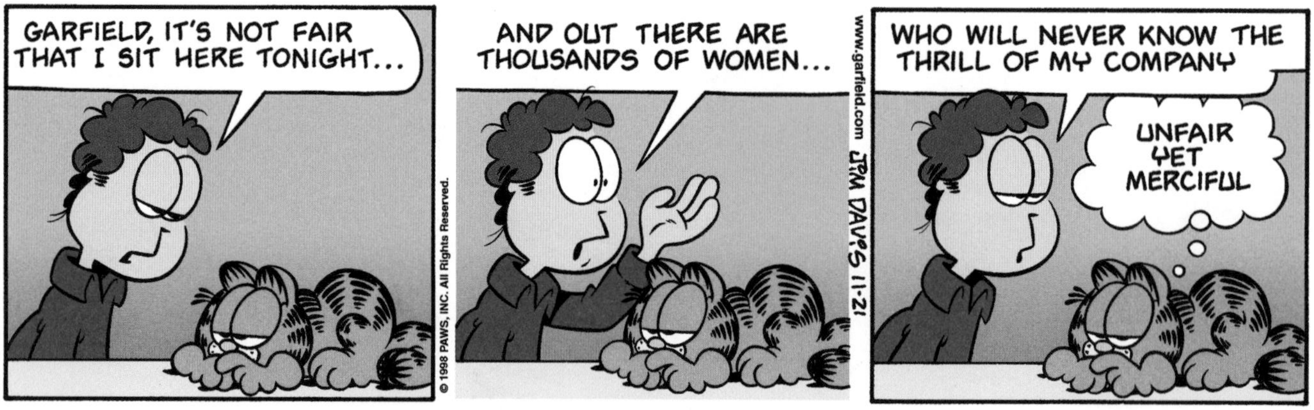
GARFIELD, IT'S NOT FAIR THAT I SIT HERE TONIGHT...
© 1998 PAWS, INC. All Rights Reserved.
AND OUT THERE ARE THOUSANDS OF WOMEN...
www.garfield.com
JIM DAVIS 11-21
WHO WILL NEVER KNOW THE THRILL OF MY COMPANY
UNFAIR YET MERCIFUL

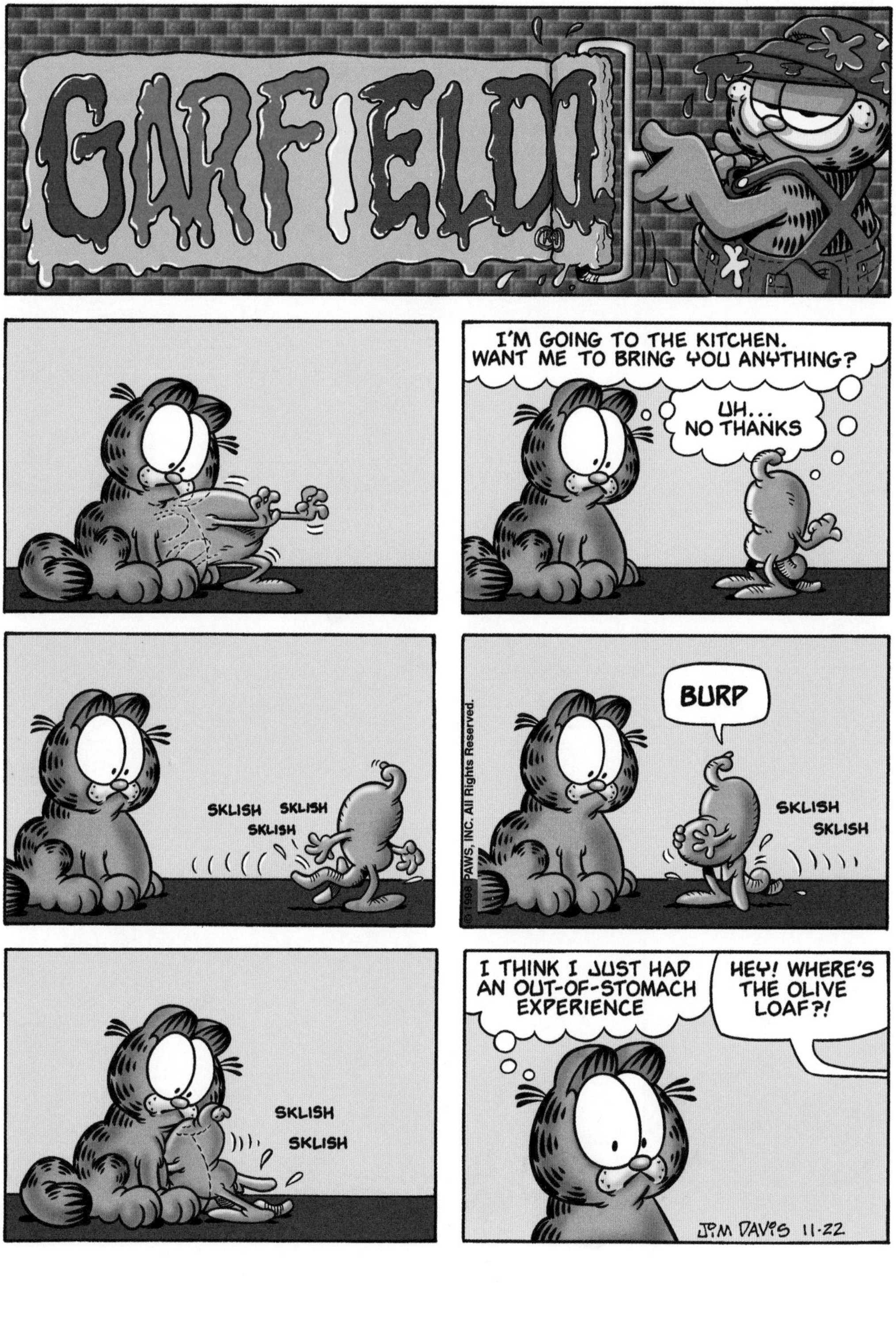
GARFIELD®
I'M GOING TO THE KITCHEN. WANT ME TO BRING YOU ANYTHING?
UH... NO THANKS
SKLISH SKLISH
SKLISH
© 1998 PAWS, INC. All Rights Reserved.
BURP
SKLISH
SKLISH
SKLISH
SKLISH
I THINK I JUST HAD AN OUT-OF-STOMACH EXPERIENCE
HEY! WHERE'S THE OLIVE LOAF?!
JIM DAVIS 11-22

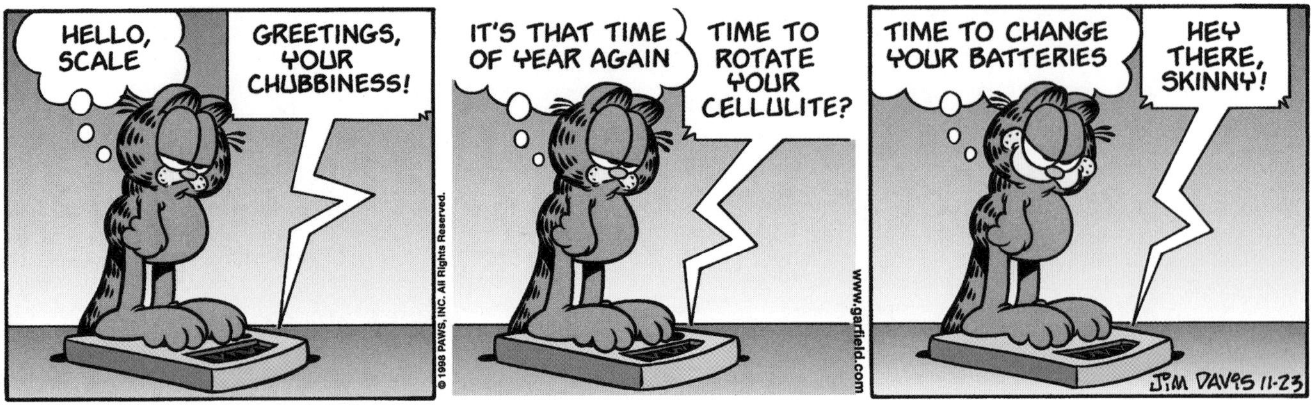
HELLO, SCALE
GREETINGS, YOUR CHUBBINESS!
IT'S THAT TIME OF YEAR AGAIN
TIME TO ROTATE YOUR CELLULITE?
TIME TO CHANGE YOUR BATTERIES
HEY THERE, SKINNY!
© 1998 PAWS, INC. All Rights Reserved.
www.garfield.com
JIM DAVIS 11-23

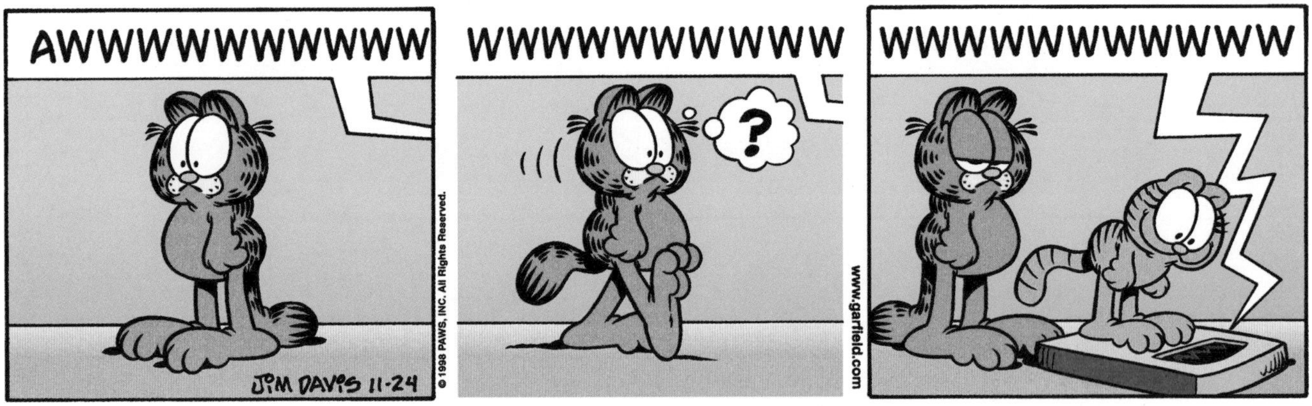
AWWWWWWWWWWW
WWWWWWWWWWWW
WWWWWWWWWWWWW
?
© 1998 PAWS, INC. All Rights Reserved.
www.garfield.com
JIM DAVIS 11-24

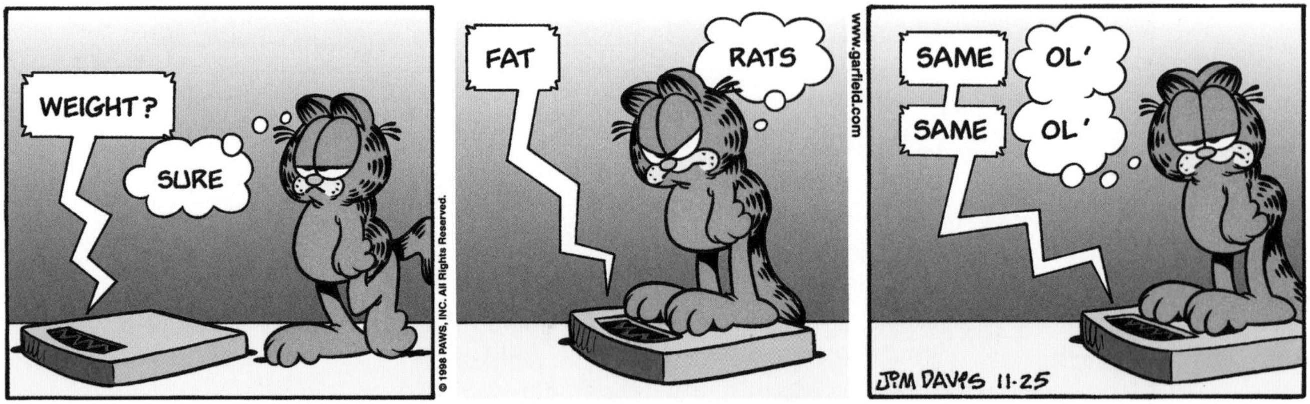
WEIGHT?
SURE
FAT
RATS
SAME
SAME
OL'
OL'
© 1998 PAWS, INC. All Rights Reserved.
www.garfield.com
JIM DAVIS 11-25

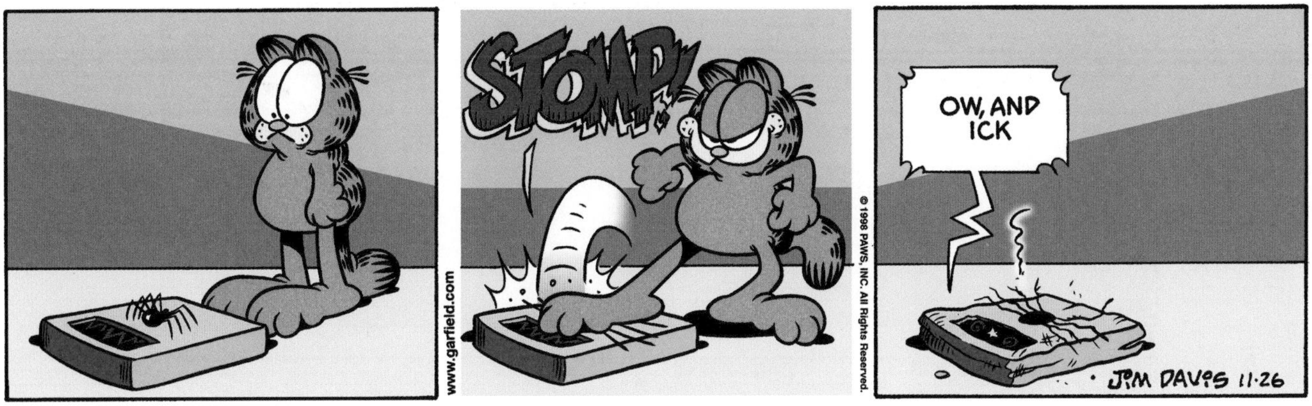
STOMP!
OW, AND ICK
JIM DAVIS 11-26
www.garfield.com
© 1998 PAWS, INC. All Rights Reserved.

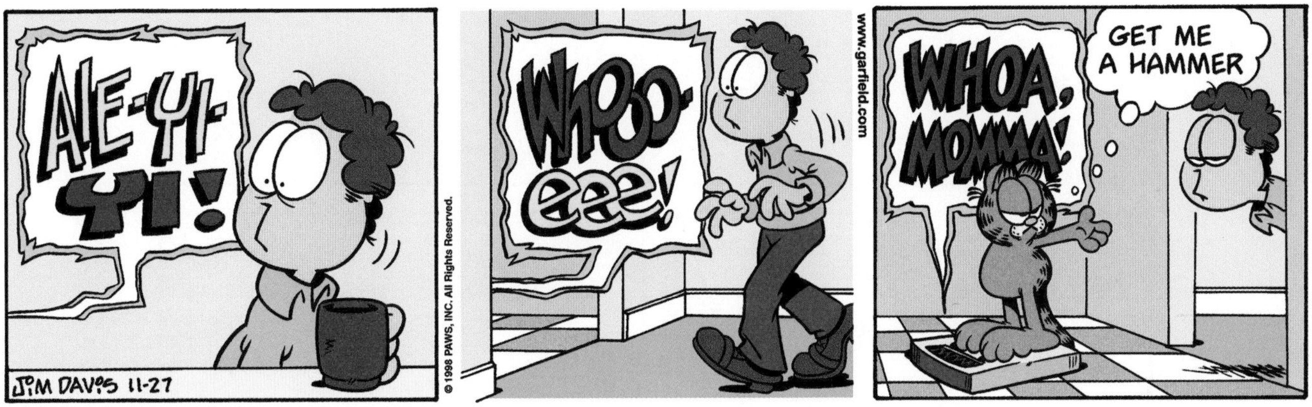
AIE-YI-YI!
JIM DAVIS 11-27
© 1998 PAWS, INC. All Rights Reserved.
WHOO-eee!
www.garfield.com
WHOA, MOMMA!
GET ME A HAMMER

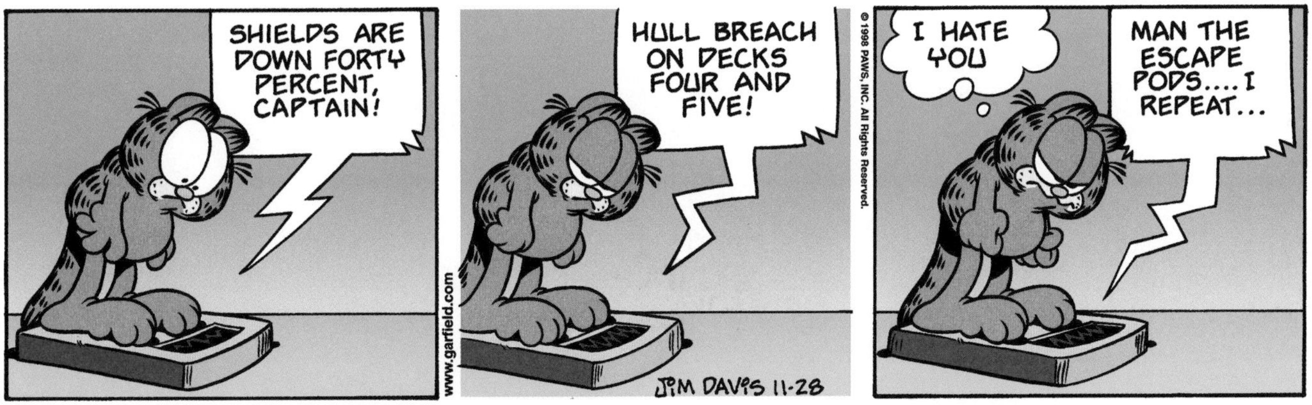
SHIELDS ARE DOWN FORTY PERCENT, CAPTAIN!
www.garfield.com
HULL BREACH ON DECKS FOUR AND FIVE!
JIM DAVIS 11-28
© 1998 PAWS, INC. All Rights Reserved.
I HATE YOU
MAN THE ESCAPE PODS.... I REPEAT...

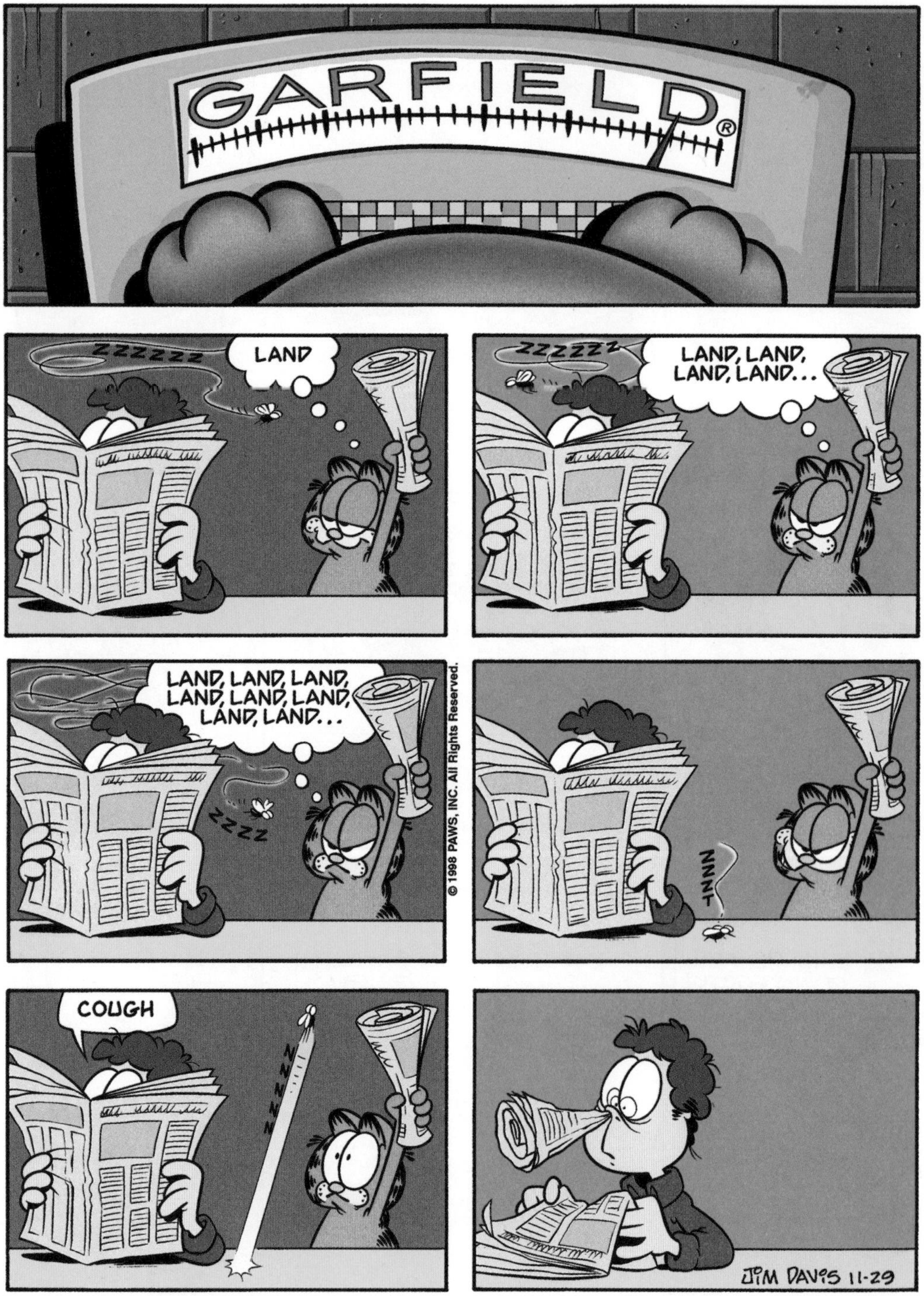
GARFIELD®
ZZZZZZZ
LAND
ZZZZZZ
LAND, LAND,
LAND, LAND...
LAND, LAND, LAND,
LAND, LAND, LAND,
LAND, LAND...
ZZZZ
© 1998 PAWS, INC. All Rights Reserved.
ZZZT
COUGH
ZZZZZ
JIM DAVIS 11-29

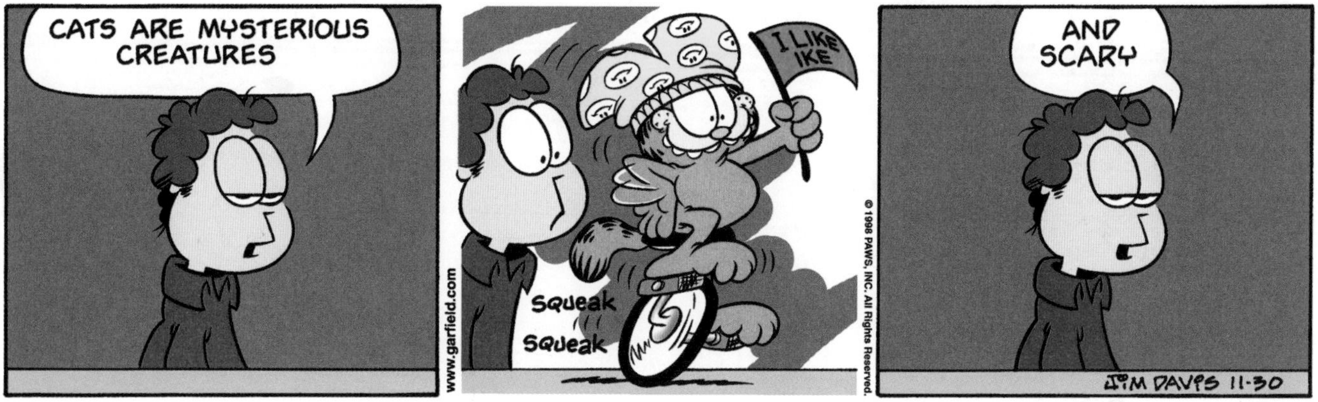
CATS ARE MYSTERIOUS CREATURES
I LIKE IKE
SQUEAK
SQUEAK
www.garfield.com
© 1998 PAWS, INC. All Rights Reserved.
AND SCARY
JIM DAVIS 11-30

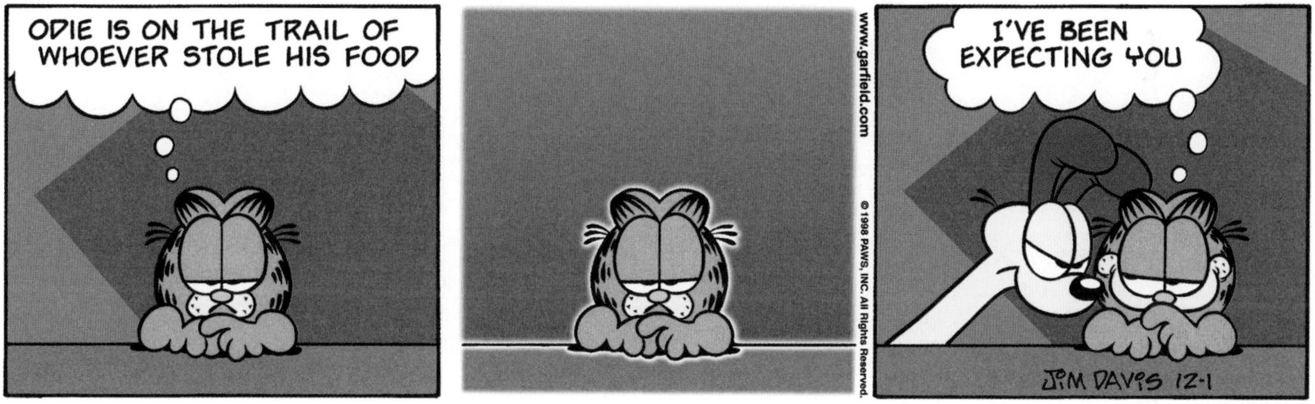
ODIE IS ON THE TRAIL OF WHOEVER STOLE HIS FOOD
www.garfield.com
© 1998 PAWS, INC. All Rights Reserved.
I'VE BEEN EXPECTING YOU
JIM DAVIS 12-1

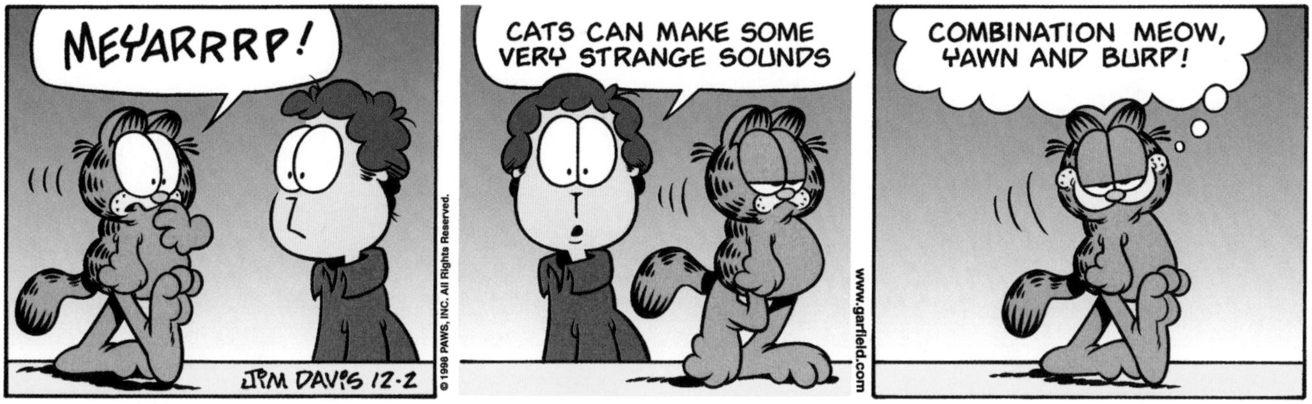
MEYARRRP!
JIM DAVIS 12-2
© 1998 PAWS, INC. All Rights Reserved.
CATS CAN MAKE SOME VERY STRANGE SOUNDS
www.garfield.com
COMBINATION MEOW, YAWN AND BURP!

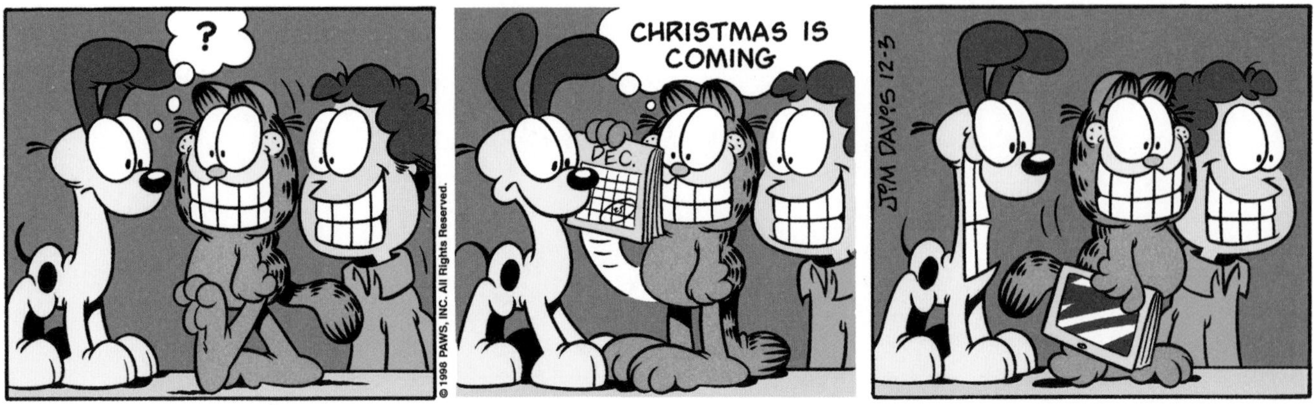
?
CHRISTMAS IS COMING
DEC.
JIM DAVIS 12-3

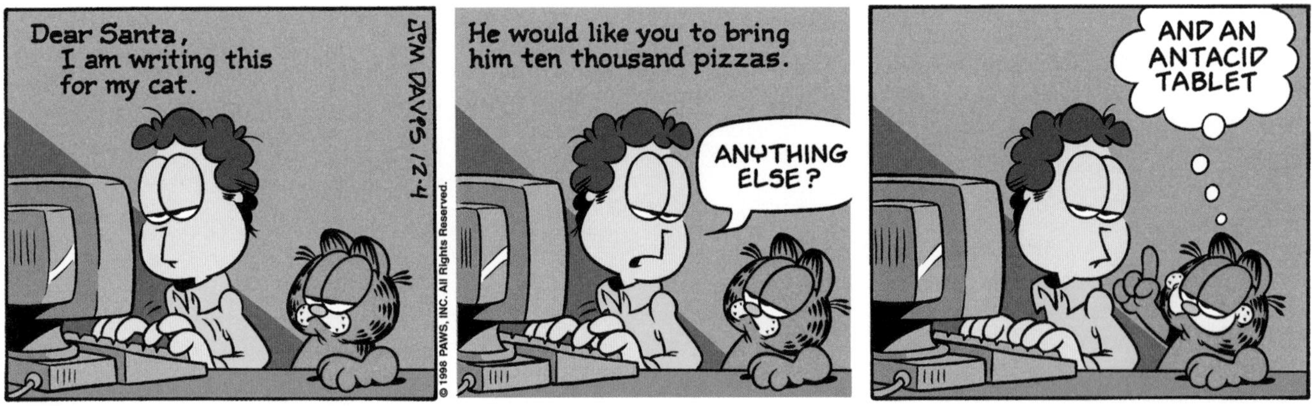
Dear Santa,
I am writing this for my cat.
JIM DAVIS 12-4
He would like you to bring him ten thousand pizzas.
ANYTHING ELSE?
AND AN ANTACID TABLET

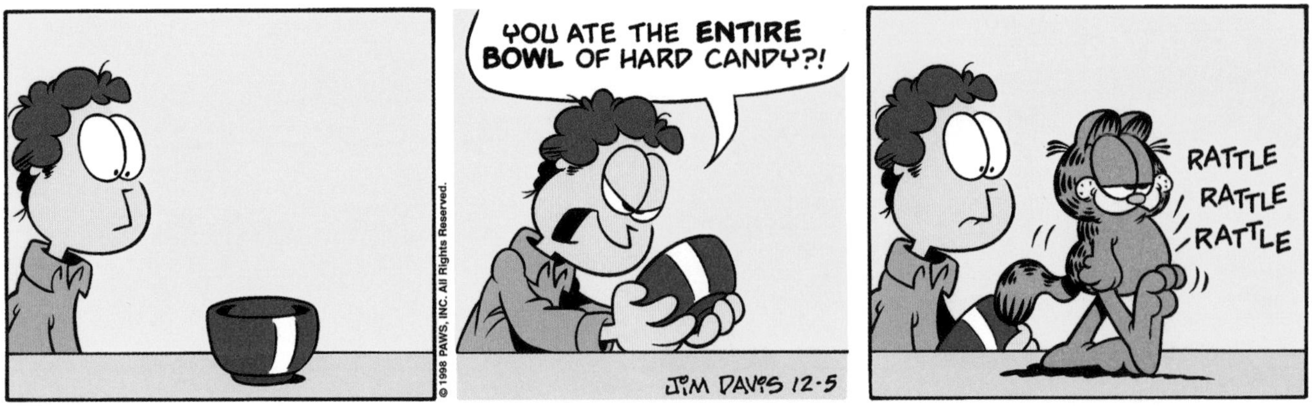
YOU ATE THE **ENTIRE BOWL** OF HARD CANDY?!
JIM DAVIS 12-5
RATTLE
RATTLE
RATTLE

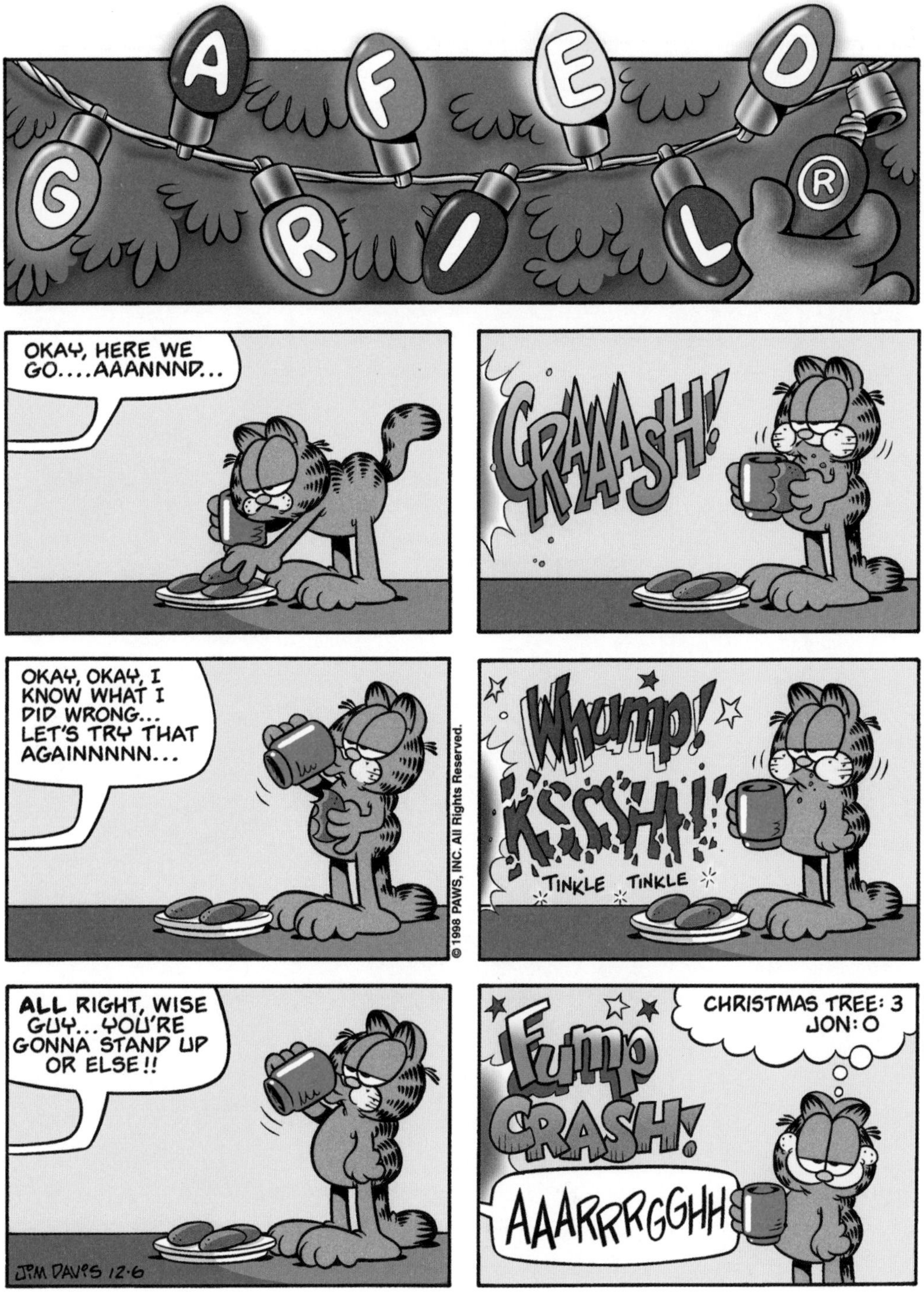
GARFIELD®
OKAY, HERE WE GO....AAANNND...
CRAAASH!
OKAY, OKAY, I KNOW WHAT I DID WRONG... LET'S TRY THAT AGAINNNNN...
Whump!
KSSSH!
TINKLE TINKLE
ALL RIGHT, WISE GUY... YOU'RE GONNA STAND UP OR ELSE!!
JIM DAVIS 12-6
Fump
CRASH!
AAARRRGGHH
CHRISTMAS TREE: 3 JON: 0
© 1998 PAWS, INC. All Rights Reserved.

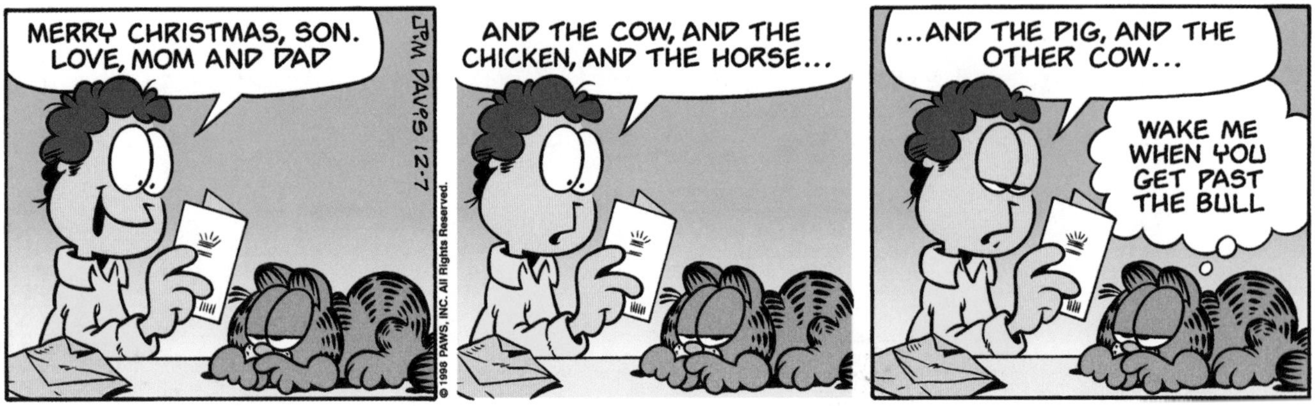
MERRY CHRISTMAS, SON. LOVE, MOM AND DAD
JIM DAVIS 12-7
© 1998 PAWS, INC. All Rights Reserved.
AND THE COW, AND THE CHICKEN, AND THE HORSE...
...AND THE PIG, AND THE OTHER COW...
WAKE ME WHEN YOU GET PAST THE BULL

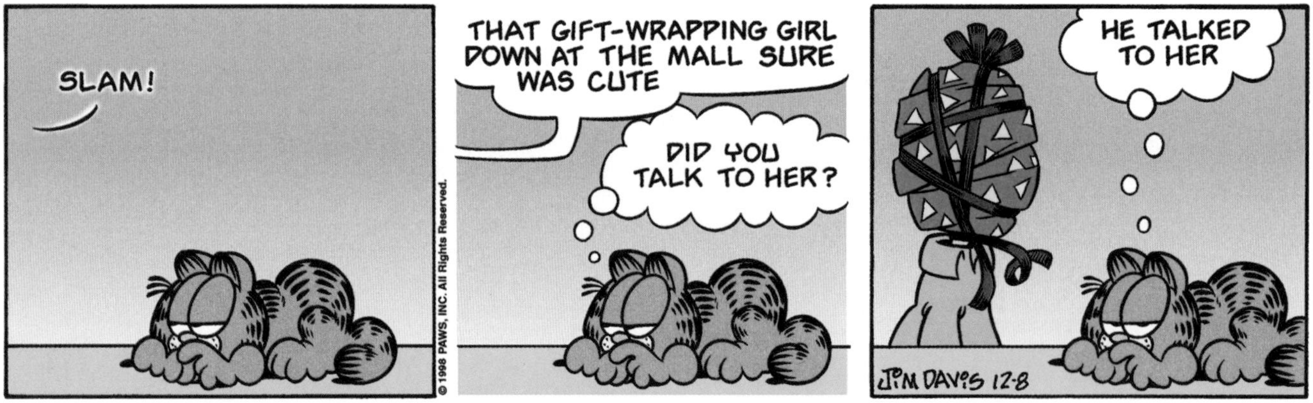
SLAM!
© 1998 PAWS, INC. All Rights Reserved.
THAT GIFT-WRAPPING GIRL DOWN AT THE MALL SURE WAS CUTE
DID YOU TALK TO HER?
HE TALKED TO HER
JIM DAVIS 12-8

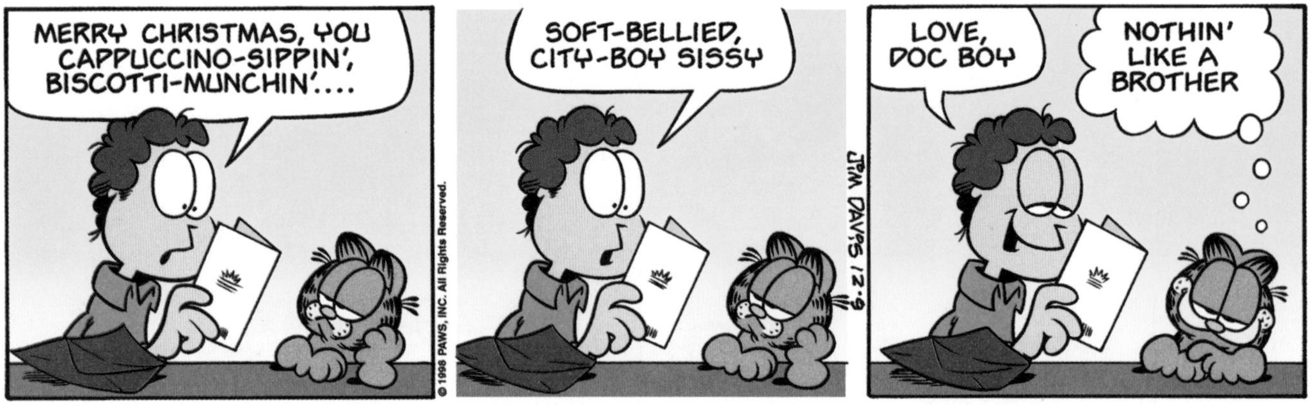
MERRY CHRISTMAS, YOU CAPPUCCINO-SIPPIN', BISCOTTI-MUNCHIN'....
© 1998 PAWS, INC. All Rights Reserved.
SOFT-BELLIED, CITY-BOY SISSY
JIM DAVIS 12-9
LOVE, DOC BOY
NOTHIN' LIKE A BROTHER

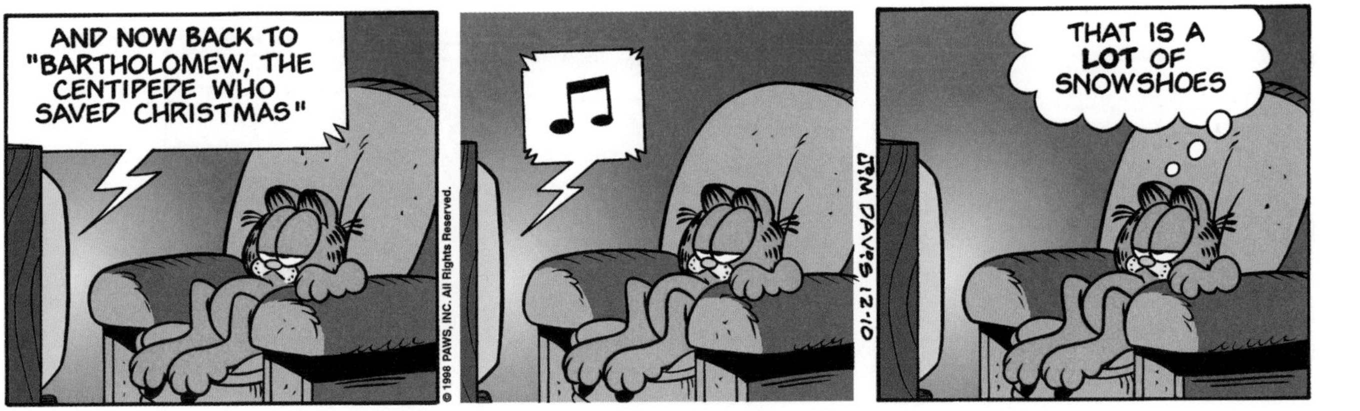
AND NOW BACK TO "BARTHOLOMEW, THE CENTIPEDE WHO SAVED CHRISTMAS"
© 1998 PAWS, INC. All Rights Reserved.
JIM DAVIS 12-10
THAT IS A LOT OF SNOWSHOES

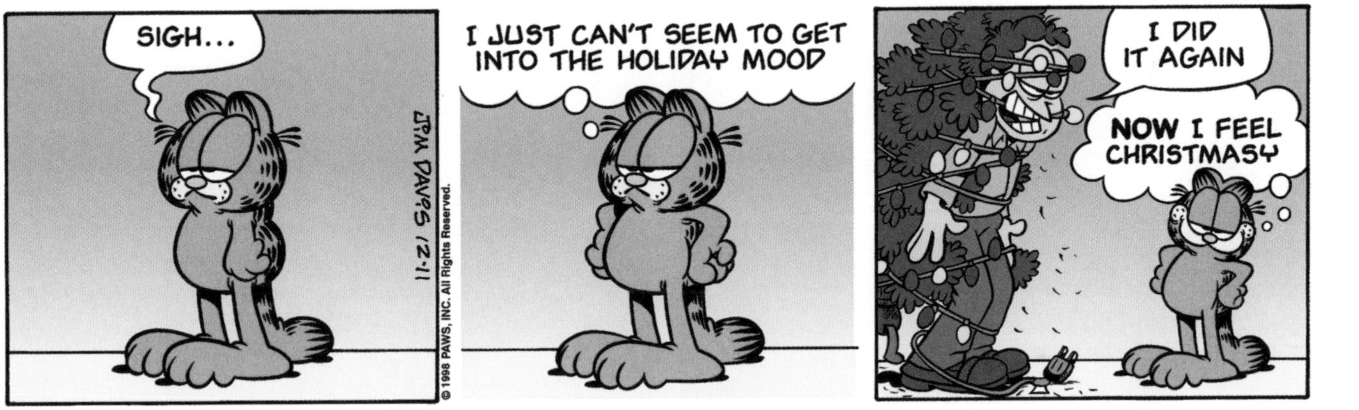
SIGH...
JIM DAVIS 12-11
© 1998 PAWS, INC. All Rights Reserved.
I JUST CAN'T SEEM TO GET INTO THE HOLIDAY MOOD
I DID IT AGAIN
NOW I FEEL CHRISTMASY

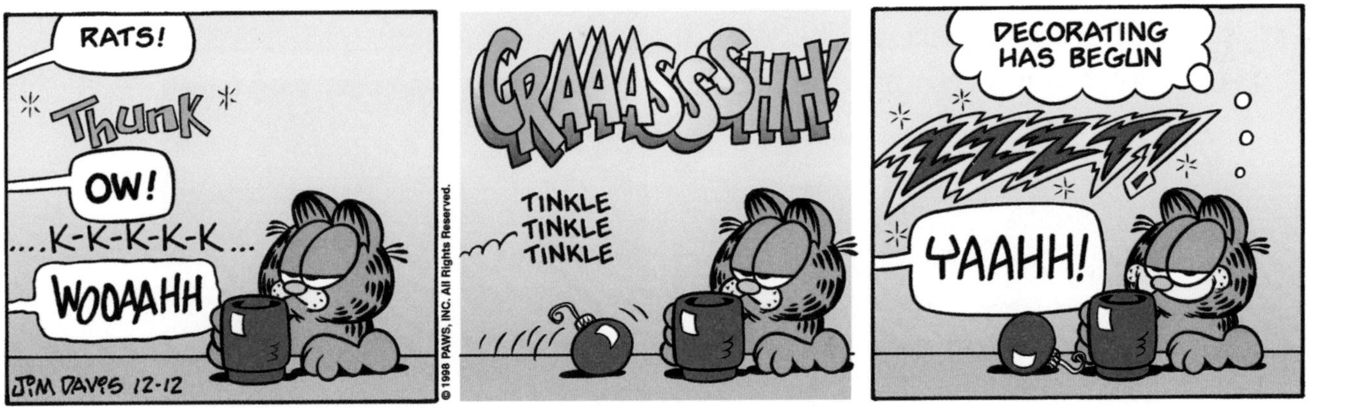
RATS!
Thunk
OW!
....K-K-K-K-K....
WOOAAHH
JIM DAVIS 12-12
© 1998 PAWS, INC. All Rights Reserved.
CRAAASSSHH!
TINKLE TINKLE TINKLE
DECORATING HAS BEGUN
ZZZT!
YAAHH!

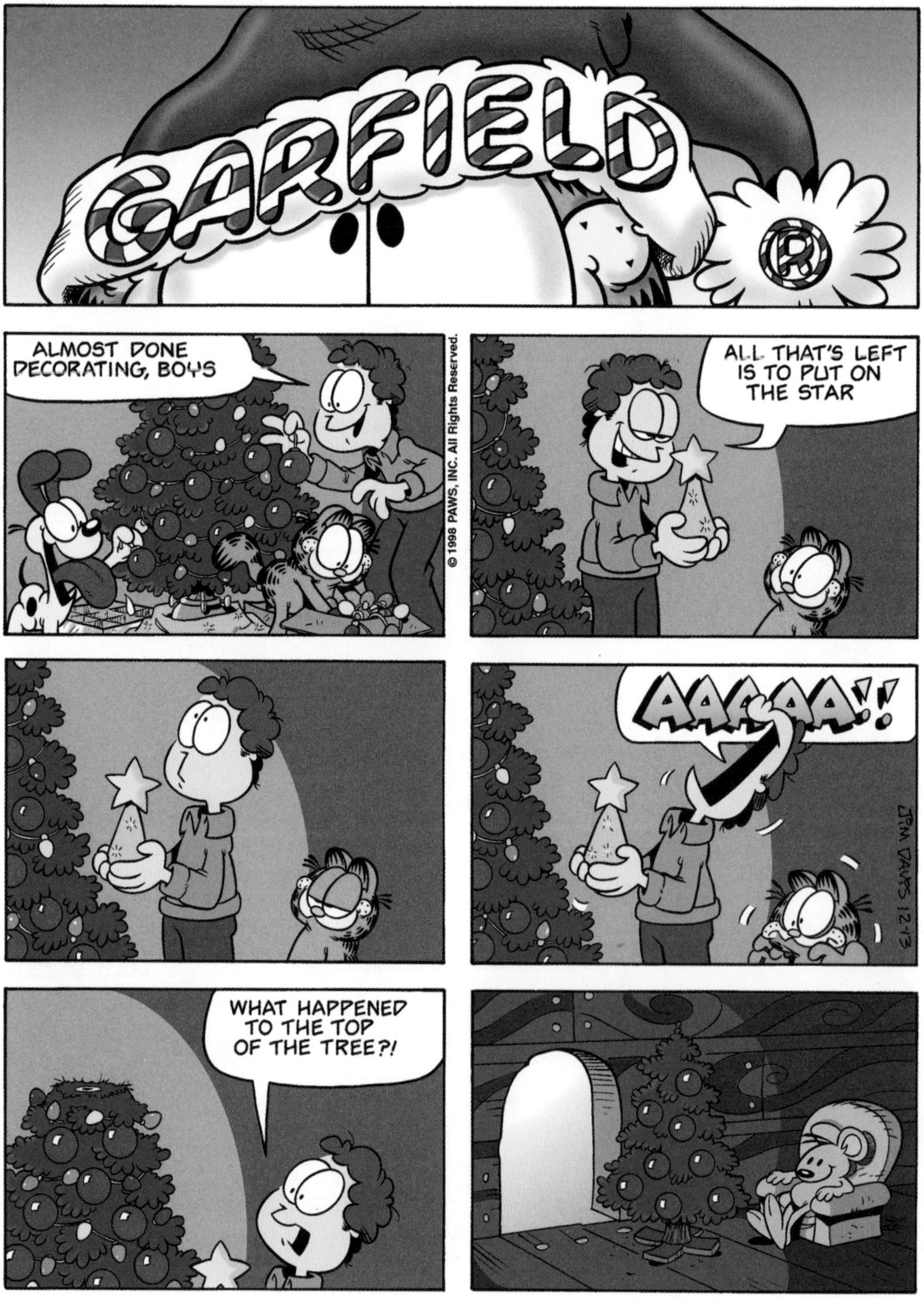
GARFIELD®
ALMOST DONE DECORATING, BOYS
© 1998 PAWS, INC. All Rights Reserved.
ALL THAT'S LEFT IS TO PUT ON THE STAR
AAAAA!!
JIM DAVIS 12-13
WHAT HAPPENED TO THE TOP OF THE TREE?!

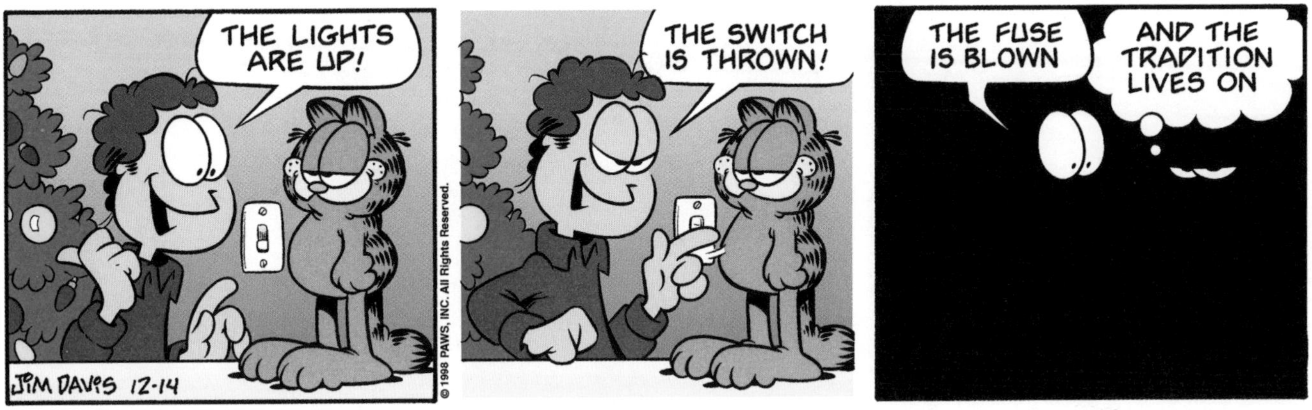
THE LIGHTS ARE UP!
JIM DAVIS 12-14
© 1998 PAWS, INC. All Rights Reserved.
THE SWITCH IS THROWN!
THE FUSE IS BLOWN
AND THE TRADITION LIVES ON

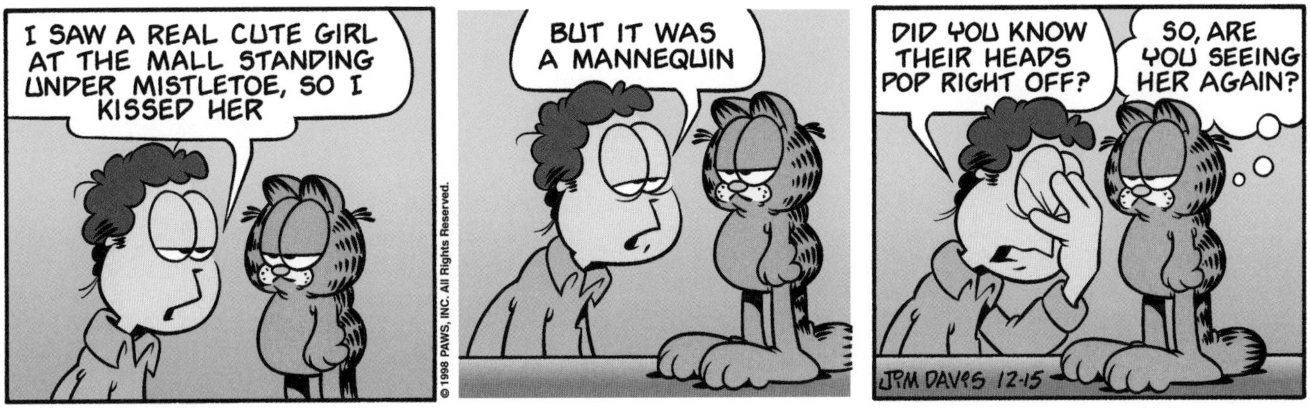
I SAW A REAL CUTE GIRL AT THE MALL STANDING UNDER MISTLETOE, SO I KISSED HER
© 1998 PAWS, INC. All Rights Reserved.
BUT IT WAS A MANNEQUIN
DID YOU KNOW THEIR HEADS POP RIGHT OFF?
SO, ARE YOU SEEING HER AGAIN?
JIM DAVIS 12-15

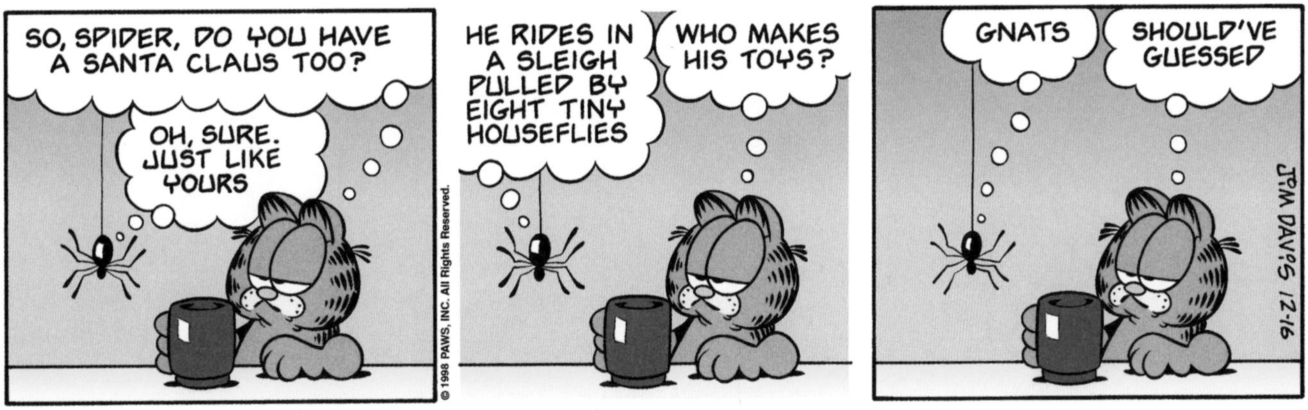
SO, SPIDER, DO YOU HAVE A SANTA CLAUS TOO?
OH, SURE. JUST LIKE YOURS
© 1998 PAWS, INC. All Rights Reserved.
HE RIDES IN A SLEIGH PULLED BY EIGHT TINY HOUSEFLIES
WHO MAKES HIS TOYS?
GNATS
SHOULD'VE GUESSED
JIM DAVIS 12-16

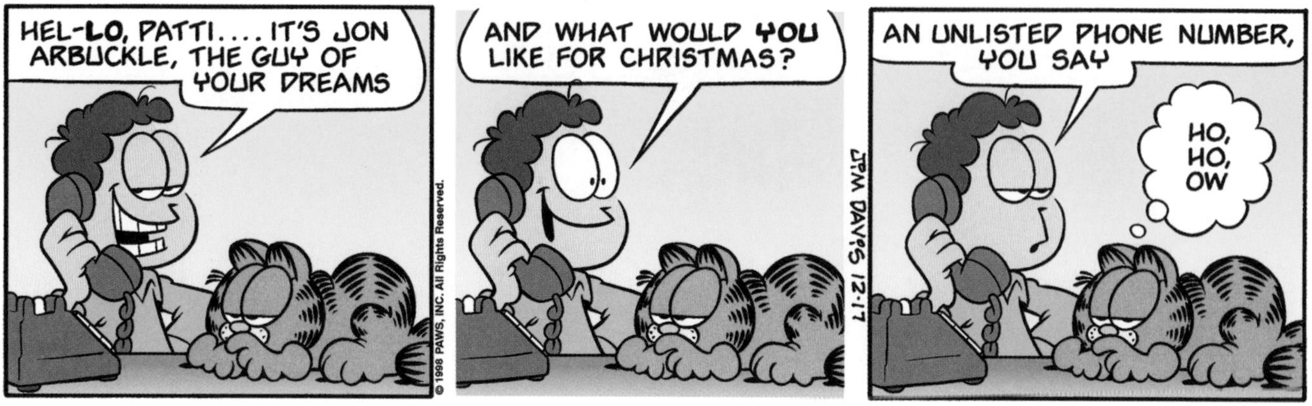
HEL-LO, PATTI.... IT'S JON ARBUCKLE, THE GUY OF YOUR DREAMS
AND WHAT WOULD YOU LIKE FOR CHRISTMAS?
AN UNLISTED PHONE NUMBER, YOU SAY
HO, HO, OW
JIM DAVIS 12-17
© 1998 PAWS, INC. All Rights Reserved.

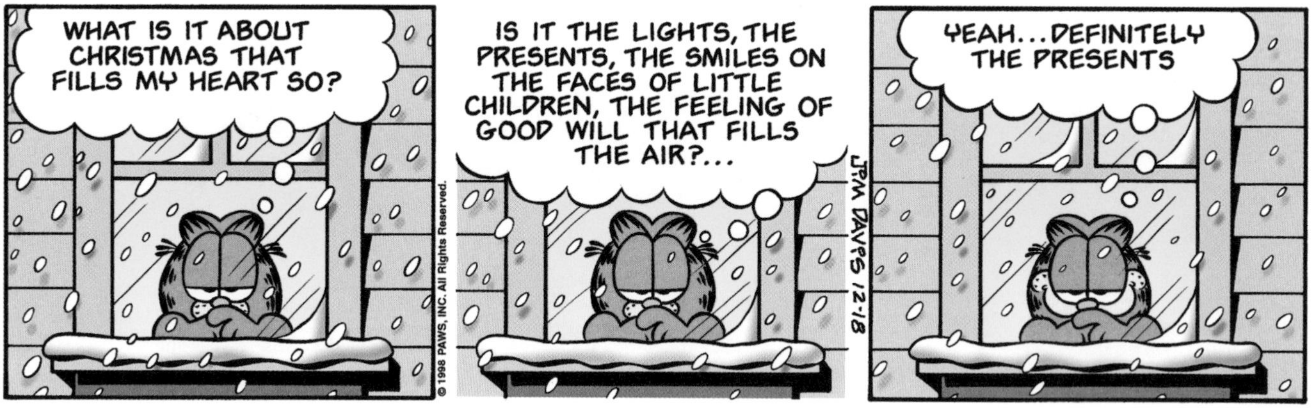
WHAT IS IT ABOUT CHRISTMAS THAT FILLS MY HEART SO?
IS IT THE LIGHTS, THE PRESENTS, THE SMILES ON THE FACES OF LITTLE CHILDREN, THE FEELING OF GOOD WILL THAT FILLS THE AIR?...
YEAH...DEFINITELY THE PRESENTS
JIM DAVIS 12-18
© 1998 PAWS, INC. All Rights Reserved.

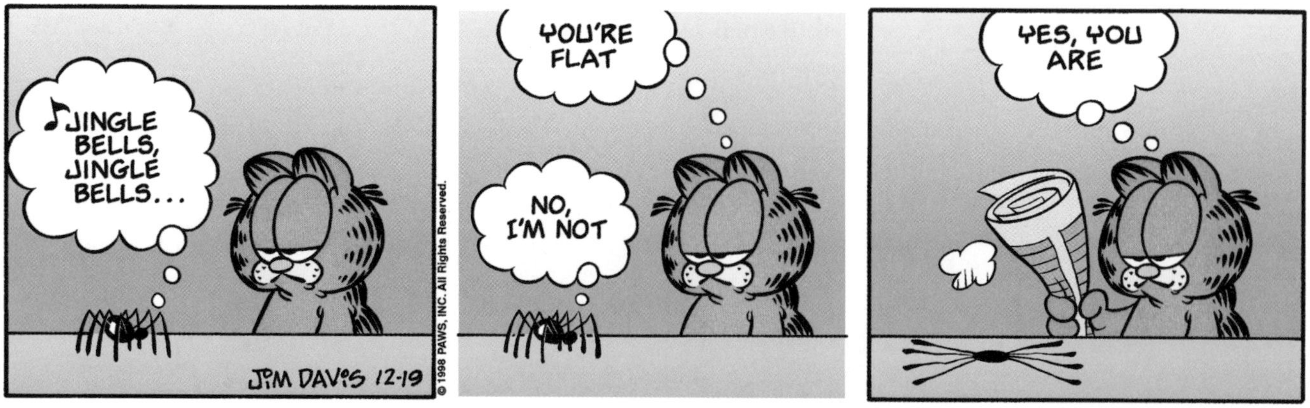
♪JINGLE BELLS, JINGLE BELLS...
YOU'RE FLAT
NO, I'M NOT
YES, YOU ARE
JIM DAVIS 12-19
© 1998 PAWS, INC. All Rights Reserved.

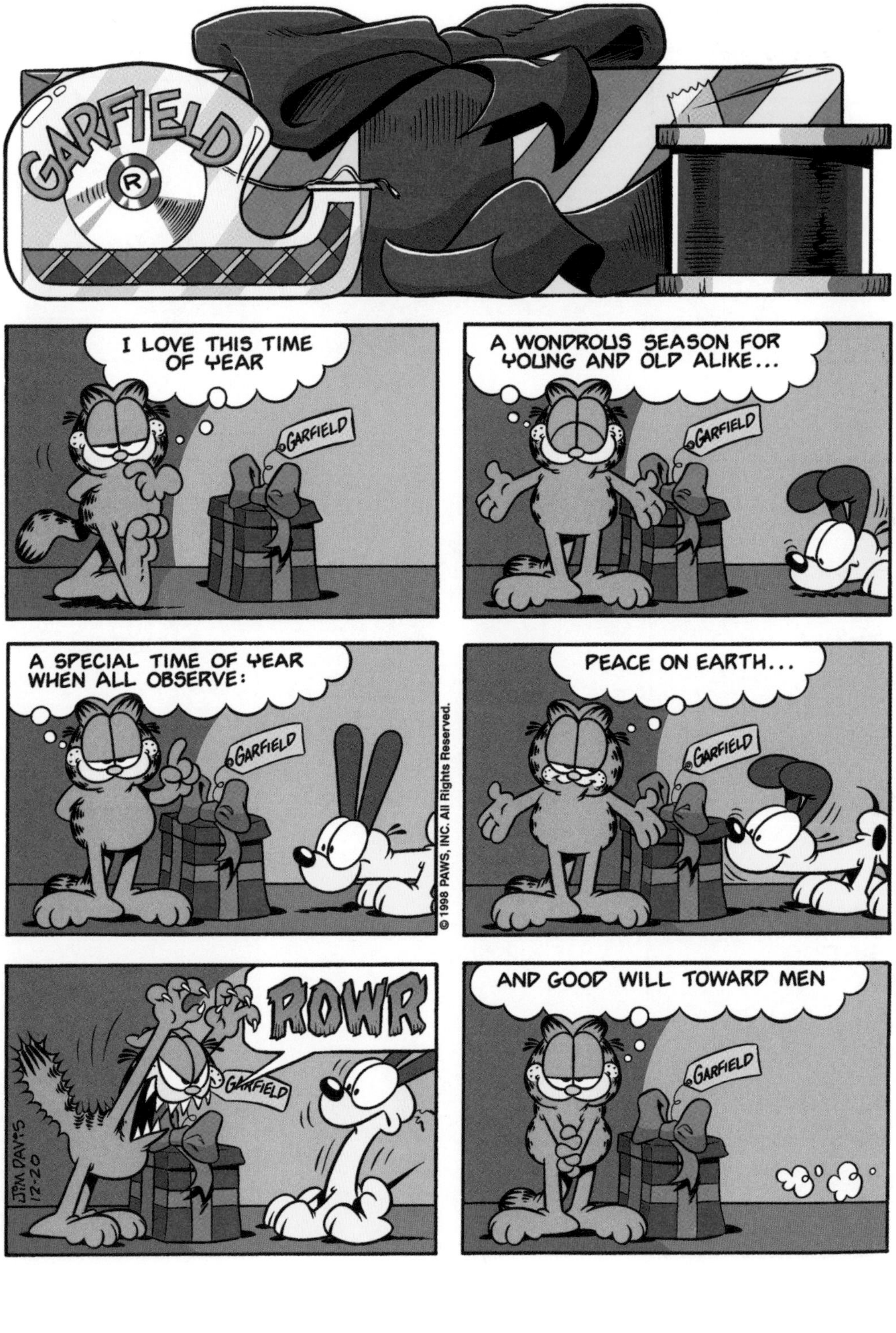
GARFIELD
I LOVE THIS TIME OF YEAR
A WONDROUS SEASON FOR YOUNG AND OLD ALIKE...
A SPECIAL TIME OF YEAR WHEN ALL OBSERVE:
PEACE ON EARTH...
ROWR
AND GOOD WILL TOWARD MEN
JIM DAVIS 12-20

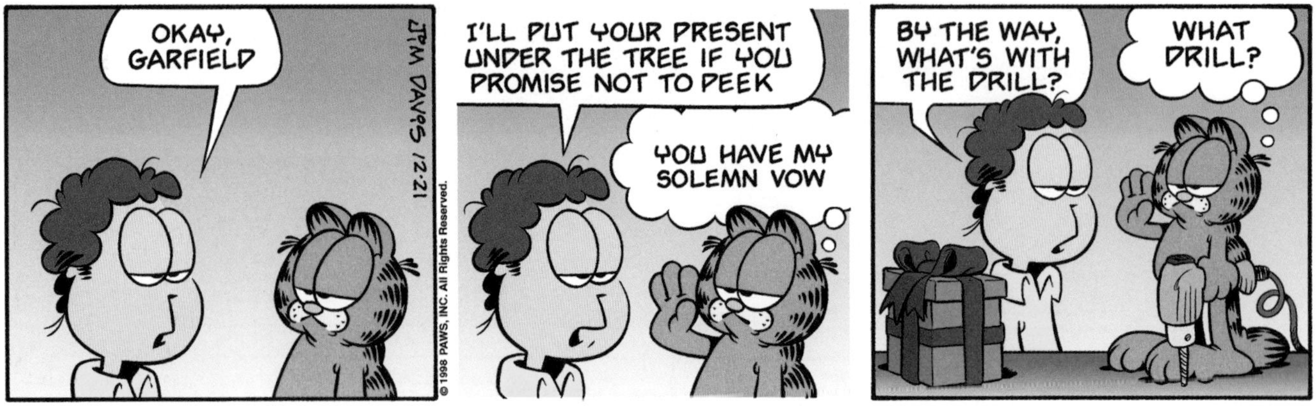
OKAY, GARFIELD
JIM DAVIS 12-21
© 1998 PAWS, INC. All Rights Reserved.
I'LL PUT YOUR PRESENT UNDER THE TREE IF YOU PROMISE NOT TO PEEK
YOU HAVE MY SOLEMN VOW
BY THE WAY, WHAT'S WITH THE DRILL?
WHAT DRILL?

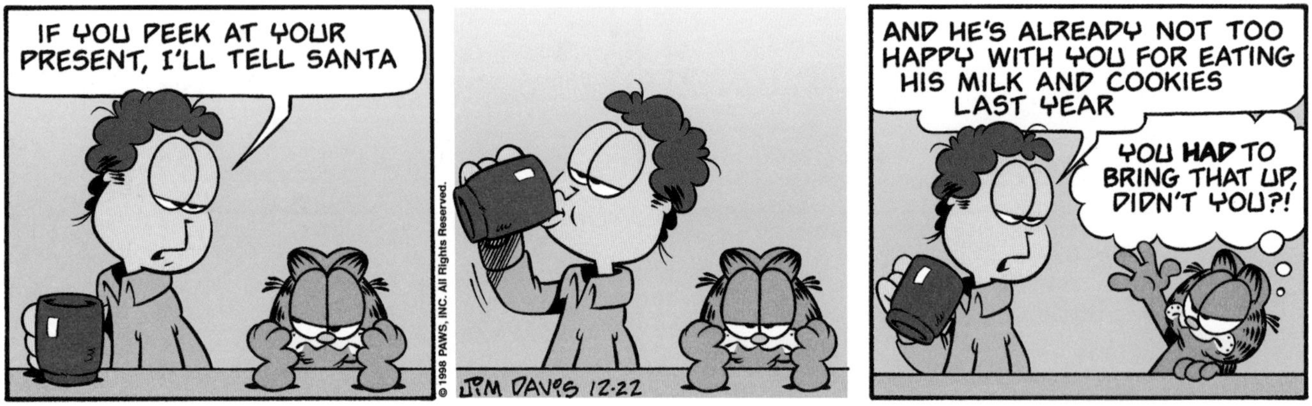
IF YOU PEEK AT YOUR PRESENT, I'LL TELL SANTA
© 1998 PAWS, INC. All Rights Reserved.
JIM DAVIS 12-22
AND HE'S ALREADY NOT TOO HAPPY WITH YOU FOR EATING HIS MILK AND COOKIES LAST YEAR
YOU HAD TO BRING THAT UP, DIDN'T YOU?!

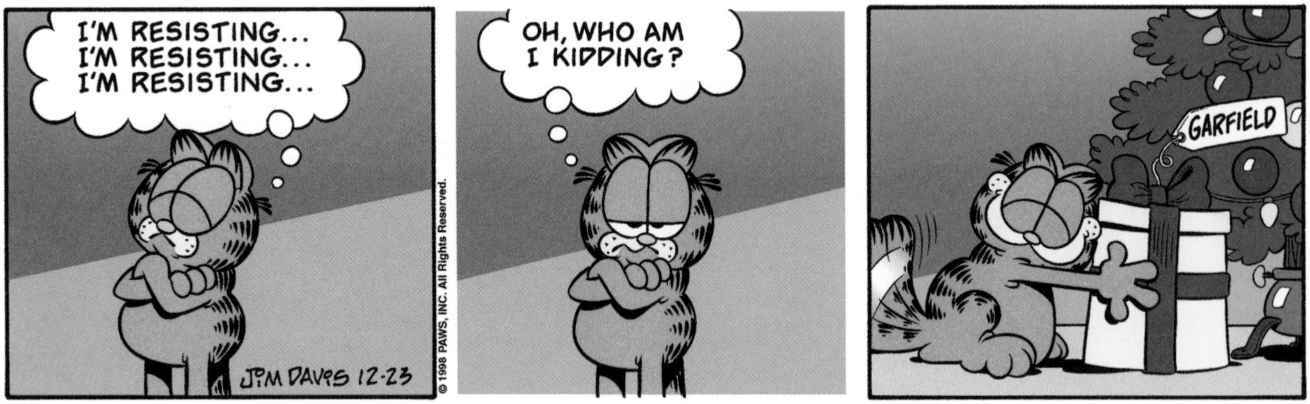
I'M RESISTING... I'M RESISTING... I'M RESISTING...
JIM DAVIS 12-23
© 1998 PAWS, INC. All Rights Reserved.
OH, WHO AM I KIDDING?
GARFIELD

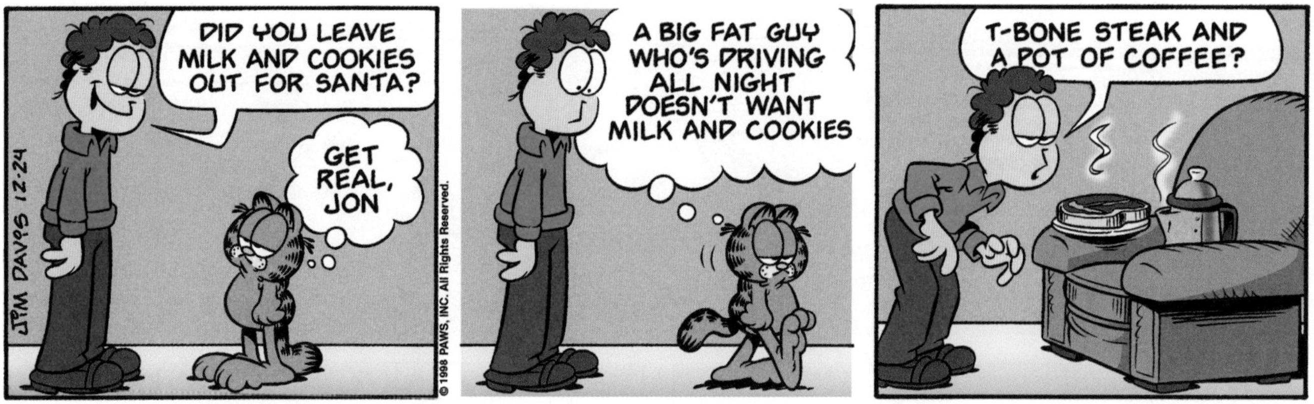
DID YOU LEAVE MILK AND COOKIES OUT FOR SANTA?
GET REAL, JON
A BIG FAT GUY WHO'S DRIVING ALL NIGHT DOESN'T WANT MILK AND COOKIES
T-BONE STEAK AND A POT OF COFFEE?
JIM DAVIS 12-24
© 1998 PAWS, INC. All Rights Reserved.

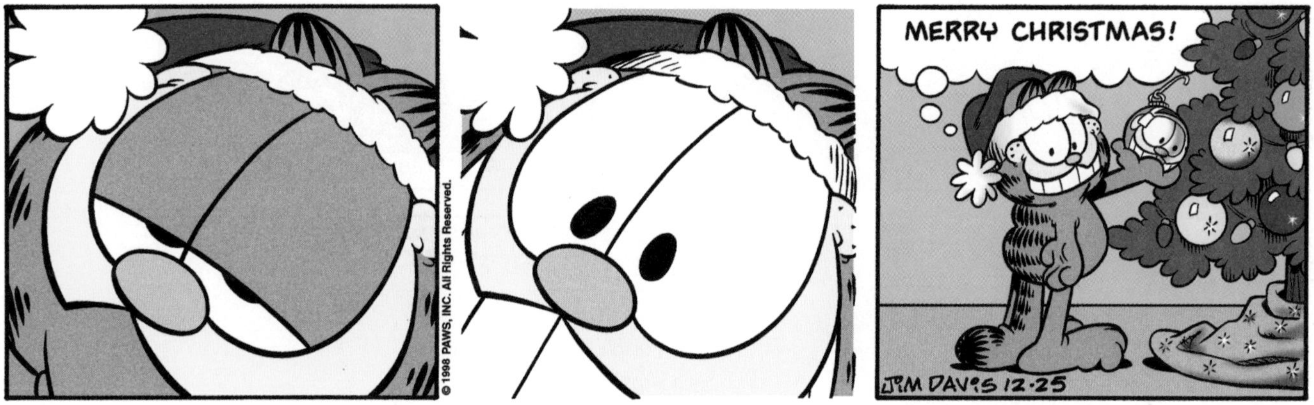
MERRY CHRISTMAS!
JIM DAVIS 12-25
© 1998 PAWS, INC. All Rights Reserved.

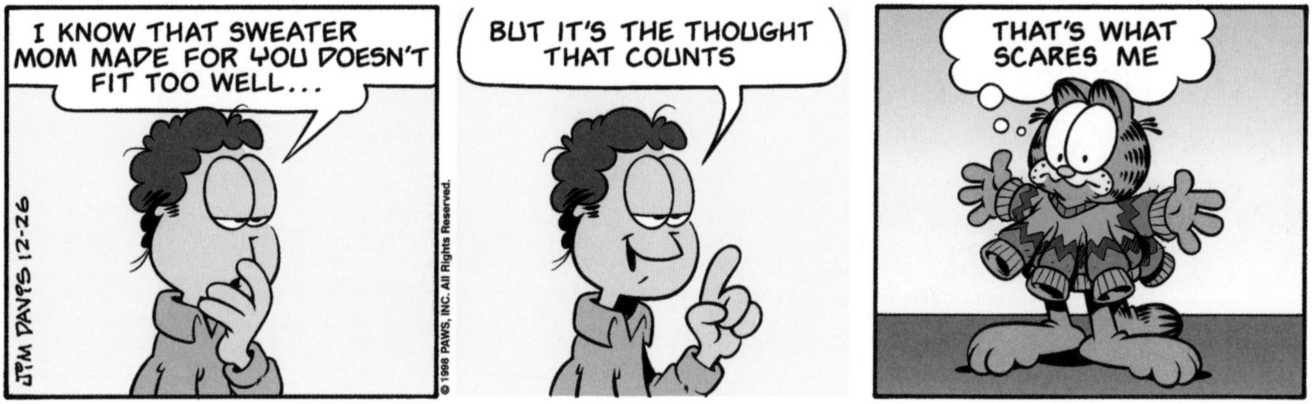
I KNOW THAT SWEATER MOM MADE FOR YOU DOESN'T FIT TOO WELL...
BUT IT'S THE THOUGHT THAT COUNTS
THAT'S WHAT SCARES ME
JIM DAVIS 12-26
© 1998 PAWS, INC. All Rights Reserved.

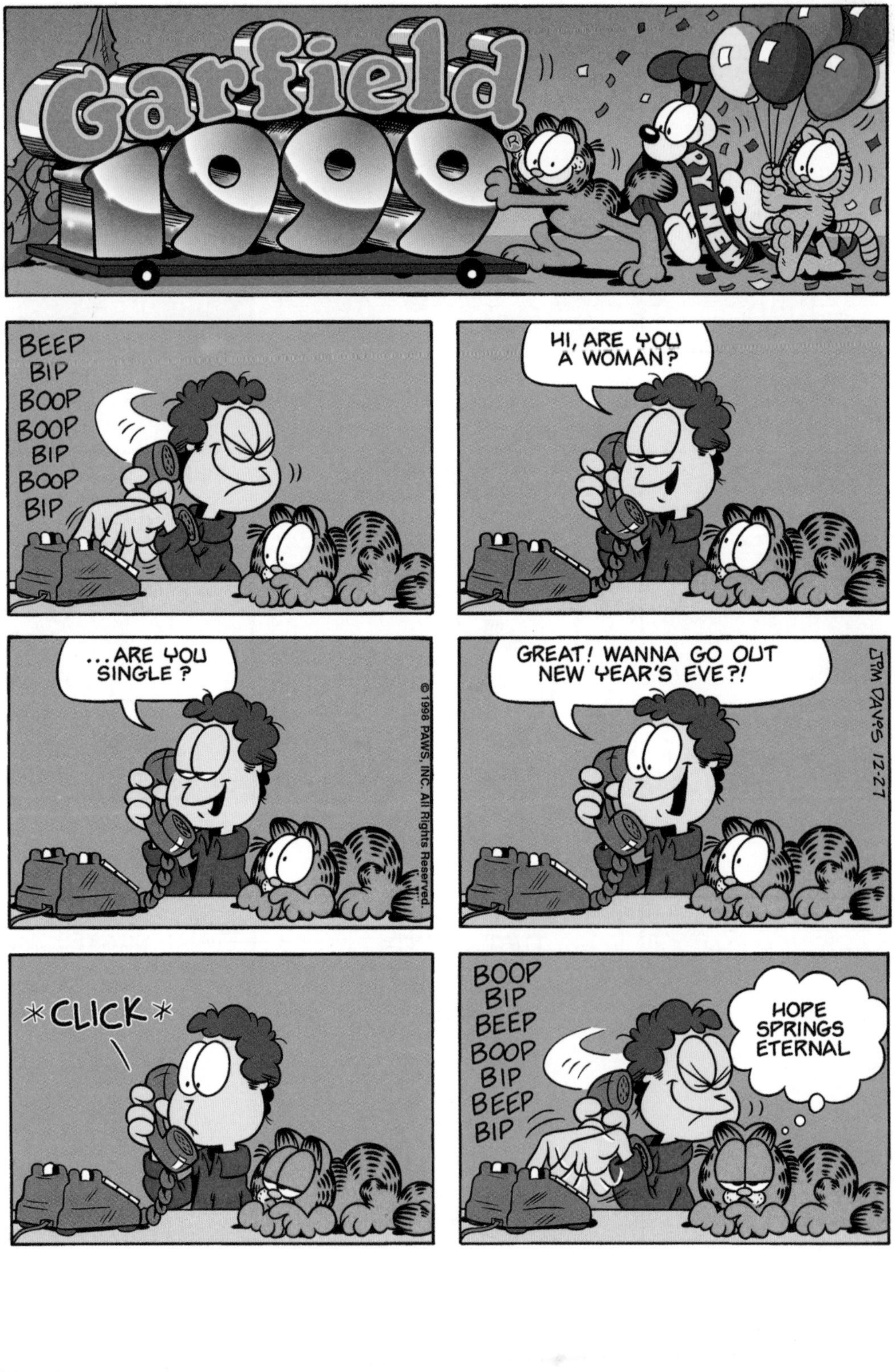
Garfield
1999
HAPPY NEW
BEEP BIP BOOP BOOP BIP BOOP BIP
HI, ARE YOU A WOMAN?
...ARE YOU SINGLE?
GREAT! WANNA GO OUT NEW YEAR'S EVE?!
JPM DAVPS 12-27
CLICK
BOOP BIP BEEP BOOP BIP BEEP BIP
HOPE SPRINGS ETERNAL

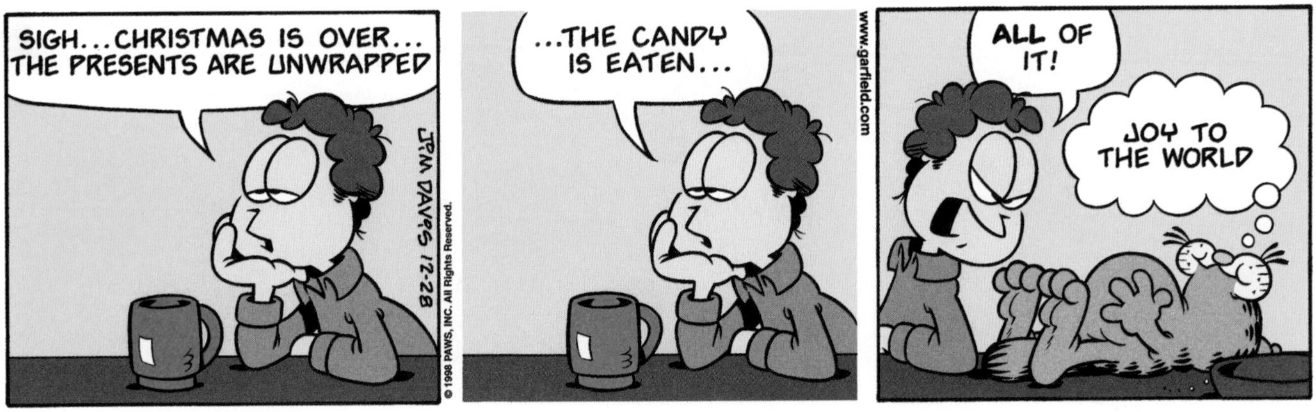
SIGH... CHRISTMAS IS OVER... THE PRESENTS ARE UNWRAPPED
JIM DAVIS 12-28
© 1998 PAWS, INC. All Rights Reserved.
...THE CANDY IS EATEN...
www.garfield.com
ALL OF IT!
JOY TO THE WORLD

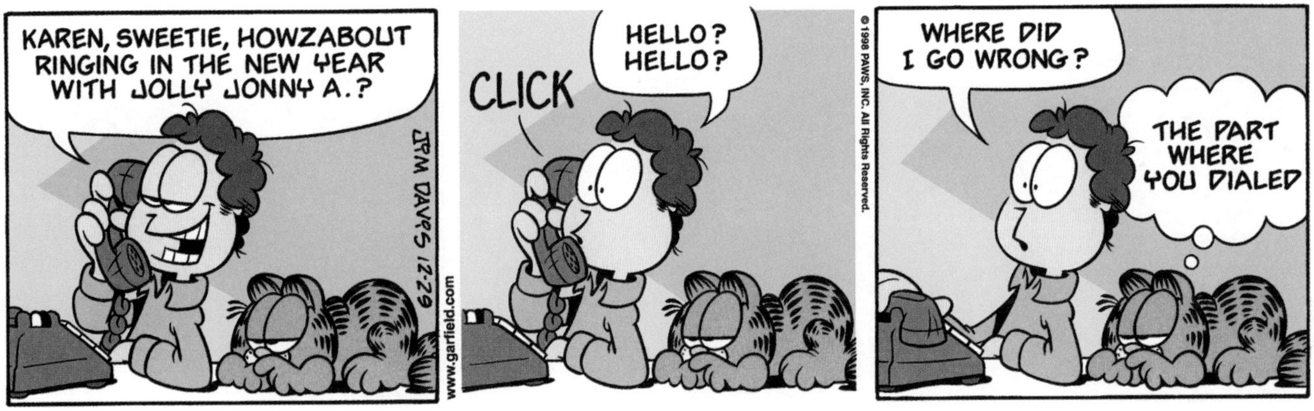
KAREN, SWEETIE, HOWZABOUT RINGING IN THE NEW YEAR WITH JOLLY JONNY A.?
JIM DAVIS 12-29
www.garfield.com
CLICK
HELLO? HELLO?
© 1998 PAWS, INC. All Rights Reserved.
WHERE DID I GO WRONG?
THE PART WHERE YOU DIALED

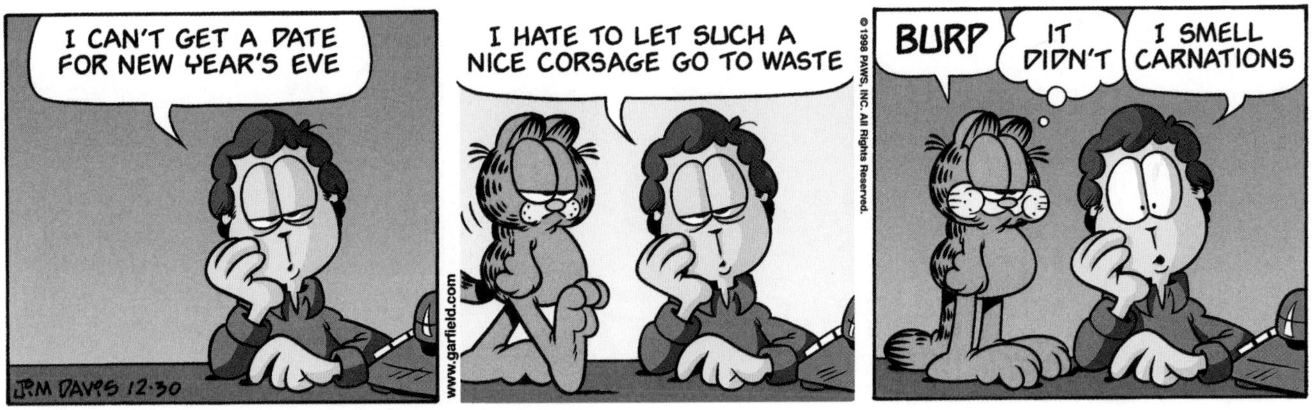
I CAN'T GET A DATE FOR NEW YEAR'S EVE
JIM DAVIS 12-30
www.garfield.com
I HATE TO LET SUCH A NICE CORSAGE GO TO WASTE
© 1998 PAWS, INC. All Rights Reserved.
BURP
IT DIDN'T
I SMELL CARNATIONS

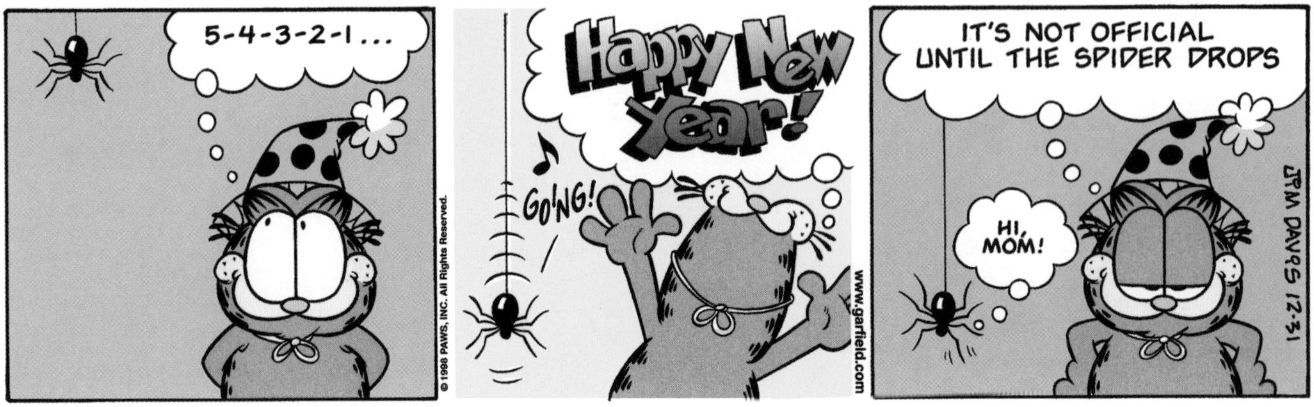
5-4-3-2-1...
Happy New Year!
GOING!
IT'S NOT OFFICIAL UNTIL THE SPIDER DROPS
HI, MOM!
JIM DAVIS 12-31
© 1998 PAWS, INC. All Rights Reserved.
www.garfield.com

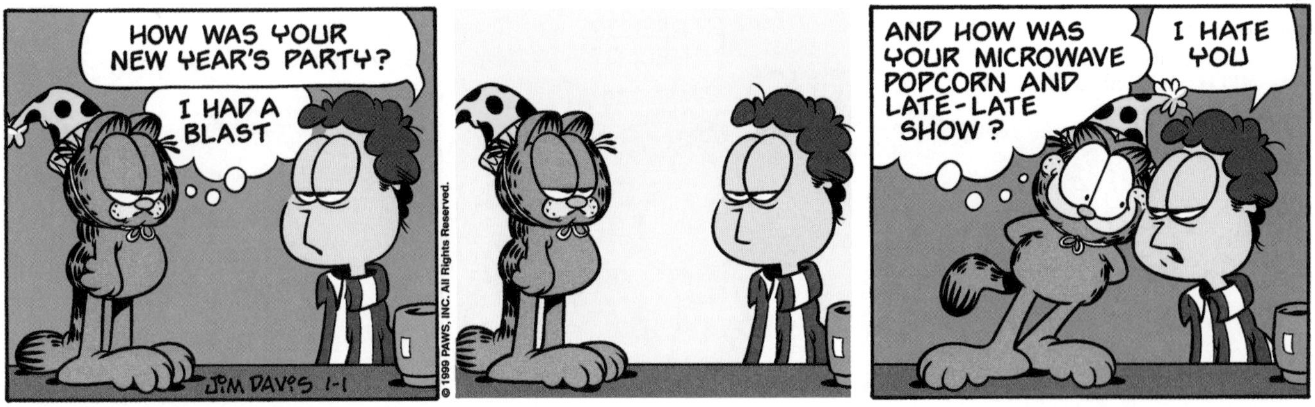
HOW WAS YOUR NEW YEAR'S PARTY?
I HAD A BLAST
JIM DAVIS 1-1
AND HOW WAS YOUR MICROWAVE POPCORN AND LATE-LATE SHOW?
I HATE YOU
© 1999 PAWS, INC. All Rights Reserved.

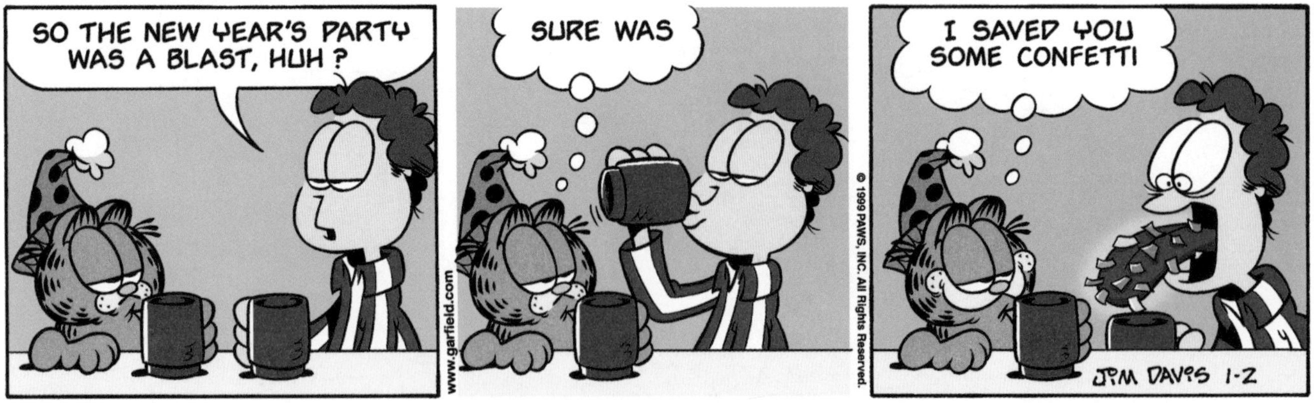
SO THE NEW YEAR'S PARTY WAS A BLAST, HUH?
SURE WAS
I SAVED YOU SOME CONFETTI
JIM DAVIS 1-2
www.garfield.com
© 1999 PAWS, INC. All Rights Reserved.

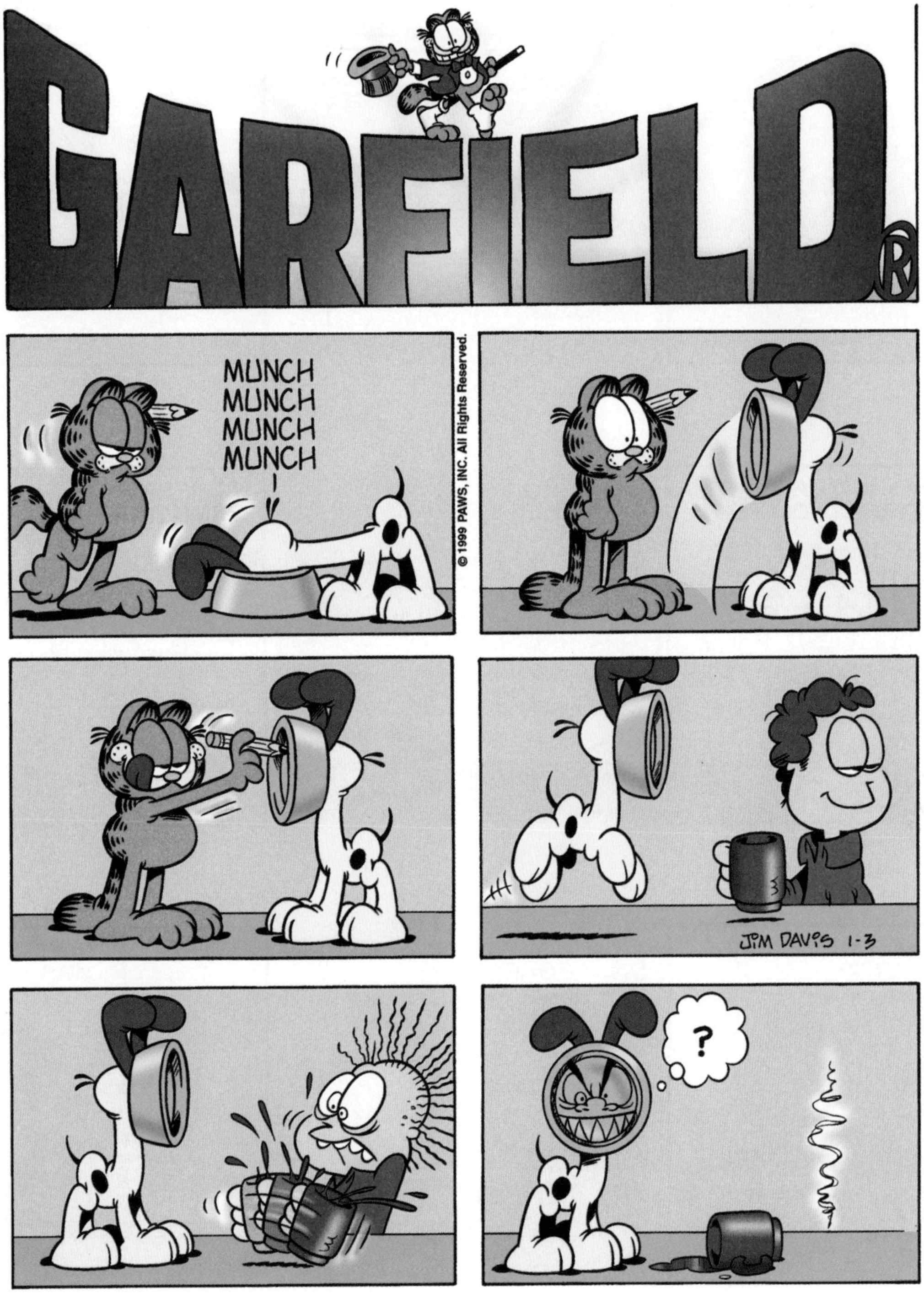
GARFIELD®
MUNCH
MUNCH
MUNCH
MUNCH
© 1999 PAWS, INC. All Rights Reserved.
JIM DAVIS 1-3
?

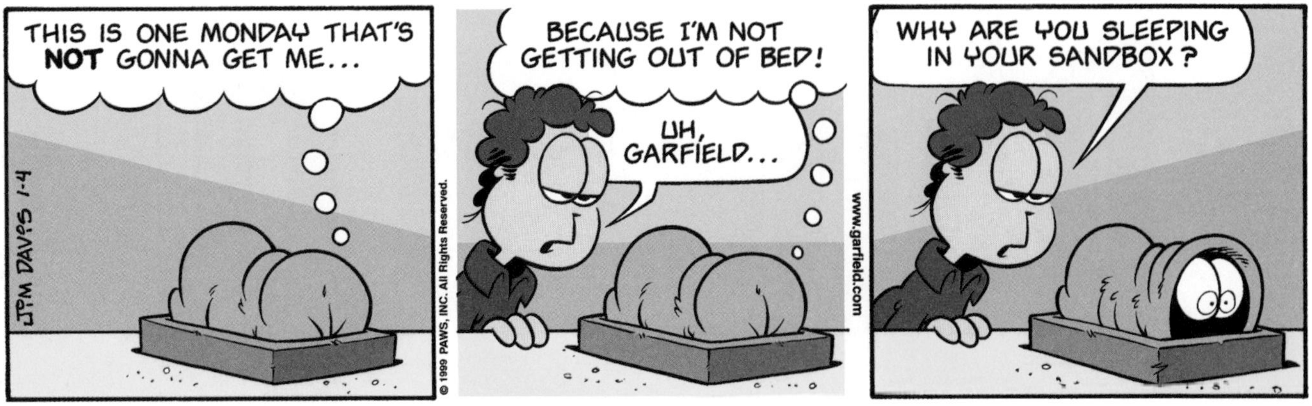
THIS IS ONE MONDAY THAT'S **NOT** GONNA GET ME...
JIM DAVIS 1-4
© 1999 PAWS, INC. All Rights Reserved.
BECAUSE I'M NOT GETTING OUT OF BED!
UH, GARFIELD...
www.garfield.com
WHY ARE YOU SLEEPING IN YOUR SANDBOX?

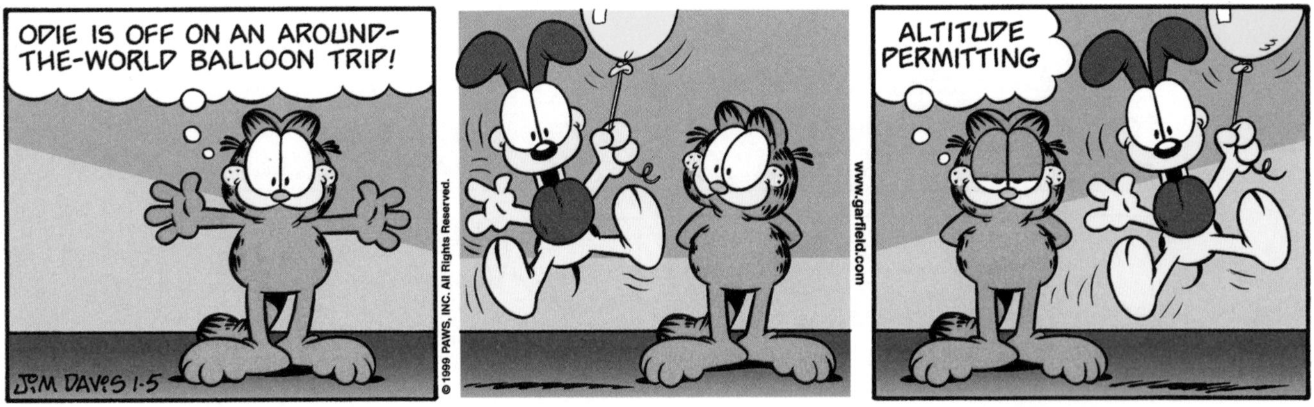
ODIE IS OFF ON AN AROUND-THE-WORLD BALLOON TRIP!
JIM DAVIS 1-5
© 1999 PAWS, INC. All Rights Reserved.
www.garfield.com
ALTITUDE PERMITTING

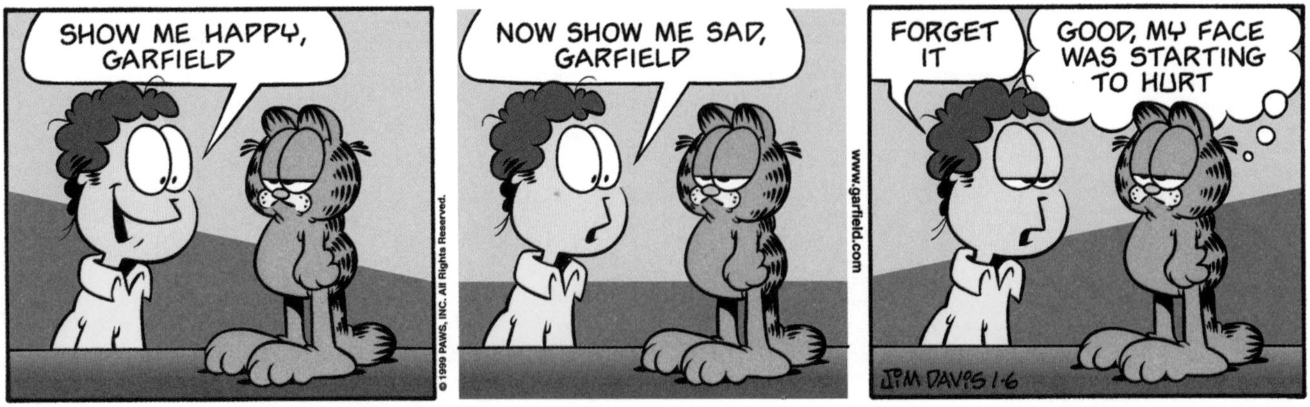
SHOW ME HAPPY, GARFIELD
© 1999 PAWS, INC. All Rights Reserved.
NOW SHOW ME SAD, GARFIELD
www.garfield.com
FORGET IT
GOOD, MY FACE WAS STARTING TO HURT
JIM DAVIS 1-6

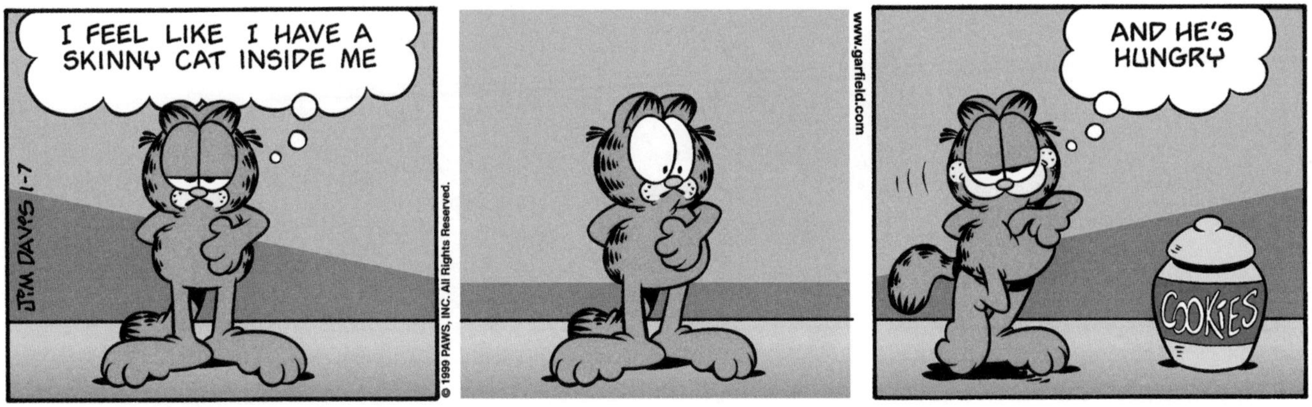
I FEEL LIKE I HAVE A SKINNY CAT INSIDE ME
AND HE'S HUNGRY
COOKIES
JIM DAVIS 1-7
© 1999 PAWS, INC. All Rights Reserved.
www.garfield.com

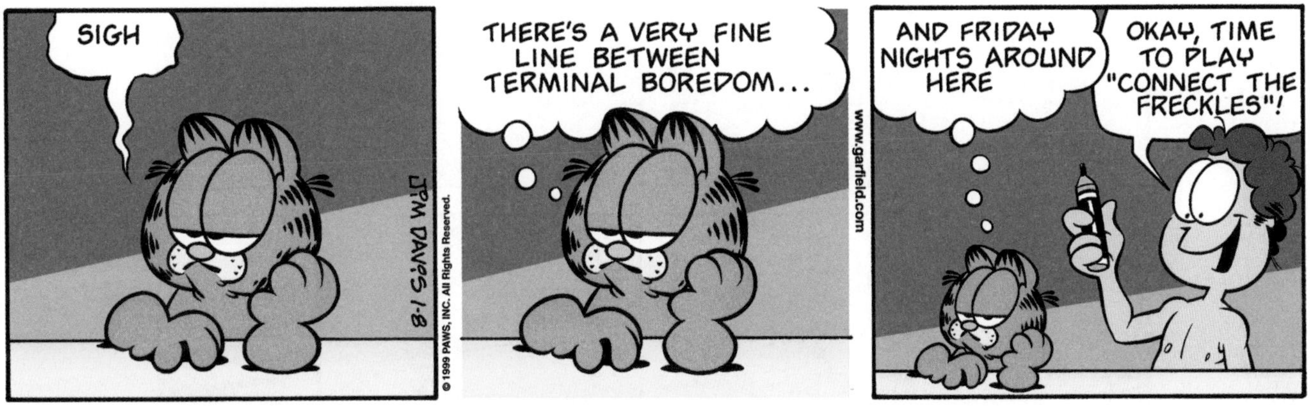
SIGH
THERE'S A VERY FINE LINE BETWEEN TERMINAL BOREDOM...
AND FRIDAY NIGHTS AROUND HERE
OKAY, TIME TO PLAY "CONNECT THE FRECKLES"!
JIM DAVIS 1-8
© 1999 PAWS, INC. All Rights Reserved.
www.garfield.com

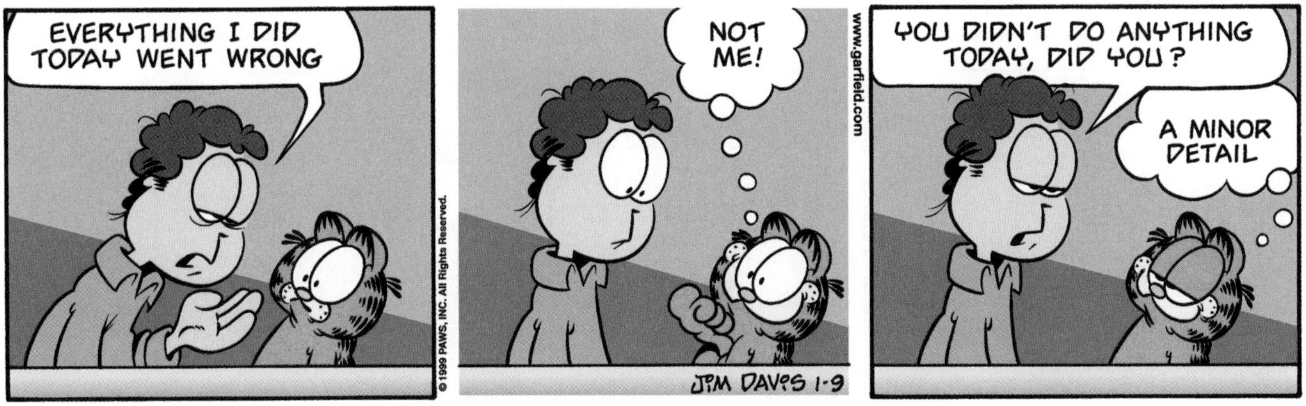
EVERYTHING I DID TODAY WENT WRONG
NOT ME!
YOU DIDN'T DO ANYTHING TODAY, DID YOU?
A MINOR DETAIL
JIM DAVIS 1-9
© 1999 PAWS, INC. All Rights Reserved.
www.garfield.com

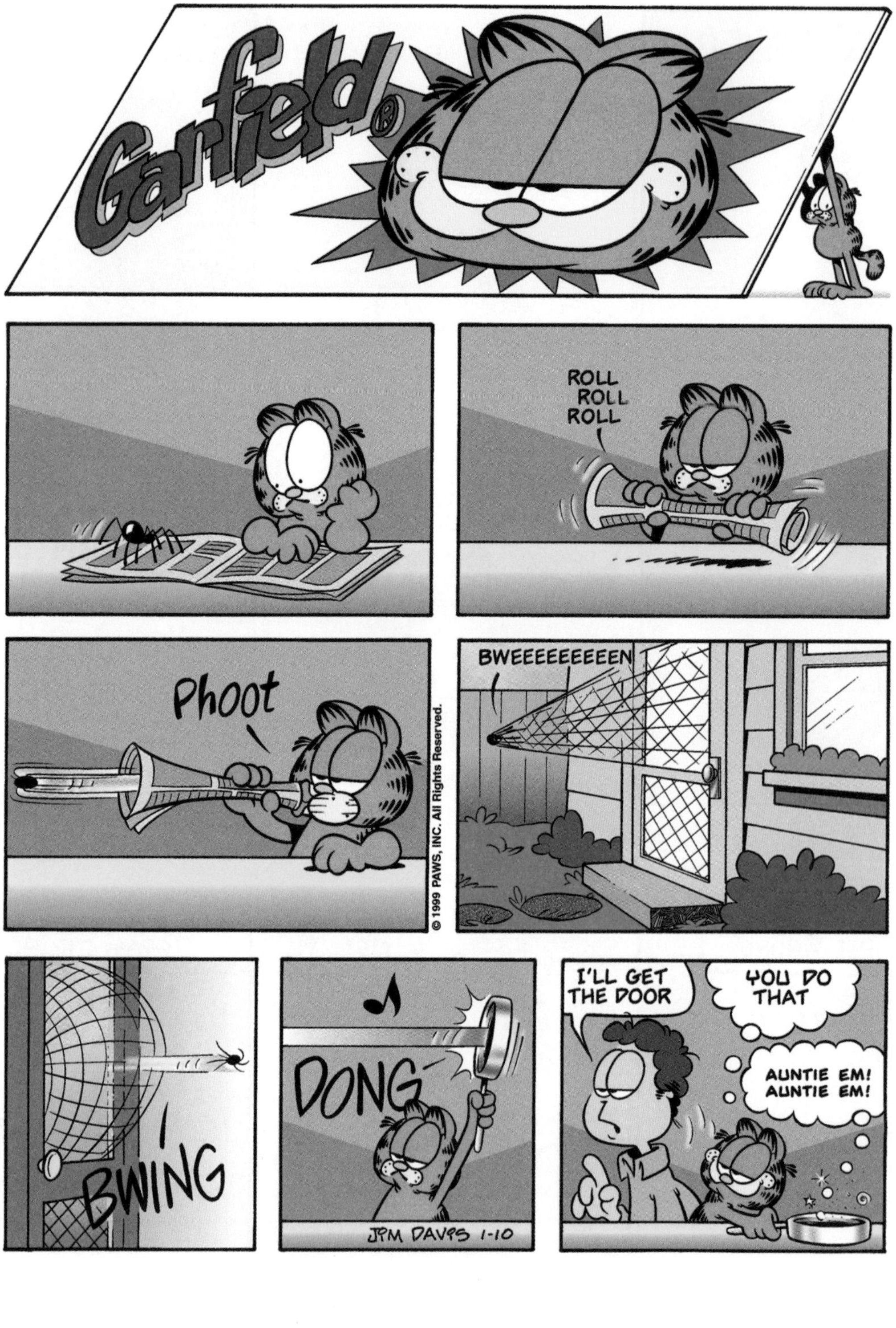
Garfield®
ROLL
ROLL
ROLL
Phoot
BWEEEEEEEEEN
© 1999 PAWS, INC. All Rights Reserved.
BWING
DONG
JIM DAVIS 1-10
I'LL GET THE DOOR
YOU DO THAT
AUNTIE EM! AUNTIE EM!

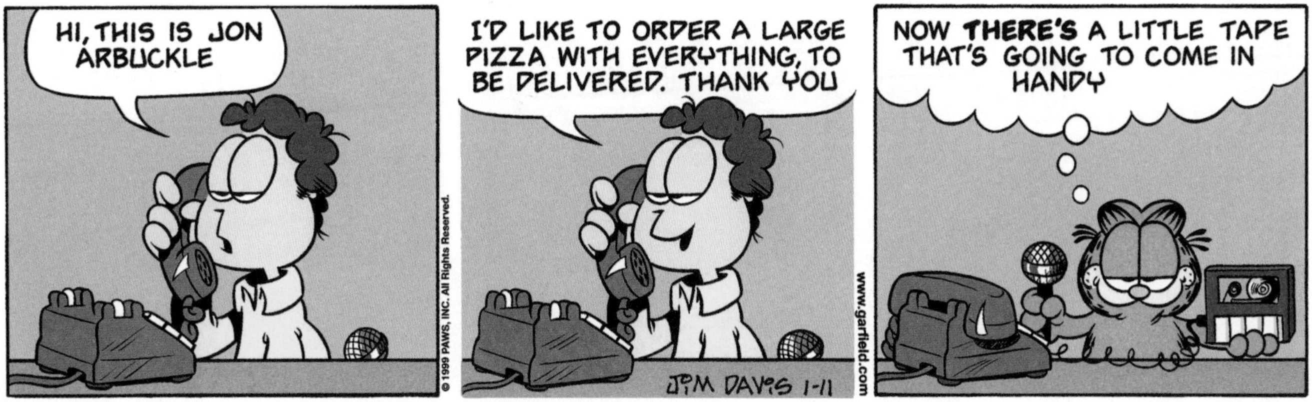
HI, THIS IS JON ARBUCKLE
I'D LIKE TO ORDER A LARGE PIZZA WITH EVERYTHING, TO BE DELIVERED. THANK YOU
NOW THERE'S A LITTLE TAPE THAT'S GOING TO COME IN HANDY
JIM DAVIS 1-11
© 1999 PAWS, INC. All Rights Reserved.
www.garfield.com

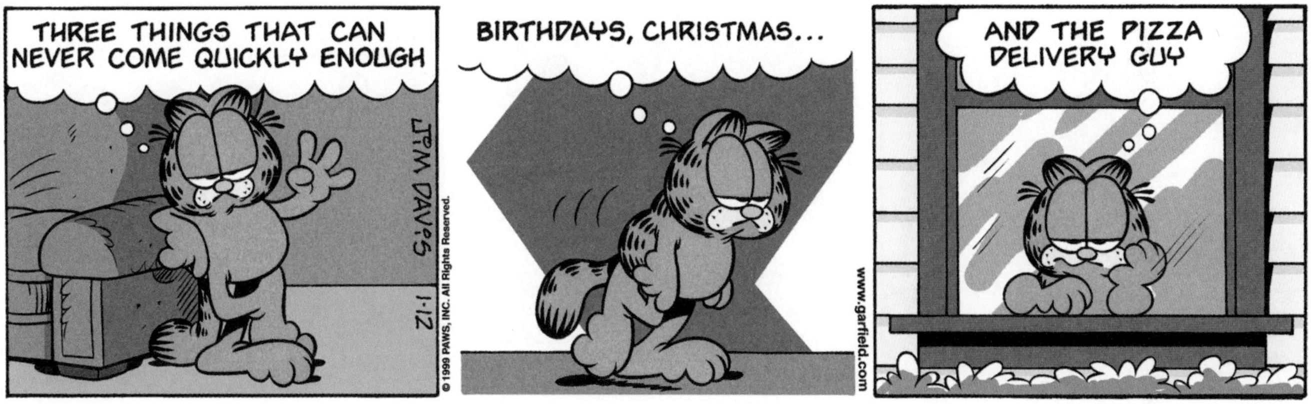
THREE THINGS THAT CAN NEVER COME QUICKLY ENOUGH
BIRTHDAYS, CHRISTMAS...
AND THE PIZZA DELIVERY GUY
JIM DAVIS 1-12
© 1999 PAWS, INC. All Rights Reserved.
www.garfield.com

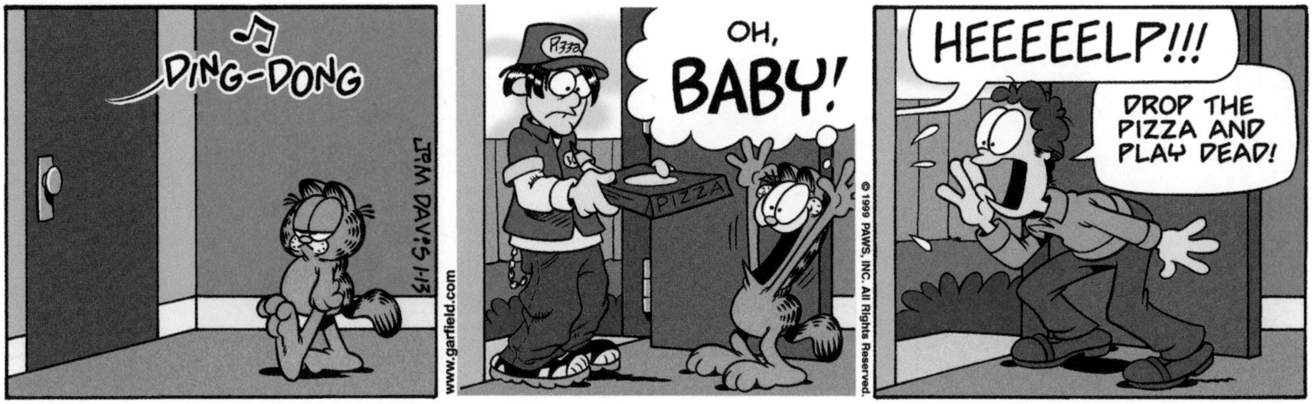
DING-DONG
OH, BABY!
HEEEEELP!!!
DROP THE PIZZA AND PLAY DEAD!
PIZZA
JIM DAVIS 1-13
www.garfield.com
© 1999 PAWS, INC. All Rights Reserved.

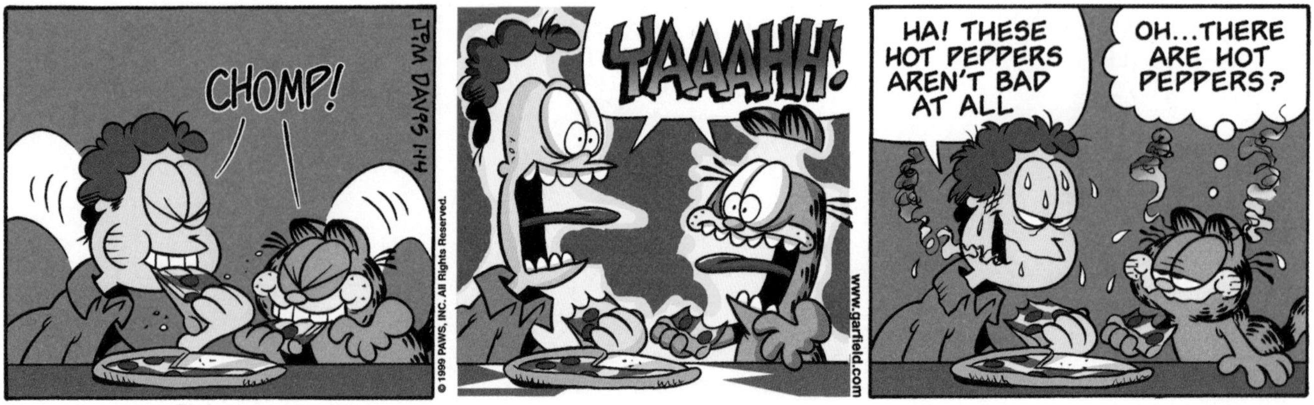
JIM DAVIS 1-14
CHOMP!
© 1999 PAWS, INC. All Rights Reserved.
YAAAHH!
www.garfield.com
HA! THESE HOT PEPPERS AREN'T BAD AT ALL
OH...THERE ARE HOT PEPPERS?

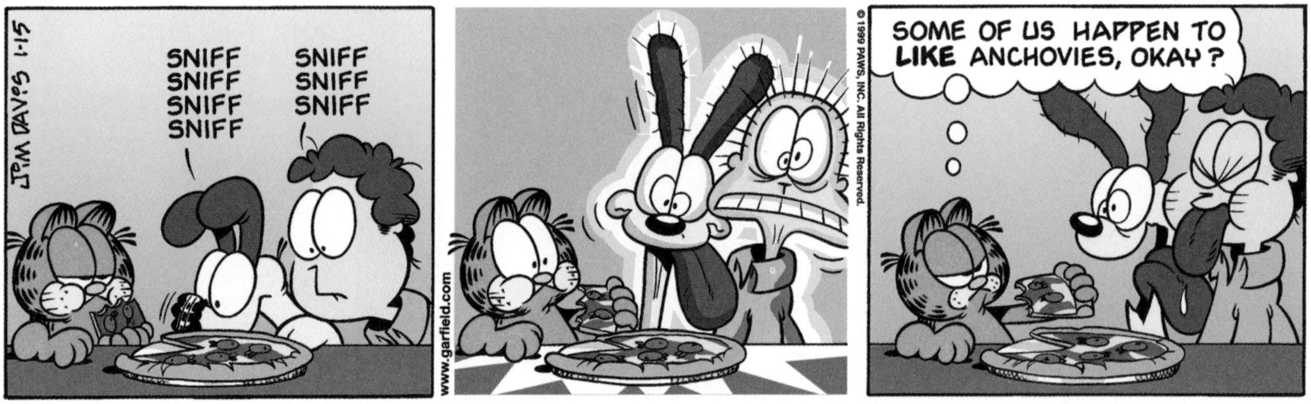
JIM DAVIS 1-15
SNIFF SNIFF SNIFF SNIFF
SNIFF SNIFF SNIFF
www.garfield.com
© 1999 PAWS, INC. All Rights Reserved.
SOME OF US HAPPEN TO **LIKE** ANCHOVIES, OKAY?

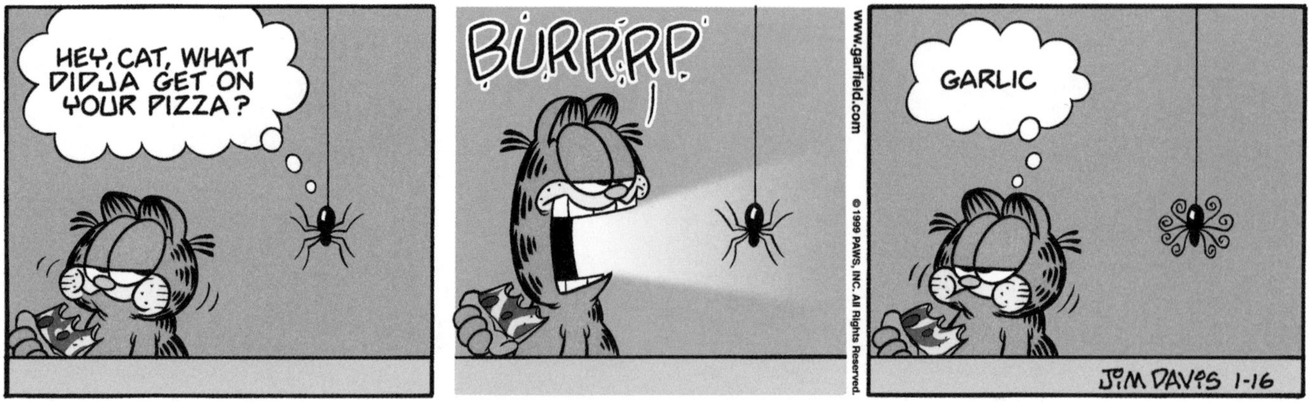
HEY, CAT, WHAT DIDJA GET ON YOUR PIZZA?
BURRRP
www.garfield.com
© 1999 PAWS, INC. All Rights Reserved.
GARLIC
JIM DAVIS 1-16

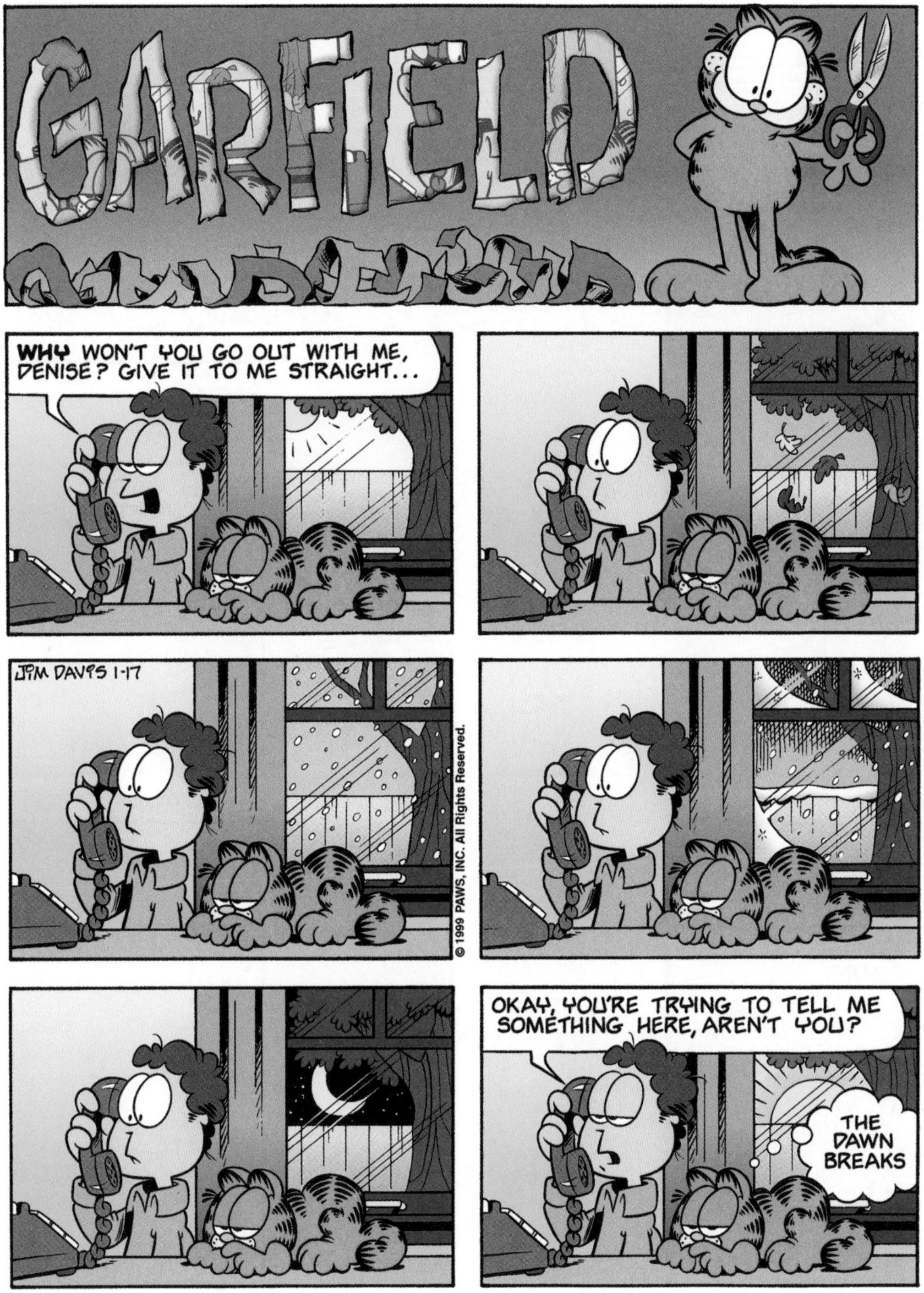
GARFIELD
WHY WON'T YOU GO OUT WITH ME, DENISE? GIVE IT TO ME STRAIGHT...
JIM DAVIS 1-17
© 1999 PAWS, INC. All Rights Reserved.
OKAY, YOU'RE TRYING TO TELL ME SOMETHING HERE, AREN'T YOU?
THE DAWN BREAKS

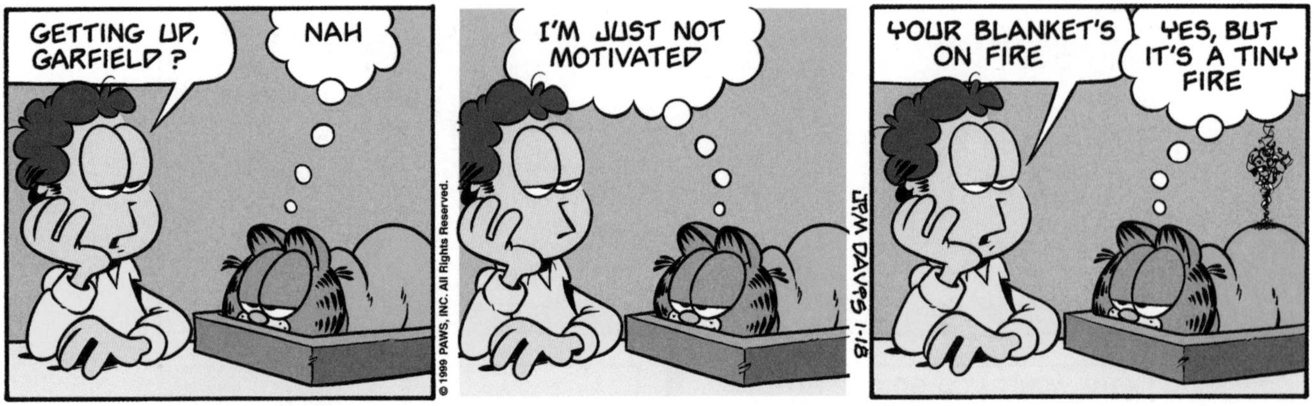
GETTING UP, GARFIELD ?
NAH
I'M JUST NOT MOTIVATED
YOUR BLANKET'S ON FIRE
YES, BUT IT'S A TINY FIRE
© 1999 PAWS, INC. All Rights Reserved.

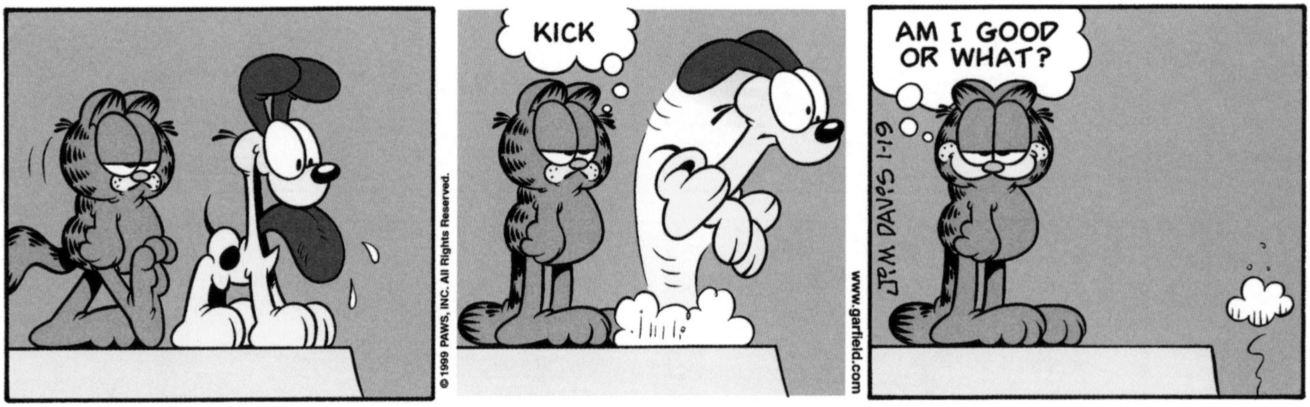
KICK
AM I GOOD OR WHAT?
© 1999 PAWS, INC. All Rights Reserved.
www.garfield.com

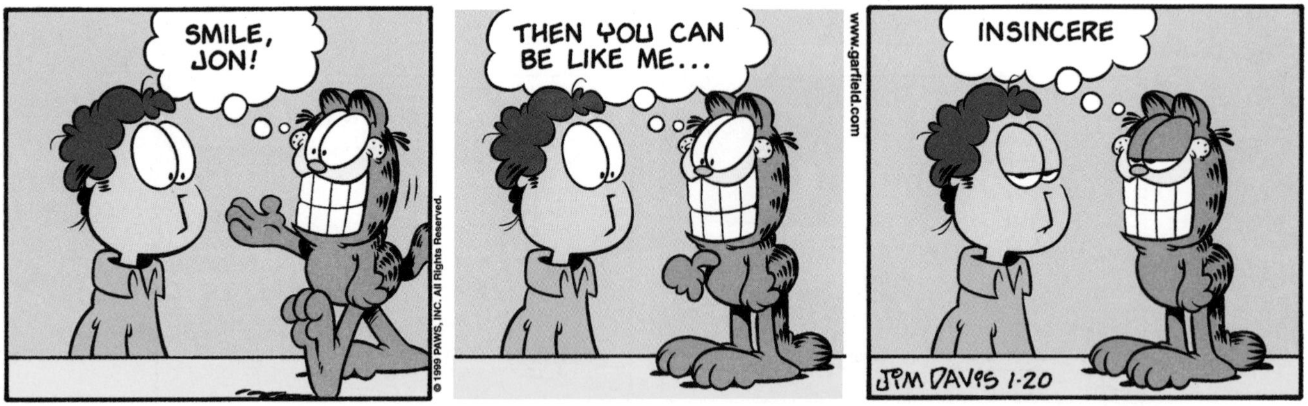
SMILE, JON!
THEN YOU CAN BE LIKE ME...
INSINCERE
© 1999 PAWS, INC. All Rights Reserved.
www.garfield.com

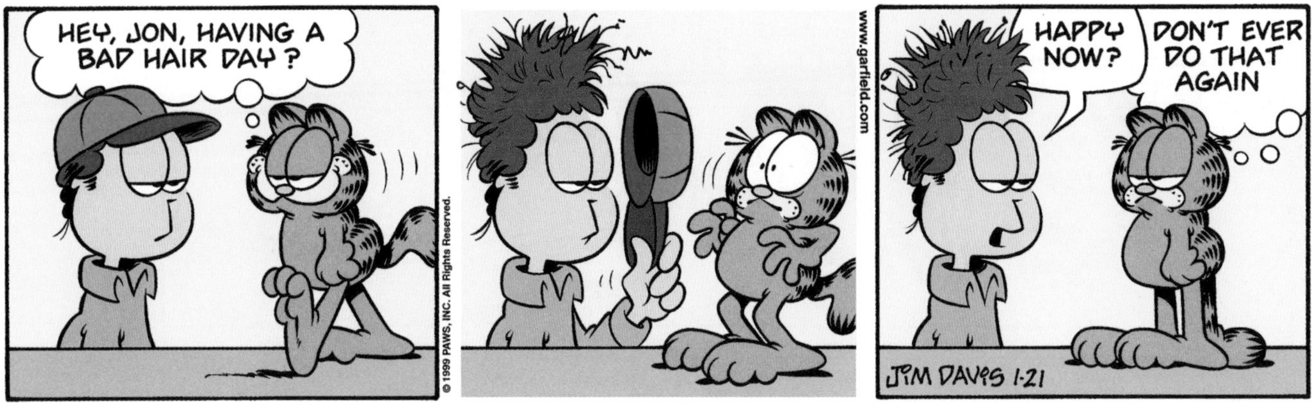
HEY, JON, HAVING A BAD HAIR DAY?
© 1999 PAWS, INC. All Rights Reserved.
www.garfield.com
HAPPY NOW?
DON'T EVER DO THAT AGAIN
JIM DAVIS 1-21

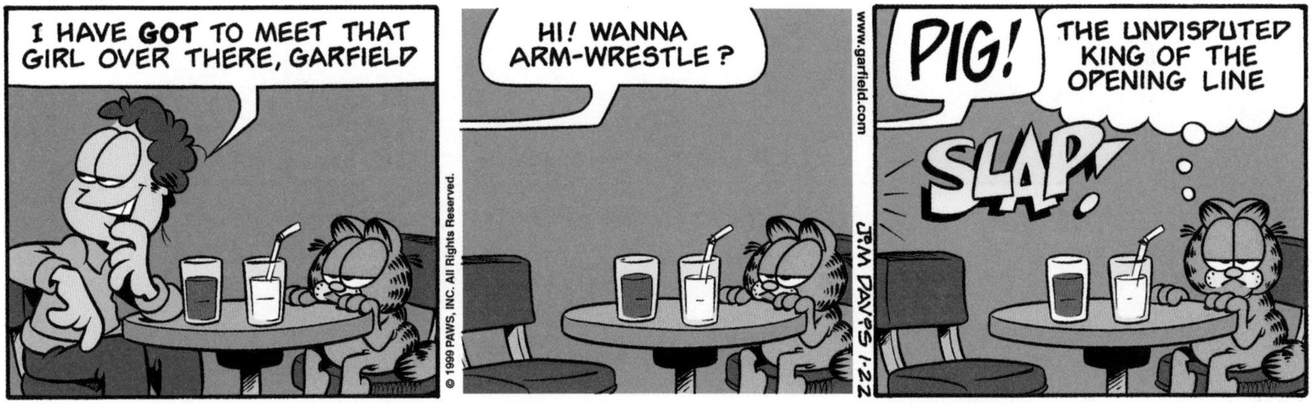
I HAVE **GOT** TO MEET THAT GIRL OVER THERE, GARFIELD
© 1999 PAWS, INC. All Rights Reserved.
HI! WANNA ARM-WRESTLE?
www.garfield.com
JIM DAVIS 1-22
PIG!
SLAP!
THE UNDISPUTED KING OF THE OPENING LINE

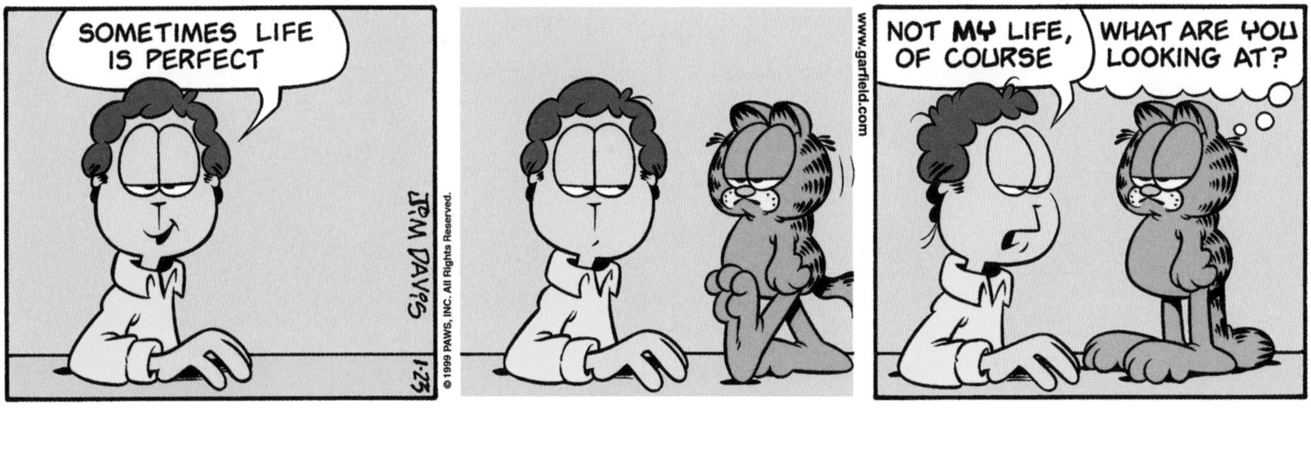
SOMETIMES LIFE IS PERFECT
JIM DAVIS 1-23
© 1999 PAWS, INC. All Rights Reserved.
www.garfield.com
NOT **MY** LIFE, OF COURSE
WHAT ARE YOU LOOKING AT?

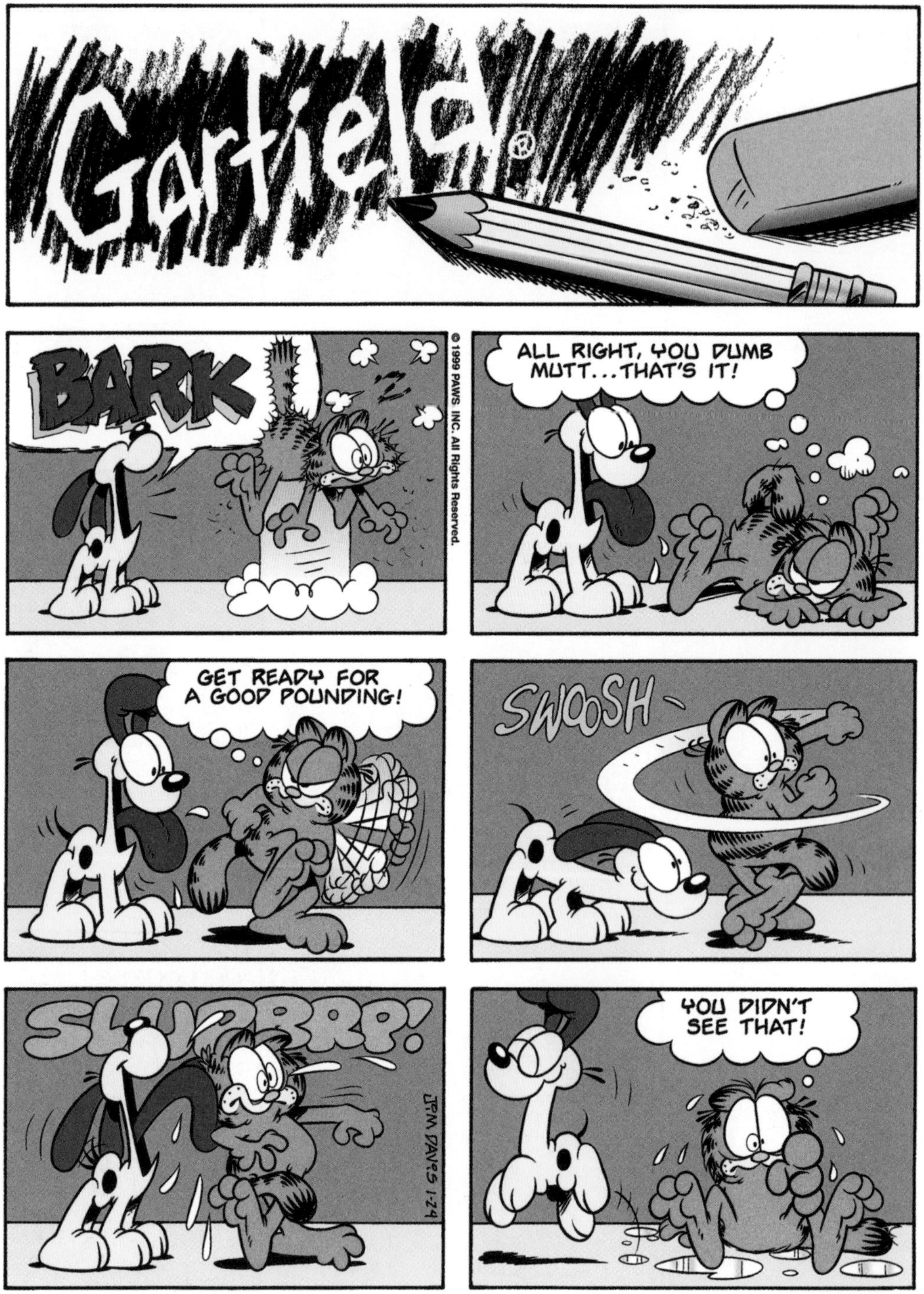
Garfield®
BARK
© 1999 PAWS, INC. All Rights Reserved.
ALL RIGHT, YOU DUMB MUTT...THAT'S IT!
GET READY FOR A GOOD POUNDING!
SWOOSH
JIM DAVIS 1-24
YOU DIDN'T SEE THAT!

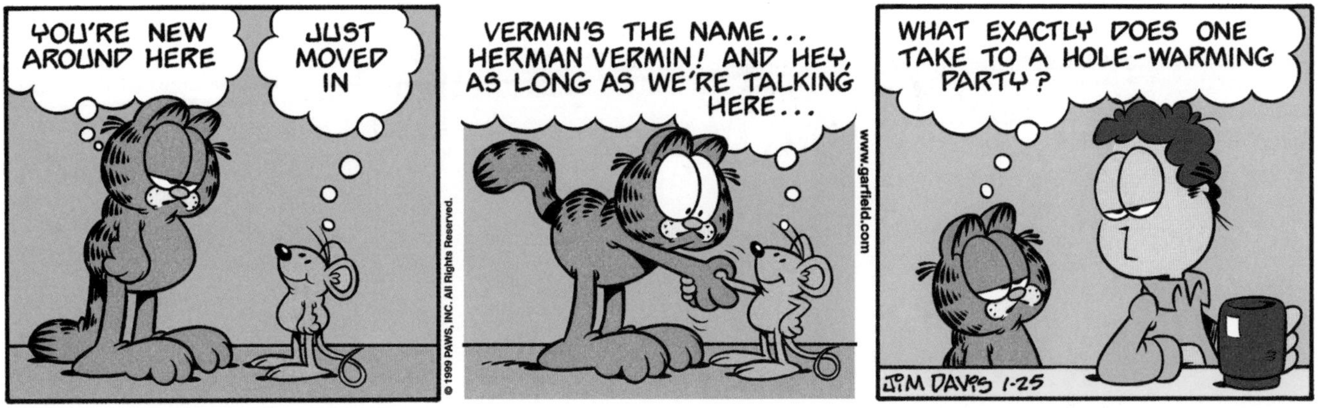
YOU'RE NEW AROUND HERE
JUST MOVED IN
VERMIN'S THE NAME... HERMAN VERMIN! AND HEY, AS LONG AS WE'RE TALKING HERE...
WHAT EXACTLY DOES ONE TAKE TO A HOLE-WARMING PARTY?
JIM DAVIS 1-25
© 1999 PAWS, INC. All Rights Reserved.
www.garfield.com

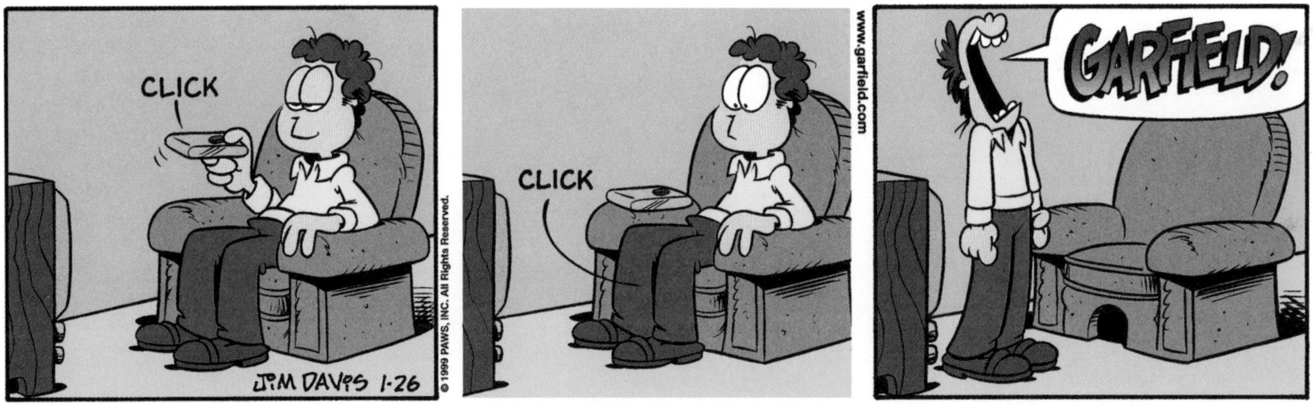
CLICK
CLICK
GARFIELD!
JIM DAVIS 1-26
© 1999 PAWS, INC. All Rights Reserved.
www.garfield.com

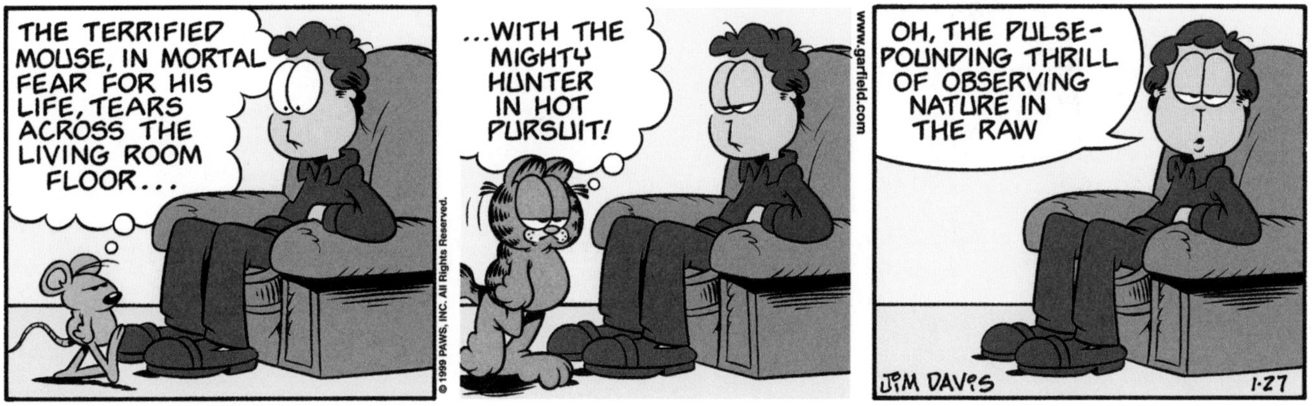
THE TERRIFIED MOUSE, IN MORTAL FEAR FOR HIS LIFE, TEARS ACROSS THE LIVING ROOM FLOOR...
...WITH THE MIGHTY HUNTER IN HOT PURSUIT!
OH, THE PULSE-POUNDING THRILL OF OBSERVING NATURE IN THE RAW
JIM DAVIS 1-27
© 1999 PAWS, INC. All Rights Reserved.
www.garfield.com

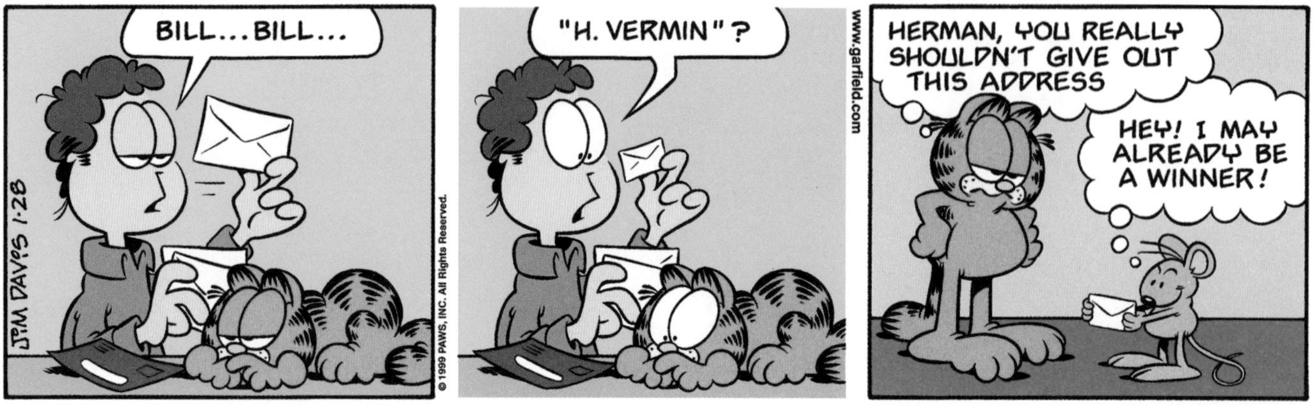
BILL... BILL...
"H. VERMIN"?
HERMAN, YOU REALLY SHOULDN'T GIVE OUT THIS ADDRESS
HEY! I MAY ALREADY BE A WINNER!
JIM DAVIS 1-28
© 1999 PAWS, INC. All Rights Reserved.
www.garfield.com

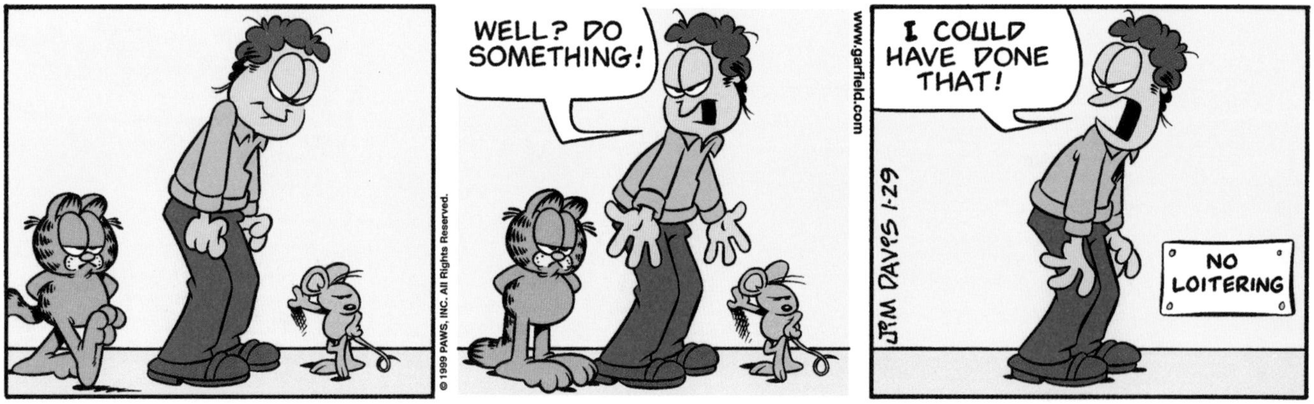
WELL? DO SOMETHING!
I COULD HAVE DONE THAT!
NO LOITERING
JIM DAVIS 1-29
© 1999 PAWS, INC. All Rights Reserved.
www.garfield.com

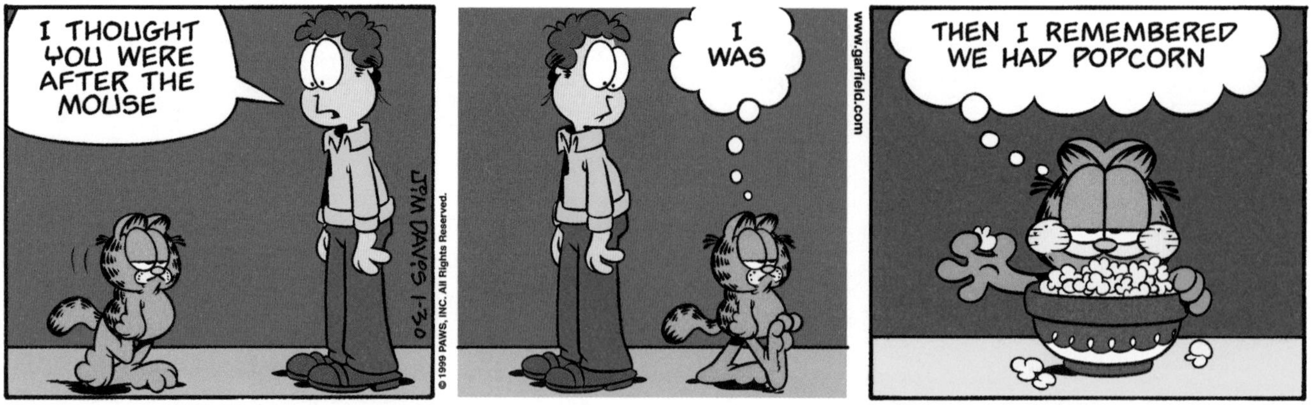
I THOUGHT YOU WERE AFTER THE MOUSE
I WAS
THEN I REMEMBERED WE HAD POPCORN
JIM DAVIS 1-30
© 1999 PAWS, INC. All Rights Reserved.
www.garfield.com

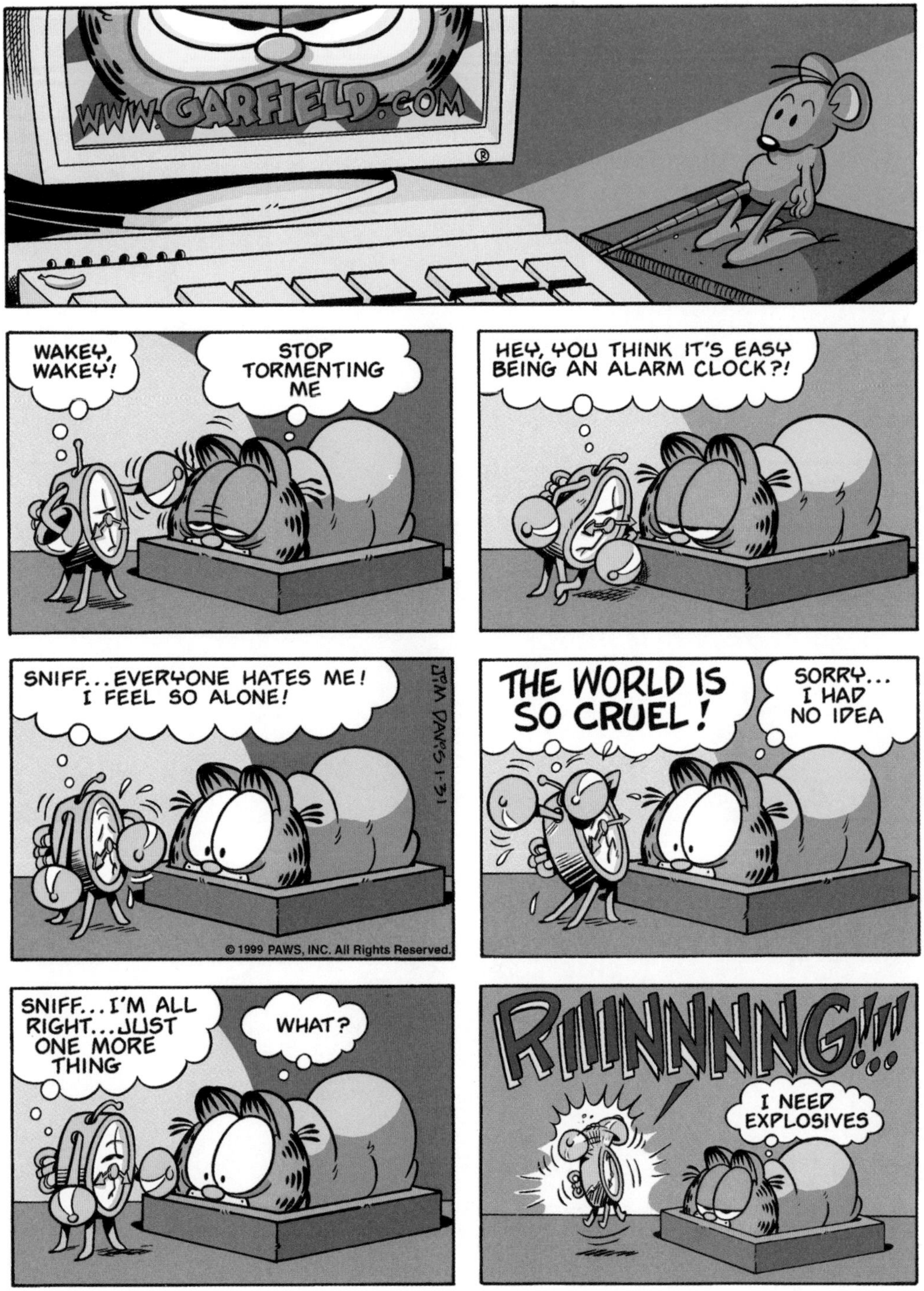
WWW.GARFIELD.COM
WAKEY, WAKEY!
STOP TORMENTING ME
HEY, YOU THINK IT'S EASY BEING AN ALARM CLOCK?!
SNIFF...EVERYONE HATES ME! I FEEL SO ALONE!
JIM DAVIS 1-31
© 1999 PAWS, INC. All Rights Reserved.
THE WORLD IS SO CRUEL!
SORRY... I HAD NO IDEA
SNIFF...I'M ALL RIGHT...JUST ONE MORE THING
WHAT?
RIIINNNNG!!!!
I NEED EXPLOSIVES

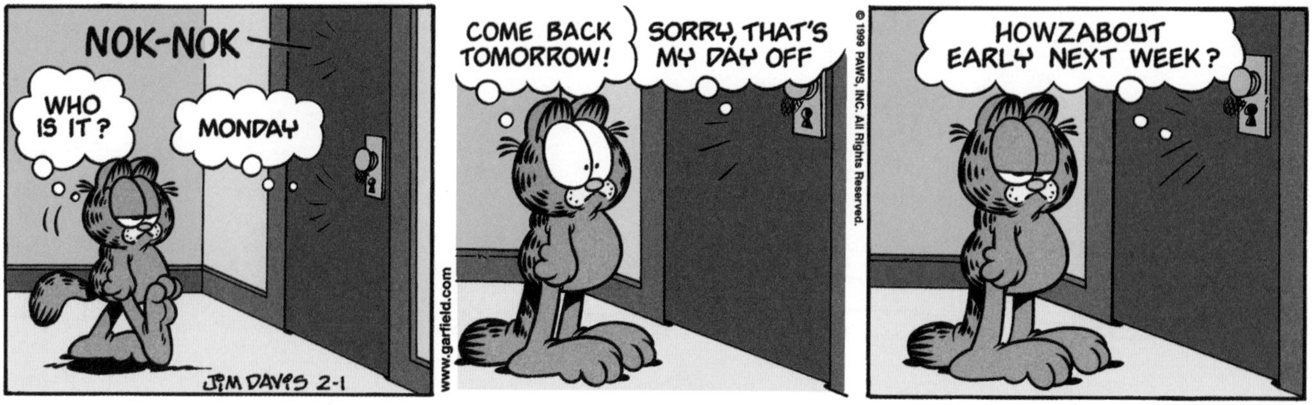
NOK-NOK
WHO IS IT?
MONDAY
JIM DAVIS 2-1
www.garfield.com
COME BACK TOMORROW!
SORRY, THAT'S MY DAY OFF
© 1999 PAWS, INC. All Rights Reserved.
HOWZABOUT EARLY NEXT WEEK?

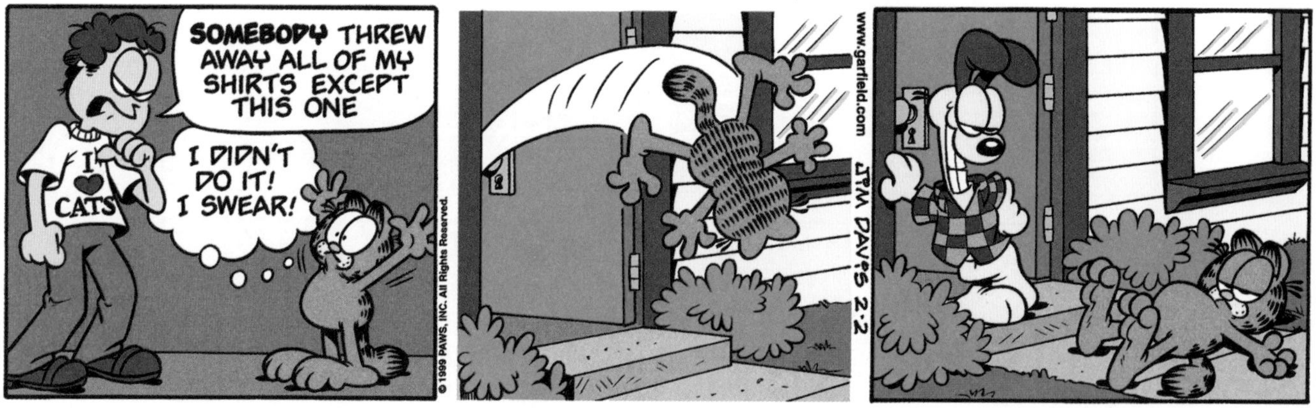
SOMEBODY THREW AWAY ALL OF MY SHIRTS EXCEPT THIS ONE
I ♥ CATS
I DIDN'T DO IT! I SWEAR!
© 1999 PAWS, INC. All Rights Reserved.
www.garfield.com
JIM DAVIS 2-2

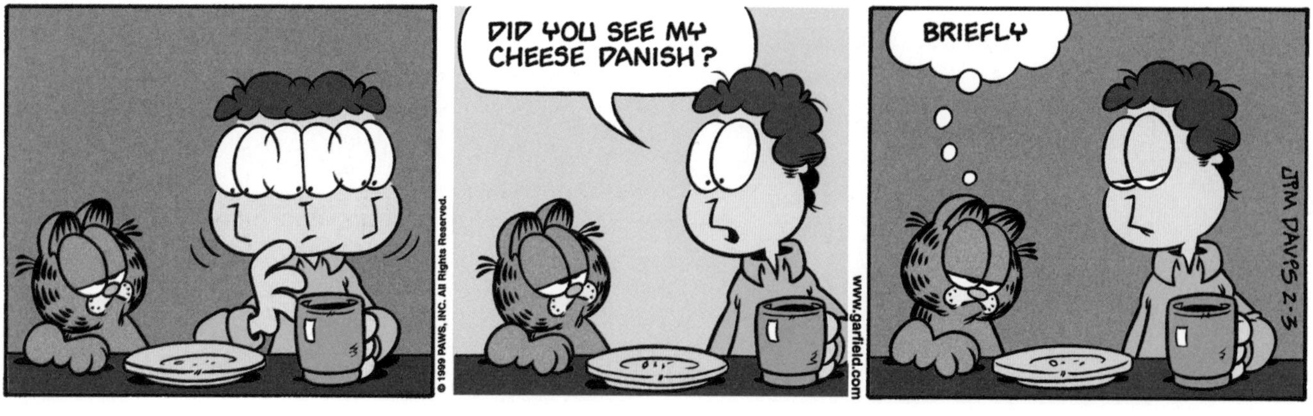
© 1999 PAWS, INC. All Rights Reserved.
DID YOU SEE MY CHEESE DANISH?
www.garfield.com
BRIEFLY
JIM DAVIS 2-3

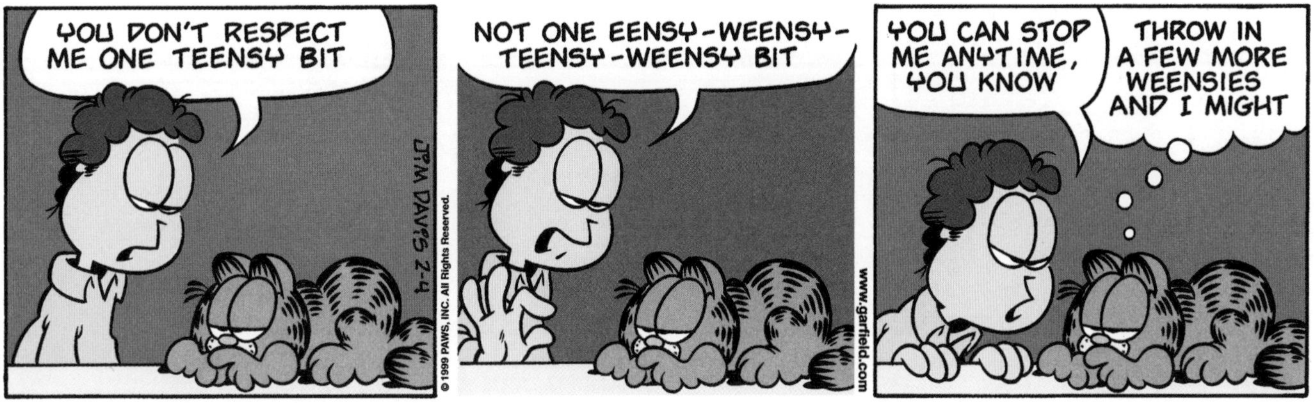
YOU DON'T RESPECT ME ONE TEENSY BIT
JIM DAVIS 2-4
© 1999 PAWS, INC. All Rights Reserved.
NOT ONE EENSY-WEENSY-TEENSY-WEENSY BIT
www.garfield.com
YOU CAN STOP ME ANYTIME, YOU KNOW
THROW IN A FEW MORE WEENSIES AND I MIGHT

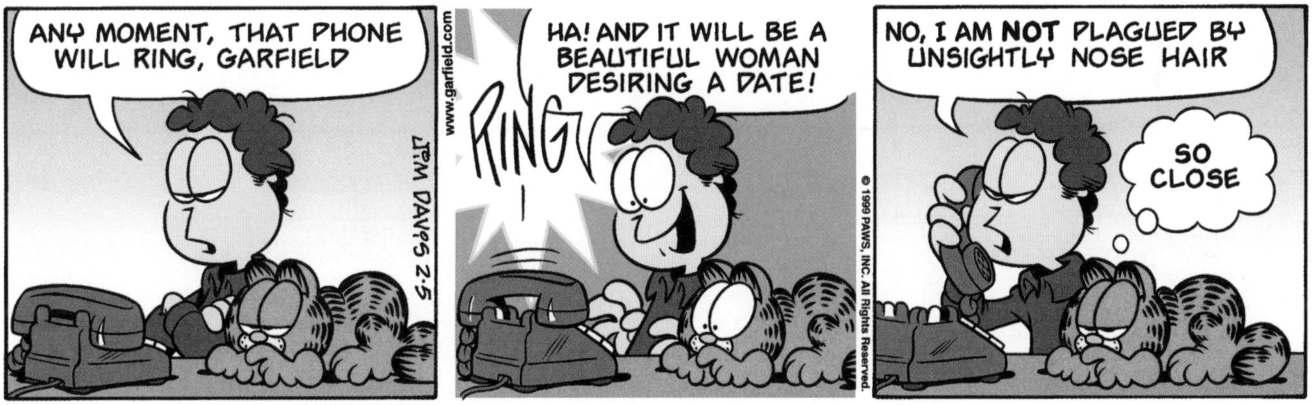
ANY MOMENT, THAT PHONE WILL RING, GARFIELD
JIM DAVIS 2-5
www.garfield.com
RING
HA! AND IT WILL BE A BEAUTIFUL WOMAN DESIRING A DATE!
© 1999 PAWS, INC. All Rights Reserved.
NO, I AM **NOT** PLAGUED BY UNSIGHTLY NOSE HAIR
SO CLOSE

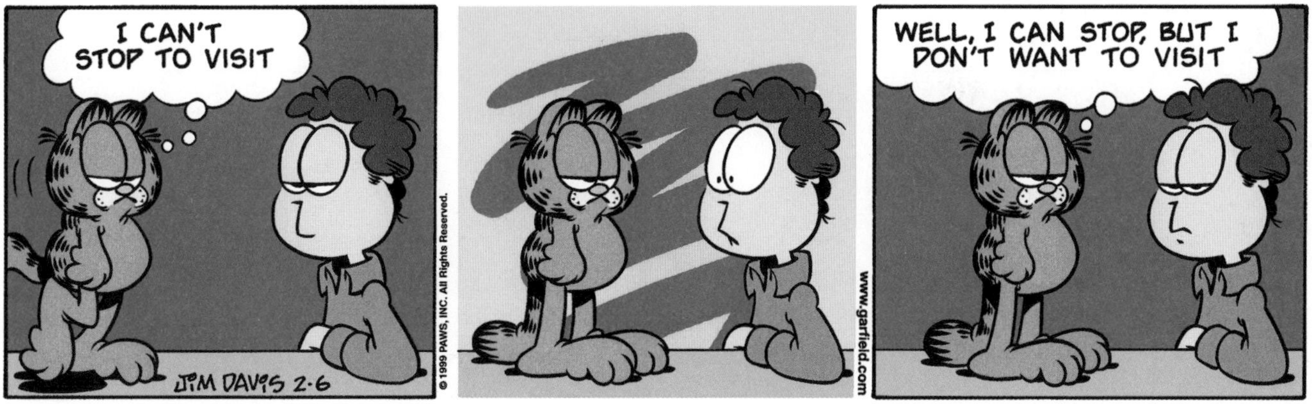
I CAN'T STOP TO VISIT
JIM DAVIS 2-6
© 1999 PAWS, INC. All Rights Reserved.
www.garfield.com
WELL, I CAN STOP, BUT I DON'T WANT TO VISIT

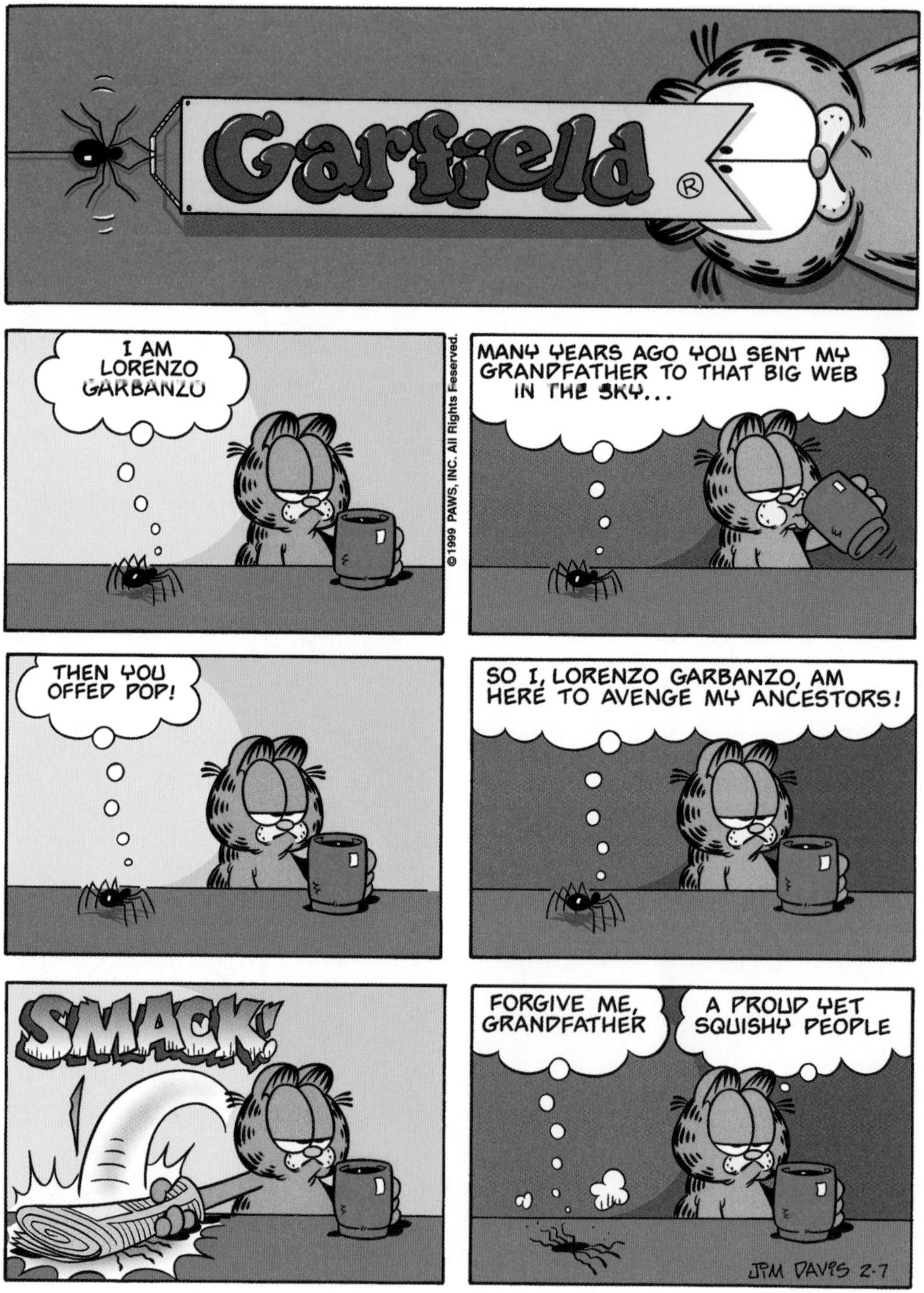
Garfield®
I AM LORENZO GARBANZO
MANY YEARS AGO YOU SENT MY GRANDFATHER TO THAT BIG WEB IN THE SKY...
THEN YOU OFFED POP!
SO I, LORENZO GARBANZO, AM HERE TO AVENGE MY ANCESTORS!
SMACK!
FORGIVE ME, GRANDFATHER
A PROUD YET SQUISHY PEOPLE
JIM DAVIS 2-7

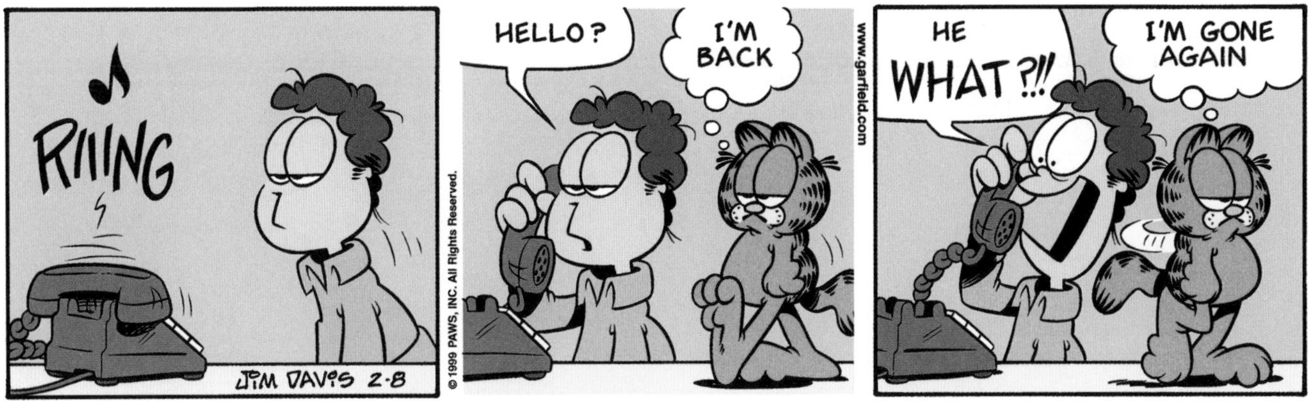
RIIING
JIM DAVIS 2-8
© 1999 PAWS, INC. All Rights Reserved.
HELLO?
I'M BACK
www.garfield.com
HE WHAT?!!
I'M GONE AGAIN

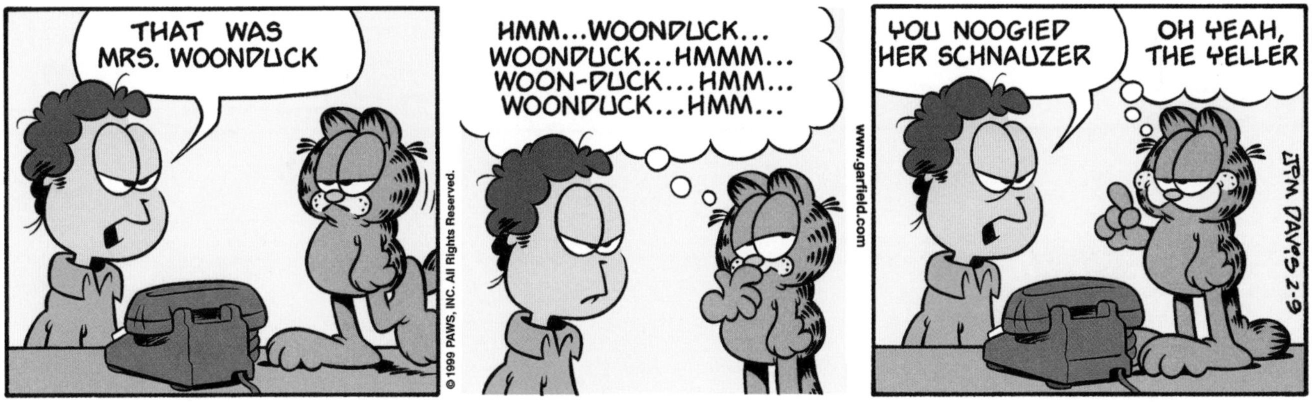
THAT WAS MRS. WOONDUCK
© 1999 PAWS, INC. All Rights Reserved.
HMM...WOONDUCK...
WOONDUCK...HMMM...
WOON-DUCK...HMM...
WOONDUCK...HMM...
www.garfield.com
YOU NOOGIED HER SCHNAUZER
OH YEAH, THE YELLER
JIM DAVIS 2-9

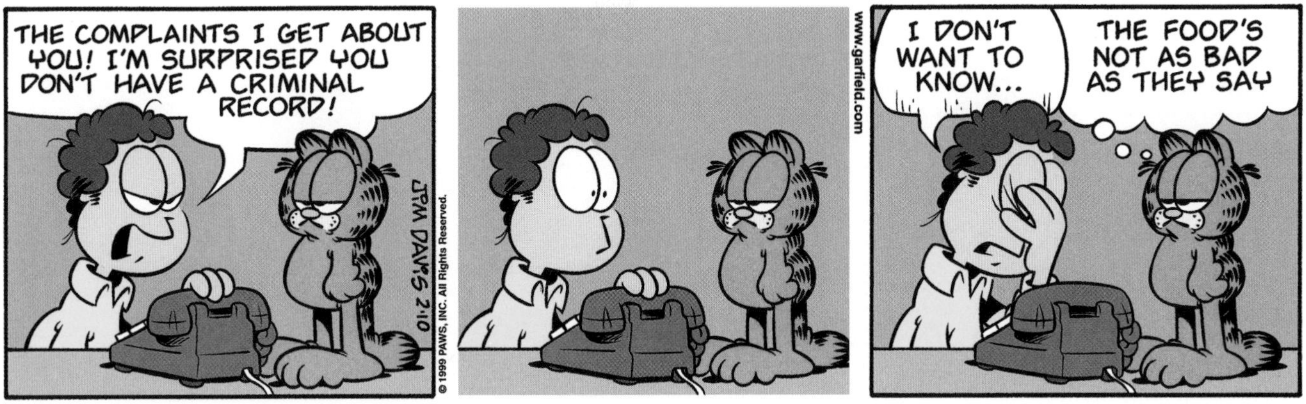
THE COMPLAINTS I GET ABOUT YOU! I'M SURPRISED YOU DON'T HAVE A CRIMINAL RECORD!
JIM DAVIS 2-10
© 1999 PAWS, INC. All Rights Reserved.
www.garfield.com
I DON'T WANT TO KNOW...
THE FOOD'S NOT AS BAD AS THEY SAY

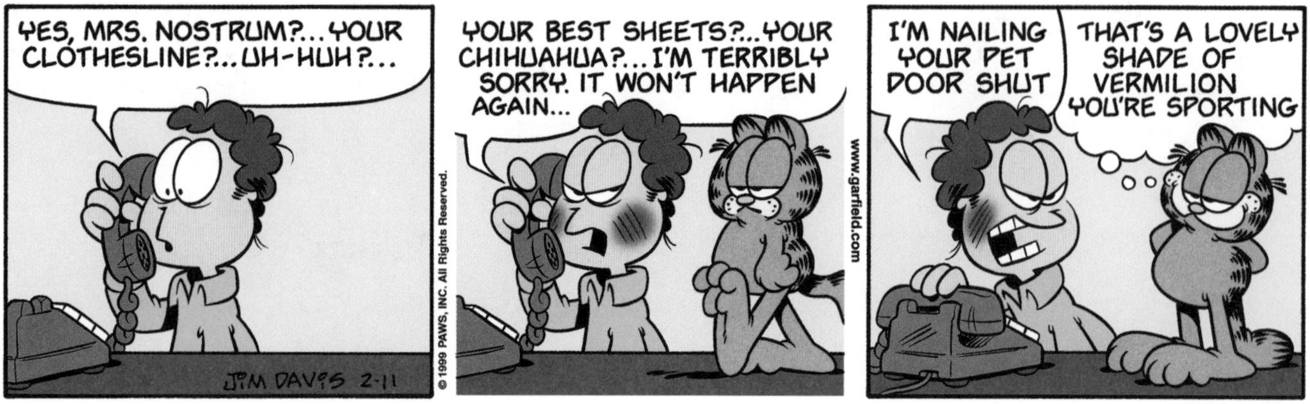
YES, MRS. NOSTRUM?... YOUR CLOTHESLINE?... UH-HUH?...
JIM DAVIS 2-11
YOUR BEST SHEETS?... YOUR CHIHUAHUA?... I'M TERRIBLY SORRY. IT WON'T HAPPEN AGAIN...
I'M NAILING YOUR PET DOOR SHUT
THAT'S A LOVELY SHADE OF VERMILION YOU'RE SPORTING

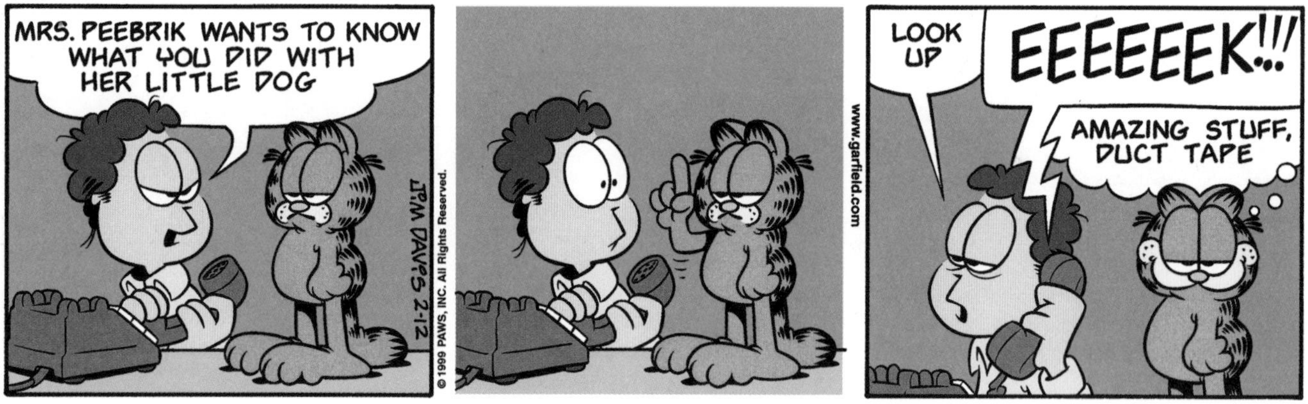
MRS. PEEBRIK WANTS TO KNOW WHAT YOU DID WITH HER LITTLE DOG
JIM DAVIS 2-12
LOOK UP
EEEEEEK!!!
AMAZING STUFF, DUCT TAPE

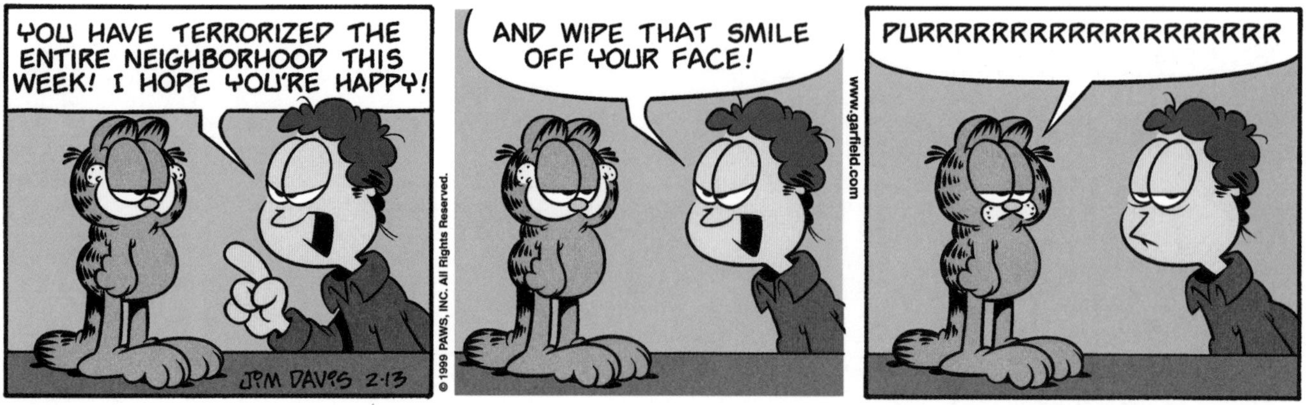
YOU HAVE TERRORIZED THE ENTIRE NEIGHBORHOOD THIS WEEK! I HOPE YOU'RE HAPPY!
JIM DAVIS 2-13
AND WIPE THAT SMILE OFF YOUR FACE!
PURRRRRRRRRRRRRRRRRRRR

REJECTED GARFIELD BOOK TITLES

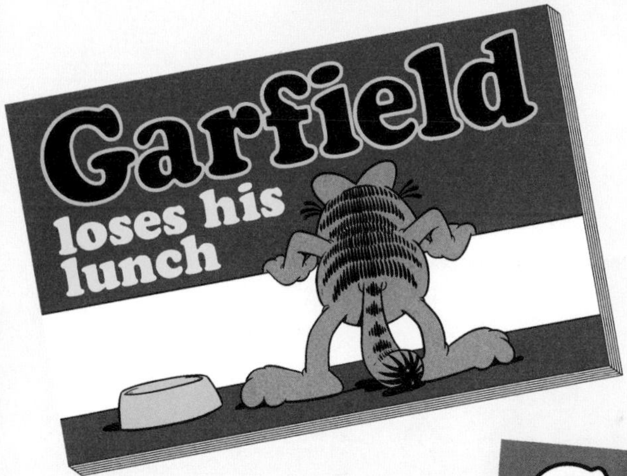
Garfield
loses his lunch

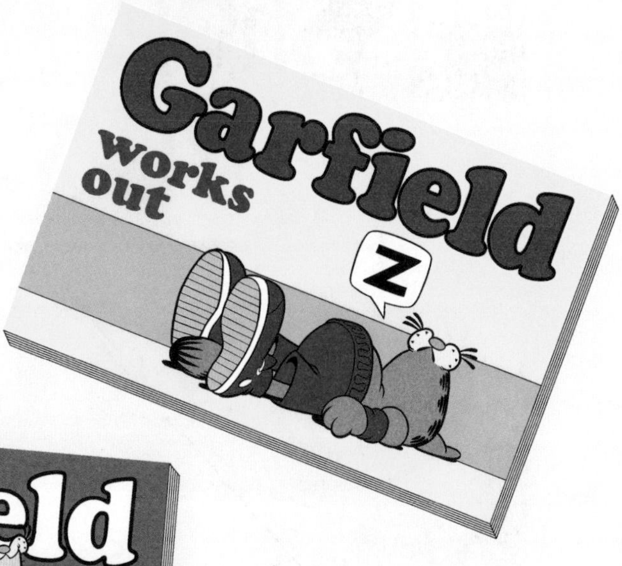
Garfield
works out
Z

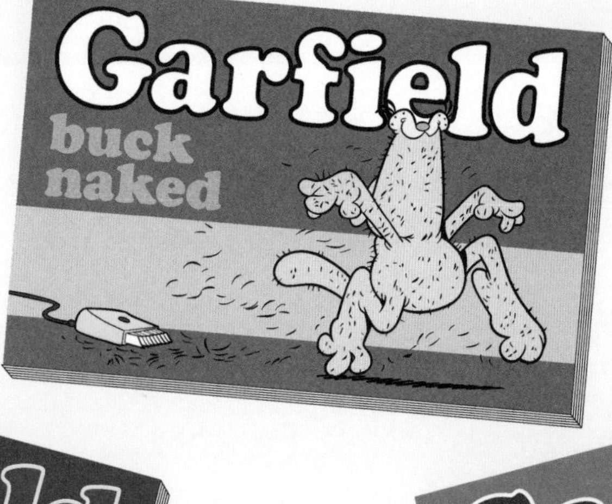
Garfield
buck naked

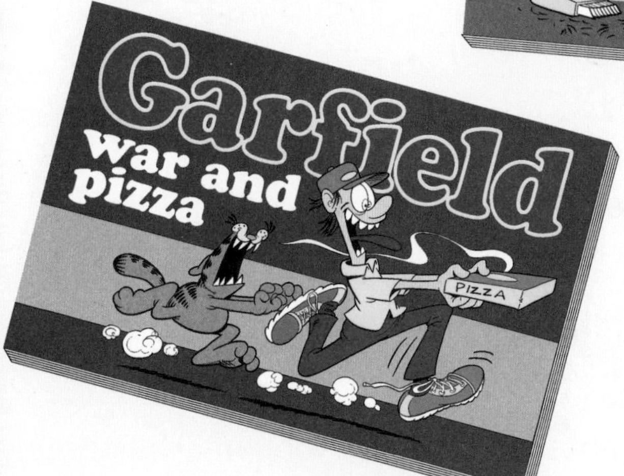
Garfield
war and pizza
PIZZA

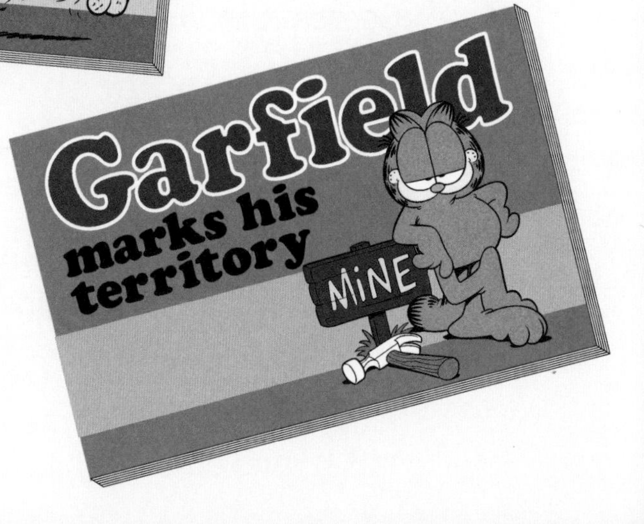
Garfield
marks his territory
MiNE

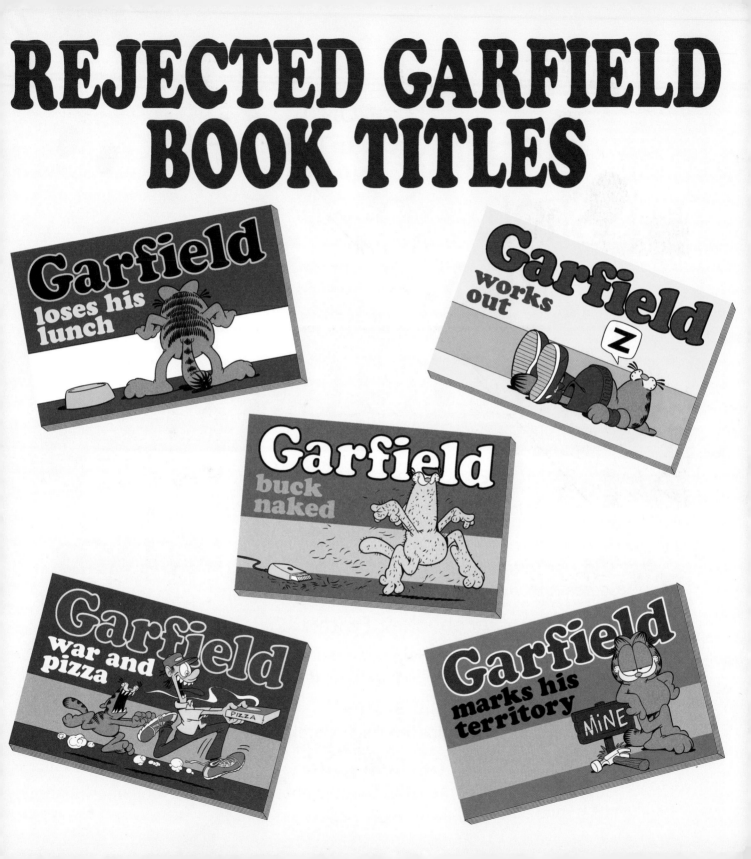